The Scent of the Father

Critical South

The publication of this series is supported by the International Consortium of Critical Theory Programs funded by the Andrew W. Mellon Foundation.

Series editors: Natalia Brizuela, Victoria Collis-Buthelezi, and Leticia Sabsay

Leonor Arfuch, *Memory and Autobiography*
Paula Biglieri and Luciana Cadahia, *Seven Essays on Populism*
Aimé Césaire, *Resolutely Black*
Bolívar Echeverría, *Modernity and "Whiteness"*
Diego Falconí Trávez, *From Ashes to Text*
Celso Furtado, *The Myth of Economic Development*
Eduardo Grüner, *The Haitian Revolution*
Premesh Lalu, *Undoing Apartheid*
Karima Lazali, *Colonia Trauma*
María Pia López, *Not One Less*
Achille Mbembe and Felwine Sarr, *The Politics of Time*
Achille Mbembe and Felwine Sarr, *To Write the Africa World*
Valentin-Yves Mudimbe, *The Scent of the Father*
Pablo Oyarzun, *Doing Justice*
Néstor Perlongher, *Plebeian Prose*
Bento Prado Jr., *Error, Illusion, Madness*
Nelly Richard, *Eruptions of Memory*
Suely Rolnik, *Spheres of Insurrection*
Silvia Rivera Cusicanqui, *Ch'ixinakax utxiwa*
Tendayi Sithole, *The Black Register*
Maboula Soumahoro, *Black is the Journey, Africana the Name*
Dénètem Touam Bona, *Fugitive, Where Are You Running?*

The Scent of the Father

Essay on the Limits of Life and Science in Sub-Saharan Africa

Valentin-Yves Mudimbe

Translated by Jonathan Adjemian

polity

Originally published in French as *L'odeur du père. Essai sur des limites de la science et de la vie en Afrique Noire* © Présence Africaine Éditions, 1982

This English edition © Polity Press, 2023

Polity Press
65 Bridge Street
Cambridge CB2 1UR, UK

Polity Press
111 River Street
Hoboken, NJ 07030, USA

All rights reserved. Except for the quotation of short passages for the purpose of criticism and review, no part of this publication may be reproduced, stored in a retrieval system or transmitted, in any form or by any means, electronic, mechanical, photocopying, recording or otherwise, without the prior permission of the publisher.

ISBN-13: 978-1-5095-5138-5 – hardback
ISBN-13: 978-1-5095-5139-2 – paperback

A catalogue record for this book is available from the British Library.

Library of Congress Control Number: 2022937999

Typeset in 10.5 on 12.5pt Sabon
by Fakenham Prepress Solutions, Fakenham, Norfolk NR21 8NL
Printed and bound in Great Britain by TJ Books Ltd, Padstow, Cornwall

The publisher has used its best endeavors to ensure that the URLs for external websites referred to in this book are correct and active at the time of going to press. However, the publisher has no responsibility for the websites and can make no guarantee that a site will remain live or that the content is or will remain appropriate.

Every effort has been made to trace all copyright holders, but if any have been overlooked the publisher will be pleased to include any necessary credits in any subsequent reprint or edition.

For further information on Polity, visit our website:
politybooks.com

For Daniel-Ange and Claude

... even as, when the surge is driven over the darkness of the deep by the fierce breath of Thracian sea-winds, it rolls up the black sand from the depths, and there is sullen roar from wind-vexed headlands that front the blows of the storm. ...

I see that from olden time the sorrows in the house of the Labdacidae are heaped upon the sorrows of the dead; and generation is not freed by generation, but some god strikes them down, and the race hath no deliverance.

For now that hope of which the light had been spread above the last root of the house of Oedipus – that hope, in turn, is brought low – by the blood-stained dust due to the gods infernal, and by folly in speech, and frenzy at the heart.

Sophocles, *Antigone*

Contents

Acknowledgments ix
Introduction – Felwine Sarr xi
Preface xiv

I. POSITIONS 1
1. A Sign, a Scent 3
2. What Order of African Discourse? 19
3. Theoretical Problems in the Social and Human Sciences .. 32
4. Christianity: A Question of Life? 41

II. ANALYSES AND TENDENCIES 55
1. Society, Education, Creativity 57
2. Cultural Cooperation and Dialogue 64
3. Universities: What Future? 79
4. Western Cultural Power and Christianity 85

III. QUESTIONS AND OPENINGS 103
1. "*Niam M'Paya*": At the Sources of an African Thinking 105

2.	On African Literature	115
3.	Sorcery: A Language and a Theory	124
4.	And What Will God Become?	136
5.	Interdisciplinarity and Educational Science	144
6.	Immediate History: An African Practice of Dialectical Materialism	152
7.	The Price of Sin	162

IV. IN LIEU OF A CONCLUSION: What Murder of the Father?   175

Notes   184
Index   200

Acknowledgments

Some of the chapters presented in this volume previously appeared, in earlier versions, as journal articles or in books:

"A Sign, a Scent": Under the title "L'Odeur du père," *Revue Zaïroise de Psychologie et de Pédagogie* 4 (1), 1975, pp. 135–49.

"Society, Education, Creativity": In a special issue of the *Revue de l'Aupelf* 13 (2), 1975, dedicated to "Creativity and the University," pp. 29–35.

"Cultural Cooperation and Dialogue," together with "Universities: What Future?": Under the title "Inter-University Cooperation and Cultural Dialogue," *Revue de l'Aupelf* 14 (1), 1976, pp. 34–54.

"'Niam M'Paya': At the Sources of an African Thinking" was published in a festschrift anthology for Alioune Diop.

"Sorcery: A Language and a Theory": *Cahiers des Religions Africaines* 8 (16), 1974, pp. 269–79.

"And What Will God Become?": *Cahiers des Religions Africaines* 8 (15), 1974, pp. 135–41.

"The Price of Sin": Published as an appendix to J. L. Vincke, *Le Prix du péché: essai de psychanalyse existentielle des traditions européenne et africaine*, Kinshasa: Éditions du Mont-Noir, 1974.

My thanks to the publishers for permitting me to republish these texts. I have modified some of them substantially in preparing them for this volume.

Four of the chapters were first presented as papers or interventions at conferences or congresses:

"Theoretical Problems in the Social and Human Sciences" is a development of a report presented at the Inter-African Meeting organized in September 1977 by the Centre des Recherches et de Documentation en Sciences Sociales Desservant l'Afrique Subsaharienne. [Mudimbe later published a revised version of this chapter in English as a section of chapter 4 in his *Tales of Faith: Religion as Political Performance in Central Africa* (London: Athlone Press, 1997). The present chapter has been translated from the original French version.]

"Christianity: A Question of Life?" was presented at the international conference on African Religions organized in January 1978 for the tenth anniversary of the Centre d›Etudes des Religions Africaines at the Faculty of Catholic Theology of Kinshasa.

"Western Cultural Power and Christianity" is a report presented at the conference on Black Civilizations and the Catholic Church organized in early September 1977 in Abidjan by the Société Africaine de Culture.

"Interdisciplinarity and Educational Science" is a reworking of a brief intervention at the seminar organized in Fall 1974 by the Centre de Recherches Interdisciplinaires pour le Développement de l'Education in Kisangani.

Introduction

The Scent of the Father, first published in French in 1982, is an essay on the situation of the social sciences in Africa in the aftermath of the independence movements and decades of political decolonization. In it, the Congolese philosopher, novelist, and philologist Valentin-Yves Mudimbe sheds light on the complex links which bind Africa to the West and determine the exercise of thought, knowledge practices, and ways of life on the African continent. In *The Scent of the Father*, Mudimbe brings together a set of texts that participate in the same questioning that he initiated in his previous essay, *L'Autre face du royaume* (1973), which focus on ethnological works produced on African countries. He examines a certain number of theoretical problems in the Western humanities and social sciences, and poses the question of what order of discourse there should be for the African social sciences and humanities, as well as the strategies to be considered for a coherence of theory and a fruitfulness of praxis in African countries.

Since colonial times, the Westernization of Africa is no longer a theoretical project, says Mudimbe; it is an action and a movement. The economic space and the teleology of development are places where this reality is most visibly expressed. Not only does the African continent hardly benefit from the positive effects of global economic exchange, but aid and the multiple forms of its cooperation with industrialized nations have contributed to the structural disorder of the economic spaces of its social formations; these expedients have rather served the imperatives of extending a mode of economic production that primarily benefits Western societies. For Africa, the challenge of unraveling the complex threads of this dependence is an important and ongoing question

How, then, does one get rid of the persistent smell of the father while avoiding the pitfall of challenging his discourse with words inspired by him? How does one erase his traces after his departure, asks Mudimbe. The father is now absent but remains present through his smell. "The father" refers to a certain epistemological paternalism that has been established and that has infantilized Africa. How can this filiation be broken to produce an African order of a scientific discourse in line with African realities?

As a reader and a critic of Michel Foucault, Mudimbe shows how scientific productions can be dependent on categories of thought that are both their own and those of others, that speak from specific geographical, but also philosophical and epistemological places. According to Mudimbe, for Africa "to truly escape from the West presupposes an exact appreciation of the price we have to pay to detach ourselves from it; it presupposes knowing to what extent the West, perhaps insidiously, has drawn close to us; it implies a knowledge, in that which permits us to think against the West, of all that remains Western." All the ambiguity and the difficulty of (the project of) epistemic decolonization is summarized in this quote. It is that of the implementation of a fertile gap, which will first have elucidated the current modalities of the integration of Africans into the myths of the West, while avoiding the need to prove its humanity in the face of the ideological, political, and symbolic violence that is opposed to it.

Instead, Mudimbe advocates to freely assume the responsibility of a thought which relates to its destiny and its environment; with the rehabilitation of its psyche as its central objective. This psyche must have the courage to rebuild, by reconstructing the genealogies of thought that were interrupted and occluded, even if the undertaking seems titanic. For Mudimbe, the constitution of an African scientific practice does not only suppose a strategy of decolonization of established knowledge, but also supposes the need to define the framework and the conditions of a true scientific practice that Africa needs most urgently, still today.

Introduction

What would be the tools, concepts, and categories as well as the methodology of such a reconstruction-rehabilitation? This is the task that the author proposes to tackle in this essay.

How to get out of the ideological traces left by the West? Through epistemological indiscipline, which becomes a strategy and a method: questioning the inner structure of Western knowledge to break out of its framework, and to get out of what Mudimbe will call, in *The Invention of Africa*, the "colonial library." It is necessary to take up the question of the "colonial library" to think from the African experience. For this, all knowledge must be reopened. The reopening for Mudimbe is not a return to a precolonial (ante-Western and ante-Islam) state of civilization or knowledge production. It is rather a question of developing a critical point of view on philosophical traditions and endogenous knowledge to raise what is relevant to preserve or to transform.

Although *The Scent of the Father* was initially published in 1982, the questions it raises are eminently current. They echo with those of decolonizing knowledge and curricula, in academic spaces and campuses in both the global South and North. The philosophical works of Mudimbe and the milestones that are *The Invention of Africa* (1988), *The Idea of Africa* (1994), and *The Scent of the Father* (published as *L'Odeur du père* in 1982) have given impetus to pressing contemporary issues around knowledge production.

Felwine Sarr

Preface

The scent of the father ... Hear that as you will. And if, to introduce these texts, I were to trace a path for the reader, I ask myself if it could really be treated as the only one. Despite the occasional peremptory assertion, throughout this book I have merely gathered together questions that seem able to illuminate the complex relations that, stronger today than in the past, tie Africa to the West, and determine not only attitudes of being but also the exercise of thought, practices of knowledge, and ways of living.

These forms of dependence are problems and need to be questioned, because the stakes are high: either continuity and blossoming through adaptation, or the reduction and pure and simple death of singular sociohistorical experiences. The contemporary situation is complex: the Westernization of Africa is now no longer a theoretical project but an activity and movement that presides over the arrangement of life and even of thought, as a function of the complex relations that connect African countries to Euro-America.

No doubt the economic is the most visible dimension. Jacques Bourrinet wrote a review of major documents on African countries' international trade, for the "dossiers Thémis" series published by the Presses Universitaires de France. He shows that before we can understand texts about the role of foreign trade in development or global perspectives promoting development, it is necessary to take note of both an increasingly marked dependence and a deterioration in the international position of the Third World. This observation is an expression of political despair and also a sign of major calamity for Africa. A glance through the important work of the Commission on International Development, under the direction of L. B. Pearson, makes the constraint measurable. In the countries of the Third World, the "question of will" with which this impressive report opens passes for a diabolical paradox.[1] On the one hand is the growing gap between the economies of the industrialized countries and those of the underdeveloped countries; on the other, the extraordinary increase in aid from rich countries to poor countries – aid which, as Tibor Mende shows in a brave book,[2] is remarkably compatible with recolonization. The Commission, whose project is to establish "lasting and constructive relations between the developing nations and the developed nations," offers normative and voluntaristic recommendations that themselves need to be untangled. They clearly describe possible actions, but at the same time they propose fatalistic-sounding prerequisites for collaboration. These constitute veritable "cruxes," given current relations between North and South and the structural disorder of economic areas in African social formations.

Even the therapeutic prescriptions that are supposed to save Africa are themselves questions. They give an account of the site from which they emerge; and we might ask if they are not better equipped to explain the particular progress of a mode of production and the conditions for its extension than they are to move non-Western societies forward – for their own good – to the point of "equilibrium" that the Euro-American world incarnates today.

The situation is the same in the ideological field. An important problem there is the question of identifying practices that might be more attentive to the African context, speak to its actual conditions, and, when faced with the paradoxes born of development, might occasionally open doors.

Upon finishing a text in which Michel Foucault describes Hegel's persistence in contemporary philosophy, I felt that I was able to understand not only the violence of the Father's existence, but also the strangeness of his scent. Here, too, it is a case of dependence, and Foucault's comments about the Hegelian heritage apply well to my subject: Africa's dependence vis-à-vis Euro-America. I thus place "the West" where Foucault puts "Hegel": for Africa, to truly escape from the West presupposes an exact appreciation of the price we have to pay to detach ourselves from it; it presupposes knowing to what extent the West, perhaps insidiously, has drawn close to us; it implies a knowledge, in that which permits us to think against the West, of all that remains Western; and a determination of the extent to which our recourse against it is still possibly one of the tricks it directs against us, while it waits for us, immobile and elsewhere.[3]

Such an embrace from the West might smother us. So we in Africa must maintain not only a rigorous understanding of the modes in which we are currently integrated into Western myths, but also an explicit questioning that will allow us to be genuinely critical in the face of this "corpus."

Even today, the West, a certain West, when it thinks of us, continues to wonder "how it is possible to be Black." Manga Bekombo puts it well:

> European scholars have a heavy responsibility – or rather, a great role – in the production of anti-Black stereotypes; these stereotypes, sometimes with accompanying paintings, are used as arguments, restored to the empty center of collective representation by literary manipulation. Here exoticism takes its full meaning: it operates like a festival, like carnival, it is the instinctive explosion that still further valorizes the prestige of reason.[4]

Confronted with this ideological violence, in my opinion it is not useful for us to expend our energies, as some of our elders have done, in trying to "prove" our humanity or the intelligence we have long been refused – and which is still, with skillful contempt, regularly and learnedly torn to pieces in the name of a reason and a science utterly at the service of political projects.

I think that we have other things to do, and urgently: to freely assume the responsibility of a thought concerned with our destiny and environment, with the goal of readapting our psyche in the wake of the violence it has suffered – this psyche which we have not always had the courage to remake because, rightly or wrongly, the project seemed titanic. Our problem, our fundamental problem, can be found in this project. Today and tomorrow, it will determine the relevance of the attitudes we develop to confront economic, political, and ideological endemics that come to us from elsewhere, or that we create ourselves.

Racialization? No. I begin from the fact that my consciousness and effort come from a place, a given space and moment; and I do not see how or why my speech, however it takes flight, cannot be first of all the cry and testimony of this singular place. Therefore, we must promote this important norm: that we stop and look at ourselves. Or more precisely, that we return constantly to who we are, with a particular eagerness and attention for our archeological setting – the setting that makes our speeches possible, while also explaining them. Particularism, you will say … Perhaps. But I would note, following Aimé Césaire: "There are two ways to lose oneself: walled segregation in the particular or dilution into the 'universal'. My conception of the universal is of a universal enriched by all that is particular, a universal enriched by every particular: the deepening and coexistence of all the particulars."[5]

The texts gathered here are occasional pieces in the proper sense of the term. These different and even apparently contradictory texts are more expressions of a questioning that pays attention to life and its vital environment than they are systematic research that follows scholarly norms. To a certain extent they express my own contradictions as an African academic. One thing unites them: the impulse of my earlier essay, *L'Autre face du royaume* [The Other Side of the Kingdom]. Each of the texts gathered here – in different ways, certainly – turns on questions I began to explore in this first essay: namely, how the human and social sciences, like ideologies, do not speak "a same" that is inoffensive and faithfully reproduced in its various expressions, on the model of logical systems. Like the ideologies that mark us today, in their application these sciences seem instead to be cut to fit certain modes of dependence. It is some of the notable traits of these types of dependence that *The Scent of the Father* addresses.

I could adapt here what Jean-Bertrand Pontalis says to introduce the texts that make up his *Après Freud* [After Freud]:[6] it may be that this ensemble of traits is purely accidental, or has no meaning other than to signify myself. It may also be – and this volume took shape around this supposition – that it is precisely in their partial character and in the reprise of the same themes, in their insertion into a personal formation, that these "chronicles" suggest something of interest to the very nature and the situation of Africanism.

If these "chronicles," with their limits, can help us to understand the equivocations of the scientific and even ethical grids that are transplanted and imposed on us in Africa, and if they can provoke even one reflection on the possible levels at which these grids can be corrected to make life and research in Africa align better with their environment, they will have achieved their objective.

I would like to thank the friends who have encouraged, sustained, and helped me in my "quest" and in the elaboration of these chronicles; in particular: Denyse de Saivre, Ilunga Kabongo, Mabika Kalanda, Barbara Kempf, Ngindu Mushete, and Benoît Verhaegen. I have benefited from their experience, their points of view, and their criticism. This books is thus a bit theirs, even though it goes without saying that I remain entirely responsible for its theses and its oversights.

V. Y. M.
Haverford, Pennsylvania
November 1981

I.
POSITIONS

1
A Sign, a Scent

Roger Bastide makes a remarkable suggestion: Georges Devereux, he writes, is a disciple of Freud. Of course, Devereux does not accept what has been rightly called "Freud's novel," *Totem and Taboo*. And, like Roheim, he thinks that an ethnologist (or historian) doing psychoanalysis must take an ontogenetic rather than phylogenetic point of view. That said, however, for him the Oedipus complex has universal value; it is linked to the existence of culture itself, considered as a form of comportment characteristic of *Homo sapiens*. It would be false to consider it a product of the Viennese bourgeois family, and not generalizable to other societies. The thesis of the psychic unity of humanity must be resolutely defended against Malinowski, and against the culturalists who want to relativize the Freudian complexes. If not, psychoanalysis will not be able to offer a valid interpretation of culture.

This point of view is developed in a book that gathers together articles written over a span of more than thirty years. Devereux notes that "the first date from the earliest days of ethnopsychiatry, when it lacked not only a theoretical armature, but even adequate concepts and technical terms. To update them, however, all that was needed was to make explicit certain things which had been merely implied ... implications that were there from the beginning, even if sometimes only as passing remarks."[1] As for content, Devereux cautiously notes that: "This book deals with disorder and at times even delirium; but it does not for a moment adopt the maxim a colleague once proposed to me: 'A delirious era calls for delirious theory.' Of course, a description of disorder or delirium must faithfully reflect the chaotic nature – or appearance – of the phenomenon under study. But a description is not a theory!"[2] This is an important remark. In effect, it introduces the following idea into Devereux's general conception of ethnopsychiatric work: as Bastide notes, if the normal is defined by adaptation, the psychiatrist will need to begin with a knowledge of the specific culture of his patients; but if the normal is defined by creative adaptation, then the psychiatrist does not need to be an ethnographer, but merely an ethnologist. That is to say, what he must know is the "universal cultural model" of which each culture is a particular version. Next, Devereux demands that psychiatrists begin from culture as lived experience, from the way in which individuals live their culture. Never mind which particular items the individual's culture presents; what is important is that neurotics and psychotics reinterpret or even deculture cultural items in terms of their own personal conflicts or delirium.[3]

I would like to take these theses, which are admirably supported by clear demonstrations and rigorous theoretical explications, as an opportunity to draw out a few practical questions: the norms of knowledge and the subjective root of ethnopsychiatry; the function of ethnopsychiatric language and practice; and, lastly, the meanings of certain universal canons.

Having followed the recent debate between Devereux and Claude Conté,[4] I know that the author of *Basic Problems of Ethnopsychiatry* would find it "strange to dedicate a very considerable part of a book review to the exegesis of the works of a different author" or authors. I have no intention of writing a "review," and would like to note from the outset that for me Devereux's book is only a pretext to reflect on a few theses often found today in certain Western settings.

Alain-Gérard Slama recently remarked that the history of epistemology may someday credit Lévi-Strauss, Dumézil, and Devereux with a revolution as significant in its field as the one ascribed to Kant in the eighteenth century.[5] One would hope that this history will also mention the particular smile of the "alienated" Africans who were confronted with this revolution.

* * *

"Each science," Devereux writes, "has its key concept, or pair of key concepts, whose precise definition is the principal problem of that science and whose analysis is the best introduction to that field of inquiry."[6] Ethnopsychiatry, "as a pluridisciplinary science, must concern itself with the key concepts and key problems of both anthropology and psychiatry." More precisely, for Devereux, psychiatric ethnology or ethnological psychiatry must "have as its key problem the coordination of the concept of 'culture' with the paired concepts 'normal' and 'abnormal.' It must be brought to bear, first of all, on the problem of determining the exact locus of the boundary between 'normal' and 'abnormal.'"[7]

These are excellent and entirely defensible choices, and in the author's metacultural perspective they lead to eminently valid conclusions. In terms of the practical meaning of the theory, it is neither shocking nor surprising to encounter this fundamental idea throughout the work:

> A real analysis of the universal culture patterns and a full specification of its nature require that, in every study of culture, one should also take into account the psychiatric perspective. Indeed, regardless of the variety of cultures, the simple fact of having a culture is a genuinely universal experience, and man functions as a "creator, creature, manipulator, and transmitter of culture" [Talayesva, *Sun Chief*] everywhere and in the same way.[8]

Nonetheless, these choices also have a reductive function. This is worth thinking about: the ethnopsychiatrist works in a particular sociohistorical context, and uses a language that is at once finite and marked by a particular cultural universe. It thus seems to me that, regardless of the scholar's good will or methodical rigor, there is one fact that distinctly influences the project, without being determinate in an absolute fashion. This is the particularity of the analysis and the sociocultural and epistemological context that "provide" it with conceptual instruments and categories. At the very genesis of all discourse on culture there would thus be what I might call a fundamental discord: the difficulty of truthfully speaking another's culture. This is because my knowledge and my experience, however open and attentive they may be, end and can only end where the other's begin. A necessary link between the "truth" of facts and the "truth" of the analyst's speech does not and cannot exist.

When Teucer breaks his bow in the *Iliad*, he is convinced that the cause was a demon who wished him ill. But here, Homer has mischievously alerted the reader to the fact that Zeus is the one responsible for the accident.[9] In this example, a subtle subterfuge unites reader and poet in the "same" complicity, since both know "the truth" – which is present in the literary context but always escapes it, leaving the actor-heroes in ignorance. The speech of ethnopsychiatry or of the ethnologist is limited to and is almost entirely supported by its context. Unlike the poet's speech, it has neither license nor means to objectively unveil the complex and subtle play of a culture's reality. It can only present an approximate weave, thanks to relatively rigorous functions that help to determine the rules and contraventions that *seem* to belong to a universe. So one can understand why Devereux, when he has to provide treatment to two "Acoma Indians" but lacks sufficient information on their culture, formulates his diagnosis in terms of culture-in-itself rather than specifically Acoma culture.

Devereux is persuaded that

> the approach that views psychiatric problems in terms of Culture rather than *cultures* is also more effective in a practical sense – that is, therapeutically – and is theoretically far superior to any other cultural approach; for it affords a deeper insight into psycho-dynamics, and this, in turn, leads to deeper ethnological insight into the nature of Culture. Moreover, it undermines once and for all the arrogant claims of the clique of neo-Freudian and pseudo-Freudian "cultural psychoanalysts" who not only boast of their greater sophistication and ethnological flair but also claim that their views are more useful to the ethnologist than those of classical psychoanalysis.[10]

Later on, I will discuss the meaning of this universalist perspective. For the moment, I would like to provisionally highlight the positive aspects of Devereux's method. To me these seem remarkably – and with such aplomb! – to negate several of ethnology's most appalling limitations. I have recently tried to show, from my point of view as an African, how and why ethnology, in itself and always, seems to me both suspect and exterior to its subject matter. As a result, it is perpetually condemned to offer only theoretical constructions pertaining to a culture, but never the culture itself.[11] Michel Foucault, who I drew on extensively in that work, offered a felicitous explanation:

> There is a certain position of the Western *ratio* that was constituted in its history and provides a foundation for the relation it can have with all other societies, even with the society in which it historically appeared. Obviously, this does not mean that the colonizing situation is indispensable to ethnology: neither hypnosis, nor the patient's alienation within the fantasmic character of the doctor, is constitutive of psychoanalysis; but just as the latter can be deployed only in the calm violence of a particular relation and the transference it produces, so ethnology can assume its proper dimensions only within the historical sovereignty – always restrained, but always present – of European thought and of the relation that can bring it face to face it with all other cultures as well as with itself.[12]

Thus the gaze toward the other and the discourses that surround it have meaning only in terms of a *ratio* that is always exterior to the object of which ethnology claims to speak. The ethnocentrism described in Michel and Françoise Panoff's thoughtful book[13] is in the end only a circumstantial barrier, which can be thrown off in certain conditions. But I do not think it is possible to exclude oneself from an epistemological field: it is a constraining order. Indeed, to return to Foucault, between, on the one hand, the region of the fundamental codes of a culture, codes which "establish for every man, from the very first, the empirical orders with which he will be dealing and within which he will be at home," and, on the other, the region of the interpretations (philosophical and scientific theories) that explain why and how there is in general an order within culture, there

> lies a domain which, even though its role is mainly an intermediary one, is nonetheless fundamental ... It is here that a culture, imperceptibly, deviating from the empirical orders prescribed for it by its primary codes, instituting an initial separation from them, causes them to lose their original transparency, relinquishes its immediate and invisible powers, frees itself sufficiently to discover that these orders are perhaps not the only possible ones or the best ones; this culture then finds itself faced with the stark fact that there exists, below the level of its spontaneous orders, things that are in themselves capable of being ordered, that belong to a certain unspoken order; the fact, in short, that order *exists* ... It is on the basis of this order,

taken as a firm foundation, that general theories as to the ordering of things, and the interpretation that such an ordering involves, will be constructed. Thus, between the already "encoded" eye and reflexive knowledge there is a middle region which ... in so far as it makes manifest the modes of being or order, can be posited as the most fundamental of all ... more solid, more archaic, less dubious, always more "true" than the theories that attempt to give those expressions explicit form, exhaustive application, or philosophical foundation.[14]

Thus, if one can generalize Foucault's model, there would be in every culture a fundamental relay and justification at work between the codes that regulate ways of being and languages of exchange, technique, or value, and philosophical and scientific theories. In a certain way, any order would be the "truth" of projections and discourses about man, an "*episteme* in which knowledge, envisioned apart from all criteria having reference to its rational value or to its objective forms, grounds its positivity and thereby manifests a history which is not that of its growing perfection, but rather that of its conditions of possibility."[15]

This observation, in its final conclusions, is the same as what Stanislas Adotévi proclaims in a book that, while its tone may seem shocking or displeasing, no less truthfully marks the limitation I am circling here: even in its finest flights, ethnology, a European science, has always been the expression of epistemological and cultural configurations that are foreign to Africa.[16] In sum, we could simply and brutally say that it has, thus far, been a "lie" – in the precise sense that, under the guise of discovering and speaking Africa, it presents Africa through a distorting prism.

But does this limitation only characterize the discourse of European specialists who speak of Africa? What site could truthfully account for theories made by Africans practicing ethnology or ethnopsychiatry today? In effect, they have been students in the school of a rationality that is entirely foreign to the fundamental codes of their cultures and the philosophical conceptions of their historical universes ...

Another serious limit to ethnology and ethnopsychiatry, like most of the human and social sciences, seems to lie in the constraining vigor of a scientific ideology whose normative function, today as in the past, blocks possible discoveries and new beginnings. An exemplary text by Engels, the Preface to the 1886 English edition of *Capital*, recently provided Louis

Althusser with a convincing illustration of scientific "blocks." The illustration is drawn from the history of chemistry:

> Priestley and Scheele, in the period dominated by phlogistic theory, "produced" (*stellt dar*) a strange gas, which the former called dephlogisticated air – and the latter: fire-air. In fact, it was the gas that would later be called oxygen. But, notes Engels, they "*had produced it without having the least idea of what they had produced*," i.e., without its *concept*. That is why "*the element which was determined to upset all phlogistic views and to revolutionize chemistry remained barren in their hands.*" Why this barrenness and blindness? Because they "*remained prisoners of the 'phlogistic' categories as they came down to them.*" Because, instead of seeing in oxygen a problem, they merely saw "*a solution.*"
>
> Lavoisier did just the opposite: "*Lavoisier, by means of this new fact, analysed the entire phlogistic chemistry*"; "*thus he was the first to place all chemistry, which in its phlogistic form had stood on its head, squarely on its feet.*" Where the others saw a solution he saw a problem. That is why, if it can be said that the first two "*produced*" oxygen, it was Lavoisier alone who *discovered* it, by giving it its concept.[17]

Althusser uses this striking example of a conceptual block to highlight Marx's contribution in relation to his predecessors. Althusser also provides a powerful image of the violence of ideology of any science. Indeed, perfectly closed in on itself and working with categories it has defined, the ideology of a science finds it challenging to provoke the irruption of new concepts, or to discover new realities that might put it into question.

Devereux claims each science has a key concept or pair of key concepts whose definition provides the essence of its problematic. If this is true, should we not also note that these key concepts or pairs of concepts, the fundamental support from which analyses and systems are established, directly contribute to the development or setting up of conceptual barriers? The only problematics that they can prescribe, the only concepts they permit to be braided or woven together, the only integration of analyses or systematization of hypotheses that they allow will be meaningless, unless supported by these keys as a sort of essential norm. And we might ask: isn't the solidity of a scientific system also an expression of dogmatism, and a measure of relative fixity?

Drawing out the lessons of Marx's revolution in political economy, Althusser claims that, among other things:

1. every revolution (new aspect of a science) in the object of a science entails a necessary revolution in its terminology;
2. every terminology is linked to a definite circle of ideas, which we might translate by saying: every terminology is a function of the theoretical system that serves as its base; all terminology brings with it a determinate and limited theoretical system.

I would say, then: a system that puts forward a problematic and a certain number of categories will certainly be faithful to the revolution that allowed it to be created; but its terminology and key concepts will account only for this moment. Without denying that it might produce valid analyses or operations, what right would such a system have to be imposed as "Science"? Confined to the truth of a single configuration, reduced to a few possibilities made possible by one foundation (a fundamental concept, a pair of concepts), it would be only one scientific discourse among other possible ones.

Devereux writes: "Adults teach *children* to be *puerile* in a particular, culturally determined, manner and then call the *study* of the *products* of this inculcated puerility 'child psychology.'"[18] Jean-Paul Sartre has shown elsewhere that psychiatry tends to logically impose a particular way of being ill on the patient, following a similar specific model.[19] For instance, this anachronism: "*Rameau's Nephew* is a subservient consciousness, open to the winds and transparent to the look of others. He is mad because that is what people tell him and because he has been treated as such: 'They wanted me to be ridiculous, so that's what I became'." His unreason is all surface; it has no depth apart from opinion. It is subjected to what is least free, and denounced by what is most precarious within reason. "Unreason is entirely on the level of the futile madness of men. It is, perhaps, nothing other than that mirage."[20] Institutionalized and analyzed, this mirage has given rise to verse and controversy,[21] and psychotherapy has been able to thematize and install itself as theory and practice. But what theory and what practice? Contemporary counter-practices, proving Sartre right (against this "interminable relation," this "dependence; the anticipated and induced transference; the feudal bond; the long confinement of a man lying prostrate ... reduced to the babbling of childhood, utterly drained"[22]), have contributed to the indictment of all models which endorse and explain fictitious relations of dependence.[23]

Here an analogy presents itself: Westerners, like adults in regard to children, or psychiatrists in regard to patients, have "imposed" on non-Westerners, according to a specific model, aberrant ways of being non-Westerners; they then gave the name "ethno-x" to the study of the *products* of this artificially induced "x."

Devereux's discourse, an "assuredly" logical discourse, is thus an ideological discourse, and eminently so. The theme of universality that runs throughout his intercultural psychiatry is one of those operations of reduction that contribute to the consolidation of models that are fully meaningful only in relation to "the bare experience of order" of the West.

* * *

It will be objected that psychoanalysis, ethnopsychiatry, and ethnology are sciences; that, despite limitations, they have real importance and efficacy. That one can hardly see individuals rising up against a science on the grounds that it is supported by a discourse which, culturally and epistemologically, comes from "outside." Are not the positions of science at once clear, prudent, and objectively articulated? Devereux writes:

> Both psychoanalysis and ethnology are branches of "Anthropology" as defined by Kant, that is, the science of that which is distinctively human in man. However ... psychoanalysis and ethnology yield complementary, not additive, insights. On the theoretical level there is actually a Heisenberg–Bohr type of indeterminacy relationship ... between the psychoanalytic and the ethnological understanding of human behaviour. In practice, convenience and economy of effort alone determine when and at what point it is desirable to discontinue further inquiry in psychoanalytic terms and to start analyzing the phenomenon under consideration in ethnological terms – and of course, vice versa.[24]

In effect, such objections and methodological questions fall short of my concerns. Their aim is either to illustrate the universal character of a science, or to establish appropriate methods that will supposedly resolve the essential – and, for the non-Westerners that we are, existential – question: under what conditions are these sciences universal sciences?

A detour here will help us address the problem in a better and more concrete way. Reflecting on Marc Soriano's study of Perrault's collection of fairy tales, Michel de Certeau notes that

> what is most instructive is the near-autobiographical architecture of the book, in which we may attempt to read how the inquiry "led" its author on. All things considered, Soriano's study informs us less about popular culture itself than about what it means for a progressive academic to speak of popular culture today. This brings us back to a ubiquitous problem we must try to answer: *From where does one speak? What can be said?* But also, in the end: From where do *we* speak? This makes the problem directly political, because it makes an issue of the social – in other words, primarily repressive – function of learned culture.[25]

Our question becomes clearer: from where does the Western scholar of ethnopsychiatry speak? What can he say, what does he say, and how does he say it?

At the least, we might suspect that the tableaux he offers inform us poorly about the behavior of non-Westerners. What they explain is rather the methods currently used by Western specialists when they speak of non-Westerners. Of course, particular behaviors do exist – and they are present in the specialist's theoretical act when he suppresses them in order to valorize universality and culture-in-itself, both projections of particular canons.

It will have been noticed that what is at question here is not the validity or efficacy of therapeutic approaches, but the *meaning* of the scientific projects these approaches assume. These projects have often, and without difficulty, been supported by the most diverse ideologies. Medicine, across eras and locales, clearly shows us that there have always been relations of non-necessity between the gleam of technical languages and real practices of healing or of consolation.[26] Further – to cite only one eloquent case from Foucault's *History of Madness* – the extension of general paralysis, moral madness, and monomania in the nineteenth century

> does not simply signify a reorganisation of nosographic space, but, underlying the medical concepts, the presence and workings of a new

structure of experience. The institutional form that Pinel and Tuke designed, the constitution around the mad of a containing asylum space where they were to admit their guilt and rid themselves of it, allowing the truth of their sickness to appear and then suppressing it, rediscovering their freedom by alienating it in the will of doctors – all this now became an *a priori* of medical perception.[27]

A young African scholar, Buakasa Tulu Kia Mpansu, offers another example; it is a bit more dense, but singularly telling for my argument.[28] Although encumbered with Western schemas and reflectors, the universe he uncovers – that of sorcery in the Kongo – is a harmony. His book is an example of the kind of research that describes a microsystem, gradually and with real originality, and determines and names the criteria of normality and abnormality, treatment and healing, in a particular culture. While the reality – or more precisely the exact borders – of the site from which Buakasa speaks may seem suspect, at least the meaning of what he says and delimits can be clearly perceived. As much and perhaps even more so than a living culture, what he reveals is an academic way of speaking. And all the concrete therapeutics and case studies are comprehensible only when situated in a particular game, in relation to a particular ideological system.

As Buakasa puts it:

> *Kindoki* (sorcery) and *nkisi* (fetishes) are a "social game," an "organized scenario." In saying this, we know well that the people who find themselves in this "game" are not lying. Because society – or better, its unthought – is not transparent to the subjects who "play," its function is to make them unconscious of the conditions of their existence, and thus the real reason for their "play" in *kindoki* and *nkisi*. The subjects believe in these as material truths, which really exist, while *kindoki* and *nkisi* have only the existence of "historical truth," that is to say of constructed reality, produced "within" the subjects, in the course of "real" history … "Organized scenario" or "social game," *kindoki* and *nkisi* are thus defined in relation to a cultural system of which they are an integral part; but they are grasped and manifested only at certain points in the system, where they denounce its flaws by revealing its contradictions.[29]

As will be evident from my recourse first to Foucault and then to Buakasa, my argument has to do with something other than therapeutics.

My argument is concerned with the discourses that structure human behavior as a function of abstract norms, conceived out of context. The theses of these discourses are discontinuous, broken, shattered, and regularly refurbished by new projects and perspectives. In spaces enunciated as scientifically universal, the theories that they affirm contain, hidden within, the disavowed figures of ruptures totally foreign to the world that they are supposed to illumine and reveal. The commonly established proximity between ethnology and psychoanalysis conflates important divergences a bit too easily. The former has up until now been defined as the science of communities "without history"; the latter, as a practice, is applied to the individual as a particular being.

Of course, when interpreted and classified, what is said by one or more particular individuals can easily be gathered as data for a theory or a formal system. This permits generalizations that formulate laws or mark tendencies said to be proper to one community or to characterize humanity as a whole. The most representative works of psychoanalysis are supported by "case studies"; and "cases" are what permeate and establish the general theory as norm and knowledge.

In his classic thesis on symbolism in Greek mythology, Paul Diel systematizes and interprets "case studies" or singular myths to name the foundation of this symbolism.[30] As Gaston Bachelard puts it: "The word that recurs in all these exercises, in the study of all the ultra-classic Greek myths discussed here, is the word *translation*. Indeed, everything that is expressed in the stories, reduced always to triteness by what Paul Diel calls 'banalization,' must be translated into the language of modern panpsychology."[31] Moving in the opposite direction, where ethnology encounters the singularity of an individual it does so by descending from overall equivocations about culture, applying the rules of a general cultural economy to a specific case.

By dreaming of a renaissance of ethnology and psychoanalysis, Michel Foucault marked the most blatant limits of both disciplines:

> One can imagine what prestige and importance ethnology could possess if, instead of defining itself in the first place – as it has done until now – as the study of societies without history, it were deliberately to seek its object in the area of the unconscious processes

that characterize the system of a given culture; in this way it would bring the relation of historicity, which is constitutive of all ethnology in general, into play within the dimension in which psychoanalysis has always been deployed. In so doing it would not assimilate the mechanisms and forms of a society to the pressure and repression of collective hallucinations, thus discovering – though on a larger scale – what analysis can discover at the level of the individual; it would define as a system of cultural unconsciouses the totality of formal structures which render mythical discourse significant, give their coherence and necessity to the rules that regulate needs, and provide the norms of life with a foundation other than that to be found in nature, or in pure biological functions. One can imagine the similar importance that a psychoanalysis would have if it were to share the dimension of an ethnology, not by the establishment of a "cultural psychology," not by the sociological explanation of phenomena manifested at the level of individuals, but by the discovery that the unconscious also possesses, or rather that it is in itself, a certain formal structure. By this means, ethnology and psychoanalysis would succeed, not in superimposing themselves on one another, nor even perhaps in coming together, but in intersecting like two lines differently oriented: one proceeding from the apparent elision of the signified in a neurosis to the lacuna in the signifying system through which the neurosis found expression; the other proceeding from the analogy between the multiple things signified (in mythologies, for example) to the unity of a structure whose formal transformations would yield up the diversity existing in the actual stories.[32]

Thus "classical" ethnology is volatilized and psychoanalysis is redefined. Reunited in a single theory, the two new disciplines, ethnology and psychoanalysis, would constitute a space of explication whose fundamental meaning begins from the point where, to cite Foucault again, they intersect at a right angle:

> For the signifying chain by which the unique experience of the individual is constituted is perpendicular to the formal system on the basis of which the significations of a culture are constituted: at any given instant, the structure proper to individual experience finds a certain number of possible choices (and of excluded possibilities) in the systems of the society; inversely, at each of their points of choice the social structures encounter a certain number of possible individuals (and others who are not) – just as the linear structure of language always produces a possible choice between several words or several phonemes at any given moment (but excludes all the others).[33]

The theoretical solidity of this project is merely apparent. It might conveniently provide a foundation and justification for new research perspectives; but how would it negate the reductionism that seems inherent in most of the sciences, or the hallucinatory ethnocentrism that takes root in every explanatory series or network established in the human and social sciences? Bachelard's remark on the psychiatrist's reductive power brings us back to the question: "What illumination does psychiatry gain by giving names to the complexes of Oedipus, Clytemnestra, Orestes, Diana ... ? Are these not so many artificial and generalized lights liable to error concerning the infinity of details, the indomitable individuality of the patient?"[34]

The sciences, in order to be sciences, presuppose another power: that of naming; whence, as we have seen, the importance of terminology. Technical frameworks, practical arrangements, ways of doing, understanding, and interpreting have been named once and for all. Terms which are univocal, in the best of cases, have come to designate wounds and defects, actions and wills, innocence and malignancy, modes of behavior and types of thoughts or dreams, etc. The power of naming organizes two superimposed systems – the system of facts and that of terminology – and an intelligent arrangement of terminology is considered the best introduction to the facts. The Greeks said "hupar" and "onar" to name distinct types of experience, which Freud believed he had reunited by establishing modes of integration, implication, and similitude.[35] But who can be sure that each experience is not rigorously unique within its proper sphere? And how should we understand that explication is supposed to be established on the basis of universal symbolic continuities, whose guarantor is a power or force completely enclosed within a terminology, within a denomination?

Jean-Bertrand Pontalis insists that, among other traits, contemporary psychoanalytic language is with few exceptions the product of one sole thinker: Freud. Its elements can thus only reveal their true function inside of Freudian "discourse."[36] That is to say, this language is the product of a particular consciousness, of a given cultural setting. Having reached a point where it functions smoothly and with relative generality, it is able to name – especially with the help of frequent metaphors – and to be questioned on the validity of its naming. But is it scientifically universal to the point that it can be considered

A Sign, a Scent

the only language able to manifest and make transparent the meaning of any given situation?

This question leads directly to another trait of psychoanalytic language mentioned by Pontalis:

> If we must maintain at once (following Conrad Stein) that Freud's psychoanalytic theory has a proper object that it cannot share with any other theory, and that this object does not coincide with any other sector of our knowledge, then this status, which remains to be defined and on which psychoanalysts are far from agreement, cannot but also reflect on the status of psychoanalytic language. One may be tempted either to accentuate its technicity – to mark its strict dependence on the location of psychopathology or the therapeutic situation – or, on the contrary, to emphasize the fecundity of Freudian concepts – in their very definition – beyond their place of origin.[37]

Cavalierly, I would say that language has no value in itself. It is not by putting psychoanalytic concepts into a few syllogisms that one does psychoanalysis, or that one can expect to explain history – as is commonly done – in terms (terminological aspect) of human nature.[38]

* * *

Devereux's discourse, which I have taken as an example (in short, what is in question is just as much ethnopsychiatric, ethnological, or psychoanalytic discourse in general), represses otherness in the silence of the "same," in the name of a human nature. The most obvious aspect of this repression is neither particular nor proper to this project. It marks any knowledge whose tendency is to take a group of humans as its object, and to establish from the beginning, explicitly or implicitly, a single location from which order is ordered, meaning is given, and the human is offered up to thought. Félix Guattari recently declared that "only a group engaged in revolutionary praxis can function as an analytical vacuole, alongside the processes of society, without any mission of leadership, without any pretention other than that of taking truth along paths from which people generally strive firmly to exclude it."[39] Concretely, what we Africans must do is to engage science, starting with the human and social sciences, and to grasp its tensions. We must reanalyze its contingent supports and sites of enunciation for ourselves, to learn what new meanings and what routes we can propose in our quest for a discourse that will justify us as singular existences engaged in a history that is itself singular. In short, we must rid ourselves of the "scent" of an abusive father: the scent of an order, of an essential region, one which is particular to a culture but is paradoxically proffered and lived as fundamental to all humanity. And in relation to this culture, if we are to fulfill ourselves, we must put ourselves in a state of major excommunication, to speak up and produce "differently."

Jacques Lacan gives me reason to hope:

> To start again from the praxis, to ask ourselves, knowing that praxis delimits a field, whether it is at the level of this field that the modern scientist, who is not a man who knows a lot about everything, is to be specified. I do not accept Duhem's demand that every science should refer to a unitary, or world, system – a reference that is always in fact more or less idealist, since it is a reference to the need of identification. I would even go so far as to say that we can dispense with the implicit transcendental element in the position of the positivist, which always refers to some ultimate unity of all the fields.[40]

2
What Order of African Discourse?

Yesterday, our older brothers – who are in fact our fathers, in literature and philosophy as in politics – demanded the right to life. Today, we know their Stations of the Cross almost by rote, and have learned to recite summaries of their discourse from memory. We know that our initiatives unfold in the literary, philosophical, or political fields that they cleared and worked. Moved by the intoxication of our speech, we believe (is this simple generosity, or naive ambition?) that we are now able to name – and so definitively negate, go around, or surpass – the essential paradox that marked the liberation of "*la parole nègre*." Léopold Sendor Senghor outlined this paradox well: our ancestors are those who saved us from despair by revealing to us our own riches.

We thus know that négritude, that extraordinary protest against the reification of the Black, emerged from the problematic of a particular turn in European history, characterized among other traits by the principle of cultural relativism. Centered on the subject, focusing by preference on subjective awareness, promoting the concrete in opposition to the abstract tradition, developing skepticism, relativism, and the meaning and value of freedom and the existential – the great philosophical systems in fashion in Europe between 1920 and 1945 seemed to negate the order of traditional truths. They gave the impression of radically questioning the claim to universality of the absolute canons of

Western Christian civilization. In this atmosphere, new perspectives could emerge and be presented – in particular, cultural values and systems of any origin, as Senghor shows in his *Pierre Teilhard de Chardin et la politique africaine* [Pierre Teilhard de Chardin and African Politics]. Senghor emphasizes the role of anthropology, and more precisely of anthropological perspectives. With their attention to difference, the Frobeniuses and Delafosses offered reasons for self-affirmation, in opposition to surrounding ideology, to young Blacks who had been forced by colonization to unlearn what it truly meant to be African. "This was far-reaching," Senghor writes:

> We had rediscovered our pride. Supported by the work of anthropologists, prehistorians, ethnologists ... we proclaimed ourselves, with the poet Aimé Césaire, "the Elder sons of the Earth." Had we not dominated the world up to and including the Neolithic, and fertilized the civilizations of the Nile and the Euphrates, before we became innocent victims of white Barbarians, nomads flowing out of their frozen Euroasiatic plateaus? I confess, our pride could quickly transform into racism. Even Nazism might be accepted if it strengthened our refusal to cooperate.[1]

Négritude is a claiming of the rights of the African; but as Senghor notes in this book, it is just as much an affirmation, founded on Geography and History, of the totality of values – political, moral, social, cultural – of the Black World. It is thus a formation of strategies for a "coherence of theory" and a "fecundity of praxis."

* * *

In exemplary fashion, Senghor's discourse shows us the problems we run against today when dealing with foundations of the social and human sciences in Africa.

In order to better mark what might be involved in a reformulation of these sciences, I would like to make a detour. First, I will analyze the general argument of the inaugural lecture given at the Collège de France by Michel Foucault. It will easily be agreed, given the importance, originality, and influence of his works, that he can be considered a noteworthy symbol of the royalty of this Western thought we would like to be rid of. I will then list several contemporary questions, to help us understand what order of discourse we might dream of for more African social and human sciences.

Foucault judges that

> Ever since the sophists' tricks and influence were excluded, and since their paradoxes have been more or less safely muted, it seems that Western thought has taken care to ensure that discourse should occupy the smallest possible space between thought and speech. Western thought seems to have made sure that the act of discoursing should appear to be no more than a certain bridging between thinking and speaking – a thought dressed in its signs and made visible by means of words, or conversely the very structure of language put into action and producing a meaning-effect.[2]

So, then: in Western philosophical thought, dating back to its oldest systems, there is a remarkable and systematic elision of the reality of discourse. Despite the extreme variety of forms and themes, its many diverse currents and projects have set up discourse in a game of self-annulment. More recently, these have included: the philosophy of the founding subject – the subject "given the task of directly animating the empty forms of language with his aims," who "in his relation to meaning ... has at his disposal signs, marks, traces, letters, but does not need to pass via the singular instance of discourse in order to manifest them";[3] the philosophy of originating experience, which

> supposes that at the very basis of experience, even before it could be grasped in the form of a cogito, there were prior significations – in a sense, already said – wandering around in the world, arranging it all around us and opening it up from the outset to a sort of primitive recognition. ... If there is discourse, then, what can it legitimately be other than a discreet reading?

and, finally, the philosophy of universal mediation, another organization that elides the reality of discourse, "despite appearances to the contrary":

> For it would seem at first glance that by rediscovering everywhere the movement of a logos which elevates particularities to the status of concepts and allows immediate consciousness to unfurl in the end the whole rationality of the world, one puts discourse itself at the centre of one's speculation. But this logos, in fact, is only a discourse that has already been told, or rather it is things themselves, and

events, which imperceptibly turn themselves into discourse as they unfold the secret of their own essence.[4]

One can only be astonished by the consistency and regularity of this elision of the reality of discourse in the Western tradition. Foucault hesitates: first, might it not seem that Western civilization, par excellence, past and present, is the one that has the most respected and honored discourse? This is only appearance. "It is," he notes, "just as if prohibitions, barriers, thresholds and limits had been set up in order to master, at least partly, the great proliferation of discourse, in order to remove from its richness the most dangerous part, and in order to organise its disorder according to figures which dodge what is most uncontrollable about it."[5]

Three great types of procedures of control preside over this limitation, which in the final analysis can only be an expression of a profound logophobia. Its outline and scansion, Foucault judges, differ between societies: "In every society the production of discourse is at once controlled, selected, organised and redistributed by a certain number of procedures whose role is to ward off its powers and dangers, to gain mastery over its chance events, to evade its ponderous, formidable materiality."[6]

First, there are external systems of exclusions. Their procedures put pressure on what in the discourse is related to power or to desire. They are:

- *prohibited speech*, which is an institutionalized limitation of the exercise of speech. One cannot say just anything to anyone, at any time: "In the taboo on the object of speech, and the ritual of the circumstances of speech, and the privileged or exclusive right of the speaking subject, we have the play of three types of prohibition which intersect, reinforce or compensate for each other, forming a complex grid which changes constantly."[7]
- *the division of madness*: a distinction and exclusion, in the mode of opposition, between reason and madness. "It is curious," Foucault remarks, "to note that for centuries in Europe the speech of the madman was either not heard at all or else taken for the word of truth. ... No doctor before the end of the eighteenth century had ever thought of finding out what was said (how it was said, why it was said), in this

speech which nonetheless determines the difference." Despite the attention doctors give to this speech today, it is not at all the case that "the old division is no longer operative."[8]
- *the will to truth* is also a principle of exclusion: it governs our will to knowledge. An examination of the history of the West shows that this will, like the other principles of exclusion, "is both reinforced and renewed by whole strata of practices, such as pedagogy, of course; and the system of books, publishing, libraries; learned societies in the past and laboratories now. But it is also renewed, no doubt more profoundly, by the way in which knowledge is put to work, valorised, distributed, and in a sense attributed, in a society."[9]

A second category of procedures that control and delimit discourse is more internal. These procedures function "as principles of classification, or ordering, of distribution, as if this time another dimension of discourse had to be mastered: that of events and chance."[10]

- *commentary*: "We may suspect that there is in all societies, with great consistency, a kind of gradation among discourses: those which are said in the ordinary course of days and exchanges, and which vanish as soon as they have been pronounced; and those which give rise to a certain number of speech-acts, which take them up, transform them or speak of them, in short, those discourses which, over and above their formulation, are said indefinitely, remain said, and are to be said again. ... They are religious or juridical texts, but also those texts (curious ones, when we consider their status) which are called 'literary'; and to certain extent, scientific texts."[11]
- *the author* as a principle of the rarefaction of discourse: "What he writes and what he does not write, what he sketches out, even by way of provisional drafts, as an outline of the oeuvre, and what he lets fall by way of commonplace remarks – this whole play of differences is prescribed by the author-function, as he receives it from his epoch, or as he modifies it in his turn."[12]
- *the organization of disciplines* likewise delimits discourse: in effect, "in a discipline, unlike a commentary, what is supposed at the outset is not a meaning which had to be rediscovered,

nor an identity which has to be repeated, but the requisites for the construction of new statements. For there to be a discipline, there must be the possibility of formulating new propositions, ad infinitum."[13] But a proposition belongs to a discipline only under certain conditions: before being true or false within a discipline, every proposition must be, as Canguilhem would say, "in the true."

A third group of procedures participates just as explicitly in the subjection of discourse. Foucault writes of these procedures that

> this time it is not a matter of mastering their powers or averting the unpredictability of their appearance, but of determining the condition of their application, of imposing a certain number of rules on the individuals who hold them, and thus of not permitting everyone to have access to them. There is a rarefaction, this time, of the speaking subjects; none shall enter the order of discourse if he does not satisfy certain requirements or if he is not, from the outset, qualified to do so.[14]

These procedures of subjection that distribute and specialize speaking subjects are:

- *ritual*, which defines "the qualifications which must be possessed by individuals who speak ... gestures, behaviour, circumstances, and the whole set of signs which must accompany discourse; finally, it fixes the supposed or imposed efficacity of the words, their effect on those to whom they are addressed, and the limits of their constraining value."[15]
- *societies of discourse*: while in today's Western society it would be difficult to find secret societies whose mission, like the groups of rhapsodists in antiquity, is to conserve and produce discourse, it is still useful to note that "even in the order of 'true' discourse, even in the order of discourse that is published and free from all ritual, there are still forms of appropriation of secrets, and non-interchangeable roles."[16]
- *doctrinal norms*: "Doctrine binds individuals to certain types of enunciation and consequently forbids them all others; but it uses, in return, certain types of enunciation to bind individuals among themselves, and to differentiate them by that very fact from all others."[17]

What Order of African Discourse? 25

- *the social appropriation of discourse*: "Although education may well be, by right, the instrument thanks to which any individual in a society like ours can have access to any kind of discourse whatever, this does not prevent it from following, as is well known, in its distribution, in what it allows and what it prevents, the lines marked out by social distances, oppositions and struggles. Any system of education is a political way of maintaining or modifying the appropriation of discourses, along with the knowledges and powers which they carry."[18]

These three complementary and powerful groups of procedures contribute directly and very concretely to the subjection of discourse. This, Foucault believes, is because "no doubt there is in our society, and, I imagine, in all others ... a sort of mute terror against ... the surging up of all these statements, against all that could be violent, discontinuous, pugnacious, disorderly as well, and perilous about them – against this great incessant and disordered buzzing of discourse."[19]

Foucault, giving himself the task of discussing this order, tells us that he made three firm decisions: "to call into question our will to truth, restore to discourse its character as an event, and finally throw off the sovereignty of the signifier."[20] To accomplish this, he operates in light of four methodological rules:

- *a principle of reversal*: contrary to tradition, where the origin of discourse is usually recognized he sees "the negative action of a cutting-up and a rarefaction of discourse."[21]
- *a principle of discontinuity*: discourses, he believes, should be treated as discontinuous practices that intersect and sometimes adjoin, but also may ignore or exclude each other.
- *a principle of specificity*: "We must conceive discourse as a violence which we do to things ... and it is in this practice that the events of a discourse find the principle of their regularity."[22]
- *a principle of exteriority*: contrary to the classical method that tends to bring forth meaning from discourse, one should rather "on the basis of discourse itself, its appearance and its regularity, go towards its external conditions of possibility, towards what gives rise to the aleatory series of these events, and fixes its limits."[23]

These four rules put forward four concepts: the *event*, the *series*, *regularity*, and *conditions of possibility*, which are opposed, respectively, to the classical operators of *creation*, *unity*, *originality*, and *signification*.

As I said, I chose Foucault's project because, within an African problematic, it helps us to think through the profusion of regulated discourses that surround and include us. In particular, I wanted to learn, from this mirror, what order and field our own analyses derive from. As I said, Foucault is a symbol; he is an excellent actualization of the Western knowledge of which we would like to rid ourselves. Posing him here at the entrance to our path is, to me, a blunt way of posing the most important problems we have to work on. For example: we may say that we wish to exercise a speech that is totally liberated, in line with a radically new perspective. But in this case, isn't the order of our discourse engaging methodological questions that preexist it – and many of which function according to the critical operations described by Foucault, following Hegel and Marx – without moving away from their problematic by even one iota? This question seems to me very close to another, more usual one: what conditions would allow an authentic African thinking to be "unblocked"? Such a thinking, on the one hand, would faithfully describe the order and norms of African discourses. On the other, it would substantiate Frantz Fanon's generosity of spirit in writing that "the density of history determines none of my acts. I am my own foundation."[24]

Confronted with Foucault's model, the initial temptation is to establish rules of application that could draw corresponding principles from African experience. By following Foucault's model and defining and circumscribing levels of language, frames of analysis, practical references, and concepts, we could mark divergences and resemblances between Western and African practices.

The methodology would be straightforward to establish. Set in the context of African culture, procedures like prohibition, the division of madness, the will to truth, rituals of speech, societies of discourse, doctrinal groups, and social appropriations of language would all lead to explicit formulations and concrete practices of subjecting discourse. These would seem to validate Foucault's analysis and prove the universality of his model.

On the other hand, applying the principles of commentary, the author, and scientific discipline as possible procedures of exclusion and control of discourse in African cultures might bring out notable differences. Any given culture might make use of one of these, or even two or all three principles; in some other culture, all might be absent. Among other questions – I am taking the easiest route here – these differences might seem to allow a certain type of hypothesis: given "evidence of linearity," either it can be concluded that the exercise of these principles is a function of determinate phases in the historical development of a people – here we would see the old thesis reappear on the horizon: "savages, contemporary ancestors of the West" – or else the stabilization of one or several of these principles as operators of control within a culture can be explained by the alterity of historical experience. In this case, the problem of universality would be posed starting from differences between the principles put into action in each culture.

We have reproached, and often quite violently, some of our elders for succumbing to this temptation – in particular, specialists in African religions and philosophies like Kagamé, Lufulwabo, Mulago, and to a lesser extent Mbiti. As we tell it, they simply and faithfully took up Western categories, concepts, schemas, and symbols and then drew out African "entities" from them. Their methodology and presuppositions were similar to those of ethnology or anthropology at the start of the century. Yes, their works tended to explicitly valorize African countries and societies – unlike the projects of evolutionary and primitivist anthropology and ethnology, which established hierarchies between human societies on the pretext of describing how savages organized their worlds. But, we tell ourselves, this was merely so that they could obtain a pedigree from the West for societies that had been disparaged, despised, and unjustly and definitively established in a position of absolute inferiority. So be it. Senghor has shown us how and for what reasons such an approach seemed justified. But whatever the case, criticism of these initiators of our African social and human sciences is generally either poorly formed or unfounded. It glides too easily over a central question: what does it mean to set the West at a distance, and what is the true cost of this distancing?

Once again Foucault, writing in relation to the Hegelian heritage, provides sentences that apply admirably to my argument. Where he writes "Hegel," I put "the West": to truly escape from the West presupposes an exact appreciation of the price we have to pay to detach ourselves from it; it presupposes knowing to what extent the West, perhaps insidiously, has drawn close to us; it implies a knowledge, in that which permits us to think against the West, of what remains Western; and a determination of the extent to which our recourse against the West is still possibly one of its tricks directed against us, at the end of which it waits for us, immobile and elsewhere.[25]

Precisely: the syncretic tendencies of the African initiators of our social and human science, like the reductive arrangements of racist ethnology; the fraternal generosity of the ethnophilosophy of Tempels and his disciples, like the methodological systems of contemporary anthropology; the rigor of the applications of neo-Marxism to the world of archaic and feudal production, like the violent demands of the "new African science" incarnated by Cheikh Anta Diop, Théophile Obenga, Ki-Zerbo, and many others – it seems to me that all of these are marked by a constant: they all aestheticize African culture, on the basis of and in terms of a "critical gaze" that, since the eighteenth century, has been the particular property of the West. The order of Western discourse, a perfectly delimited space, a function of a socio-economic structure and a cultural archaeology, accounts for and can only account for other cultures or other systems by reference to itself – and, it seems to me, not at all within the specificity of an experience that is irreducible to it.

In a recent book, *The Mirror of Production*, Jean Baudrillard's comments on materialism and ethnocentrism seem to lead in this direction. For instance:

> Western culture was the first to critically reflect upon itself (beginning in the eighteenth century). But the effect of this crisis was that it reflected on itself as a culture *in the universal*, and thus all other cultures were entered in its museum as vestiges of its own image. It "estheticized" them, reinterpreted them on its own model, and thus precluded the radical interrogation these "different" cultures implied for it. The limits of this culture "critique" are clear: its reflection on itself leads only to the universalization of its own principles.[26]

In presenting another order and other rules for the structuration and historicity of our societies, even as substitutes for ethnological speech the discourses of the social sciences in sub-Saharan Africa cannot avoid the most remarkable aestheticization. For instance: in the study of art, by both European and

African scholars of our generation, it is when they have tried to "restore" "works" to their magical and religious "context" that, as Baudrillard suggests, they have – in the most gentle but the most radical way in the world – transformed them into museum pieces. By inoculating them with the aesthetic category, they have neutralized objects which were not art at all, and whose non-aesthetic character might have been precisely, if seriously envisioned, the starting point for a *perspectivization* of Western culture that would be radical (rather than an *internal critique* that would lead only to expanded reproduction). Even when apparently set up as a counter-discourse – think of the beautiful despair of Diawara's *Manifeste de l'homme primitif* [Manifesto of Primitive Man] – these studies are situated in the critical space of an epistemological field and are under the sign of a totality, an order of discourse that they at once reflect and overflow.

Is it not significant that every classification of the sciences leads, inevitably, to the archaeological field where they were born and developed: the West?

What should we think of the fact that the "Africanization" of the sciences is thought only in terms of modes of application? The sciences of education, like the psychological sciences, merely revise parameters and analytical hypotheses, aiming for more specific performance measures and competencies. The practice of economic science seems to be nothing but a reproduction of the themes of unequal relations of dependence between international metropoles and African countries, at least when it does not become enmired in problematics of necessity and freedom. Do the juridical and moral sciences in our societies truly and functionally respond to the demands posed by the intersection of our past social formations, the contemporary context of modernity, and the effects of their complex articulation on individual behavior? Between sociology and anthropology, for more than a century, there has been an opposition – more ideological than scientific, in Jean Poirier's sense – between a science of collectivities based on rationalist motivations and a science of collectivities based on traditional motivations. These major ambiguities are held within a fundamental ambiguity: perhaps the meaning of the eclipse of the sociology of Saint-Simon and Auguste Comte during the age of Durkheim is very similar, in its reductive tendencies, to the waning of colonial sociological and anthropological practices.

Certainly – and this is a good thing – scholars of African history have shown in very concrete terms how to reconceive the organization of disciplines inherited from the West. Trying to remake African history from top to bottom, they have shown clever and subtle ways to de-structure doctrinal authority and the social appropriation of scientific discourse. They have even tried to reconceive the will to truth. What they are trying to accomplish is what Fanon called for when he wrote: "We would be overjoyed to learn of the existence of a correspondence between some black philosopher and Plato. But we can absolutely not see how this fact would change the lives of eight-year-old kids working in the cane fields of Martinique or Guadeloupe."[27] These new practices, following the pathways of a new kind of knowledge, may be able to advance new norms for an African will to truth. And by revising the order of discourse, they might explode the systems of exclusion and control in which the young Guadeloupean, like all the colonized, is enclosed.

Of course, as critical demands and generalities these new practices are inscribed in paths that fall methodologically under the scope of Foucault's analysis. They may support or oppose his project of the liberation of discourse. And to propose an image: perhaps the perspective of a new historical gaze, like that of Cheikh Anta Diop or Théophile Obenga, can take direction and meaning from Claude Lévi-Strauss's declaration in *Tristes Tropiques*:

> Knowledge is based neither on renunciation nor on barter; it consists rather in selecting *true* aspects, that is, those coinciding with the properties of my thought. Not, as the Neo-Kantians claimed, because my thought exercises an inevitable influence over things, but because it is itself an object. Being "of this world," it partakes of the same nature as the world.[28]

And what would be the truth of this, if not the beach of discourse where, despite differences in their temperaments, particularities, and projects, Cheikh Anta Diop offers his hand to Claude Lévi-Strauss?

Starting from this image, it is easy to see how we might study the demands of intellectual métissage, particularly in the light of the issues that Senghor so remarkably explored.

In addition, by attempting a radical linguistic revolution – the replacement of European languages by African languages – we may be able to bring about a total revision of the norms and modes of working. Will this cause a different and original order of discourse to appear? At any rate, a new, mixed, and rich world will come to light. From this perspective, when I think of the establishment of African human and social sciences – that is, as our scholars have already pointed to, practices and knowledges that are as much in harmony with the gradients of our cultures as with the postulates of our modernity – I ask myself, following Foucault: what is the status of this discourse, and what is its order? What sovereignty governs and orients it, and in what direction?

To answer these two questions would be already – very imperfectly, of course, but very concretely – a way of imagining a possible future.

By transplanting the knowledge they received from ancient Egypt into their own language, techniques, methods, and procedures, the instigators of ancient Greek thought were able to unleash a reorganization of knowledge and of life whose essential order is still alive and in motion – an order that, through the channel of the West, marks Africa today. In the same way, a change in the linguistic instruments of scientific knowledge and production in Africa will surely provoke an epistemological rupture and open the path to a new adventure.

Without doubt it would be useful for us, starting today – as a dream – to pause and think, in terms of this vector offered by language and its orders, of the possibilities that can be imagined. And we might tremble at the thought of encountering, even in imagination, systems of exclusion that express, if only symbolically, a will to truth supported by principles like the ones Foucault reminds of us, returning to ancient Greece: "Though arithmetic may well be the concern of democratic cities, because it teaches about the relations of equality, geometry alone must be taught in oligarchies, since it demonstrates the proportions within inequality."[29]

3
Theoretical Problems in the Social and Human Sciences

In the history of Western science, the social sciences are relatively young.[1] At any rate, their recognition as sciences – as rigorous disciplines working on singular objects – still seems highly uncertain, or at the very least under debate. The issue is that their objects of study are only with difficulty accepted as the precise themes of a knowledge that can be weighed, measured, and thoroughly verified, like those of the exact and natural sciences.

This uncertainty is troubling. Directly or indirectly, it means that the site where the social sciences are developed is obliged to be the reflection of another site. This other site provides the norms and rules that allow the experimental models and privileges of the so-called exact sciences to be adapted and applied. The duality of exact sciences vs. social and human sciences thus betrays a fundamental problematic, in which and by which the social sciences are only shadows of the more effective systems that haunt them.

Today as in the past, the social and human sciences, moral sciences, or sciences of the mind (*sciences de l'ésprit*, after the German *Geisteswissenschaften*) define themselves and limit their field of application and their particular methods in reference to the distance separating them from the rigor of the natural disciplines. In his *Essai sur la théorie de l'histoire en Allemagne contemporaine* [Essay on the Theory of History in Contemporary Germany], speaking as a representative of the humanist tradition,

Raymond Aron declares that "the sciences of the mind neither can nor should imitate the natural sciences, because the realities they study have a specific structure. The psychic totality is both a primary datum for observation and the condition of our consciousness. The originality of the moral sciences hangs on this fundamental fact."[2]

This exemplary appeal clearly intends to give the moral sciences a particular place and foundation. But has it not also functioned for a number of years now, as a review of certain contemporary theories would show, as a demand that we circumscribe a well-delineated space, situated at a remove from the one inhabited by the natural sciences? The demand for a difference in objects and methods curiously assumes a mistrust that, in a constant state of ambiguity, has united and separated the fields of natural science and the moral sciences. Helmholtz already noted this mistrust in the last century, commenting on Hegel's harsh attacks against Newton: the rigor of "scientists" seems to emerge from narrow-mindedness, and the finesse of humanists from a sweet reverie.

But the very violence that opposes the two fields is what, in the past and still today, provides attempts at methodological conciliation with their reason and mission. By comparing objects and methods, major differences are identified. In the process, possible analogies can be marked, clearing the way for the establishment of sets of procedures and rules that might "humanize" the natural sciences and certify the rigor and objectivity of the moral sciences. Still, we might ask to what extent these projects of synthesis are deployed only thanks to, and in terms of, the contradiction that Jules Lachelier in the nineteenth century traced back to a radical split. At root, he claimed, the opposition of Letters and Sciences is that of human subjectivity and the objectivity of nature. Similarly, despite the firmly unifying principle of his *Essai sur la philosophie des sciences* [Essay on the Philosophy of Science] (1834), Ampère established two types of parallel knowledge under two significant headings, *Mundus* and *Mens*.[3]

This duality seems to me a notable expression of the way that knowledge is covered over by culture. Or, to speak like Michel Foucault, it testifies to the vigor of a fundamental order, a positive ground on which general theories of the ordering of things are built, together with the interpretations they call for.

Even the naming of the social and human sciences leads to hesitation: human sciences? Moral sciences? Sciences of mind? What exactly do these encompass? What do they engage in, and what precisely are they meant to study? We are told that they deal with man, and a recent formulation – *les sciences de l'homme* [the sciences of man] – seems to say this clearly. But what is it that they study – and in what way are they concerned with man, and with what man?

Two recent definitions, proposed by eminent representatives of contemporary thought – Michel Foucault and Jacques Lacan – leave us perplexed.

Foucault:

> In a more general fashion, man for the human sciences is not that living being with a very particular form (a somewhat special physiology and an almost unique autonomy); he is that living being who, from within the life to which he entirely belongs and by which he is traversed in his whole being, constitutes representations by means of which he lives, and on the basis of which he possesses that strange capacity of being able to represent to himself precisely that life ... The human sciences are not, then, an analysis of what man is by nature; but rather an analysis that extends from what man is in his positivity (living, speaking, labouring being) to what enables this same being to know (or seek to know) what life is, in what the essence of labour and laws consist, and in what way he is able to speak.[4]

And Lacan: "There is no such thing as a science of man because science's man does not exist, only its subject does."[5]

I am not troubled by the meaning of these statements, which in sum privilege the observable characteristics of human behavior as the object of the social sciences. I also see that they are representative of the current Western perspective, and are enlightening when situated in the contemporary cultural context of the West. They help me understand how to justify the fact that human medicine, anatomy, or physiology are not sciences of man. They also show why the practice of the social sciences – rather than speaking of and accounting for the reality of life – is concerned only with those images and manifestations that individual or collective actions and behaviors are.

Posed as an object of science, and therefore as the object of scientific analysis and reasoning, this "social" is in principle conceived as a reality in itself. It is thus the possible object of a knowledge, which could be thought in relation to one or another of its manifestations. But wasn't this reality decomposed and cut up into layers, and very early on? First there was history, which englobed all the others. Then came sociology – for example, Le Play's – once it became necessary, particularly with the emergence of the bourgeois order, to distinguish past orders from present ones. With the discovery of "the savage," ethnology found its role and function in the West's quest for self-discovery. Finally, psychology and its therapeutic extensions emerged when it began to be clear that the meaning and value of individual or collective behavior do not necessarily express a conscious rationality.

The arbitrariness of these divisions becomes untenable from the moment we try to rigorously mark the borders of each discipline. Where does the line of demarcation pass between history and sociology, if we set aside the diachronic/synchronic dimension? What scientific justification is there for the coexistence of sociology and ethnology, apart from the imperial vocation of the West, which founded ethnology as "a science of communities, of groups centered on traditionalist motivations" in contrast to sociology, "a discipline interested in groups centered on rationalist motivations"?[6] In what way is the object of political science fundamentally different from that of sociology? At what precise moment does psychology cease to be social and become individual? Faced with the implications of these questions, we may wonder whether it will be necessary to extend to all the social sciences what Georges Politzer wrote in his *Critique of the Foundations of Psychology* in 1928: "The history of psychology in the last 50 years is not, as we are wont to assert at the beginning of psychology manuals, the history of an *organisation*, but one of *dissolution*."[7]

But the main problems of the social sciences do not only result from these divisions. More exactly, we could say that the divisions signify an essential contradiction: the pretension that the social can be reduced to an object of reasoning and theoretical mechanics, whose functioning could be calculated and predicted if its laws were mastered and its mechanisms known. But – thanks to the bankruptcy of the very investigative and interpretive techniques with which these sciences are endowed, and which they regularly but fruitlessly revise – it is becoming more and more clear that everything social evades these reductive procedures, and every other mode of objectivation. To take the social as object and claim to explain it also means to evacuate, to radically negate, the subject of experience. By doing this, as R. D. Laing writes, we "falsify our perception to adjust it to our concepts."[8] But as everyone knows, even specialists in the social sciences, "the human fact is irreducible to knowledge. It must be lived and produced."[9]

These contradictions are proper to all the social sciences. They belong particularly to sociology, whose project, to use an older definition – Auguste Comte's, which at least has the virtue of being clear – is the positive study of the totality of fundamental laws proper to social phenomena. The use of this discipline – like all the ones that flow or directly follow from it – is rarely innocent, in any society. Or better: the social order, whatever it may be, cannot remain neutral when it is "read." As well, by the exercise of its power and the complex unfolding of its prescriptions, every order also marks, orients, and determines the general line of research. This (sometimes) provokes "problems of conscience" for researchers – interior tensions that are customarily, out of convenience or ease, put down modestly and in good taste as confrontations between theoretical hypotheses.

All this is to quickly note a fact that, if analyzed attentively, might lead to a better understanding of the questionable relations that unite the researcher and their object of study. Before addressing these relations, however, it is worth considering whether a researcher's situation within a given society does not imprint a permanent mark on the work they produce. In an excellent book, Benoît Verhaegen has attempted to classify sociologists on this basis. He suggests, as a hypothesis, "that we classify sociologists into three categories: positivist, formalist, and engaged" – categories that more or less correspond to their social and geopolitical situation. He further distinguishes:

- an empirical, positivist sociology, practiced in "bureaucratic or totalitarian societies" (the United States, the Soviet Union) "whose factual results can always be reconciled with the political order";
- a formalist and uncommitted [*désengagée*] sociology, which consecrates the rupture between theory and practice (functionalism, structuralism, etc.) and is practiced in "the more liberal

zones [of the bureaucratic and totalitarian societies] and in Western societies of the second tier";
- a committed [*engagée*] sociology that tends to open onto political action, found "at the periphery of the Western and Soviet scientific worlds, among researchers whose objects of study are societies driven into change and political action in order to survive; for an engaged sociology, knowledge supposes an ever stronger reduction of the distance between the subject and object, up to their coincidence in revolutionary action."[10]

On first view, this classification is a bit facile: the schema it presents has an attractive theoretical purity, and does not seem to account for the complex and ambiguous relations that link Euro-America and the Third World. The diverse networks of economic dependence that unite the two groups are also guarantors of the cultural imperialism that ensures that, in new countries, the "boss" is a norm of scientificity elaborated, like every certified model of scientific practice, in the West. Thus in Africa empirico-positivist sociology and formalist sociology are often images and expressions of a discreet but effective power, set in action by good and brilliant students trained in the "White Man's School." Similarly, at the other end of the spectrum, the violence of totalitarian and bureaucratic structures sometimes generates practices that then become established as theories of praxis – for example René Lourau, Georges Lapassade, C. Wright Mills, etc.

The merit of this classification is that it sheds light on what we might call the "missions" of practitioners of the social sciences, viewed as a function of their social formations. Thus in Africa, under the cover of the universality of science discursive policies work, with a remarkable orthodoxy, to safeguard the gleaming surface of economic dependence and the pre-eminence of a particular order. Verhaegen's hypothetical classification also shows that in the case of empirical and formalist practices, currently seen as "scientifically exemplary," ideology adheres more or less explicitly. How, we might ask, could ideology be perfectly occluded from a territory that is not only the site from which it arises, but also its field of application par excellence: the social? Such a question is evocative in itself: it points to the function and role of social knowledge in a social body, and shows us how to understand the principle according to which "knowledge is the source of power." The usual corollary of this principle is the ignorance in which the "objects" of social knowledge are maintained, whether as mass, group, or individual.

If ideology is defined as a *ratio* that presides over and determines action, the social sciences are ideological in at least two senses. First, by their very object, to the extent that every social fact is dialectically marked by the dominant ideology and by ideology *in the making*. And second, by their discourses, which are at once mirrors and reflections of a given ideology. Indeed, everything takes place as if there were two parallel but complementary structures, of which one is base – social reality in the making – and the other surface – the discourses constructed by specialists. The problem then is to know how reality can correspond to the scholarly constructions that claim to account for it; and on the other hand, for formalist and positivist sociology, to know what "scientific" exercises might allow ideology to be evacuated.

Earlier, I connected the birth of social science to the emergence of the bourgeois order in the West. More rigorously, I would say with Pierre Lantz that

> sociology was born from an ambiguous project: to understand the reality of society in order to adapt politics to social transformation. The goal was to substitute for the "metaphysics" of the rights of man a social physiology, as Saint-Simon would say, that would make it possible to discern regressive pathological elements and sources of trouble – for example, political and economic direction by classes that have been overtaken by history – and to substitute for them ruling strata recruited from the productive elements of society.[11]

There is thus a relation between the development of social science and the affirmation of class struggle.[12] At the end of the nineteenth century, following in the wake of the drafts and theses produced under the Second Empire, sociology was a science of "Order." It was a discourse that redirected social energies toward the social ideal incarnated by bourgeois society and, in the opposite direction, invested this ideal in analyses that put constraints on social reality.

This will to power established two principles, which confirm each other in a circular reasoning: the universality of social

Theoretical Problems in the Social and Human Sciences 39

knowledge elaborated from Western societies and, as a corollary, the hierarchization of different societies on the basis of comparisons and analogies established in terms of the particular steps of European history. These principles animated the thesis of the West's civilizing mission, which among other things was used to justify the colonial enterprise, and still seems to cover neocolonial structures and projects today.

With Western society the society par excellence, Western history the history par excellence, and Western science the norm, the West then had to "invent" the primitive and thus ethnology. Social science was reserved for Western societies and their tentacles, such as urban phenomena in Africa.

The structuralist current in ethnology, by attempting to set the West at a distance, tries to be the reflection of a respectful gaze on difference, and so to study different societies for themselves and in themselves. And yet here too the fundamental problem is still the relation between Western culture and other cultures. In terms of method, as Anouar Abdel-Malek shows, a century's worth of refining the tools of analysis has not changed the nature of the analytic enterprise. During the Enlightenment as in our day, it emerges from the will to universalism, the postulate that all social phenomena can be immediately reduced to the same grid.[13]

We can see, across the questions we have pursued thus far, the problems faced by the social sciences in Africa, first to present themselves as "sciences," and then to truly be "sciences." Must the African researcher *necessarily* be positivist, formalist, or committed? Where will he or she find the criteria and reasons for such a choice? And whatever they choose, will that choice be innocent? The alienation of African specialists in the social sciences can be so strong that they may not even sense that there is a problem – their problem and their society's, but also a problem for the science that they practice. In all good faith and with exemplary rigor, it is possible that they may turn a Westerner's gaze on Africa, and all their research and publications may be nothing but reassurances of Western ideology.

When it comes to the relations between social science and economic and political power, the problems are no doubt apparently the same in the West and in Africa. This concordance has the merit of showing that, here or there, no one can maintain innocence when practicing the social sciences. This allows us to rigorously interrogate the levels at which the power–knowledge articulation is situated in Africa.

Furthermore, when any African researcher considers their scientific practice, they must pause at least briefly on the following trivialities: the West created the "savage" in order to "civilize"; "underdevelopment" in order to "develop"; "the primitive" in order to do "ethnology." These banal phrases hide crushing models, which must be accepted or rejected. To accept them implies, notably, a model of development as adjustment to the economic, social, and political evolution of the West. In this case, the role of the social sciences will be to serve as an auxiliary to this program, and to the political prospects of the dominant classes. To reject them is to choose "adventure" over "science," uncertainty over intellectual security. But it is also to opt for a promise: that of being able to produce "a science from within," of becoming integrated into the true complexity of African social formations and taking them up no longer as exact copies of Western history but in their cultural and historical specificity. It is to conceive of Africa as able to be something other than a margin of the West, as able to claim a different future than that of an underdeveloped zone, a guarantor of Western development. Finally and above all, it is to want the social sciences to be more than mere collectors of supposedly objective information; it is to want them to be a genuine revelation of social dynamism and the site of a permanent coming to consciousness and to speech.

In sum, these sciences must be remade from top to bottom, beginning by breaking open the languages that are hermetically sealed off from the people who are "objects" of their knowledge. These languages are at the service of a class power, and in Africa this is only too often the power of those installed to faithfully apply models of underdevelopment. Thus the problem of the social sciences in Africa is definitively a political problem: which master to choose? The imperialist ideology of the West, or service to the future of Africa?

4
Christianity: A Question of Life?

Today, "Christianity as seen by an African" is a well-worm theme. It is generally approached in relation either to African tradition, or to colonization or colonialism. Most of the time, it leads either to the demonstration of a serious incompatibility between Africanity and Christianity, or to the establishment of possible ways and means for a successful integration of Christianity into African cultures.

Here I would like to try to revive interest in the debate by giving full force to the idea of the encounter of differences, and so to arrive at an understanding of Christianity as a cultural phenomenon that, in Africa, actualizes the experience of conflict.

* * *

"To go," writes Michel de Certeau, "to leave the narrow borders of the countries where the Lord already lives visibly, to take a step outside of closed groups and well-established societies. To leave everything, to go and declare to the ignorant the Word that God has addressed to them, and which will open up their existence."[1] Such is the classic and traditional image of the mission. It involves three major notions: rupture with a cultural milieu, a voyage toward far-off lands, and lastly the project of converting "pagan peoples" to the truth of Christianity.

Even in the missionary's own description, rupture is the very foundation of his project and vocation. It is defined by the distance he takes from his family and his place of origin, and it becomes concretized in the particular orientation of his life project. The primacy he gives to the spiritual, and the call he feels he has received to participate in the extension of the "kingdom," explain both the objective distancing and the interior detachment he is required to perform. In the particular logic of this engagement, the foreign mission to which the missionary candidate decides to dedicate himself is not only a plan of action. Much more often, it should be considered the end point of a "personal call" that he feels at the deepest level of his being. Two breaks constitute the stringent conditions that precede his "departure." First of all, the young apostle must "exit" his family environment and "enter" a world, an "order," that will prepare him for departure. Then, after completing that preparation, he must "leave" this world, the last glimpse of his cultural universe, to "take on" and confront "his mission." From the point of departure, there are then two aspects: the departure for foreign lands itself and the announcing of the Gospel to the gentiles.

The idea of the voyage that intervenes here implies multiple values, as I have shown elsewhere:[2] the path, the journey at sea, displacement, exploration, route, trajectory, crossing, etc. These are merely so many notes in the semantic field of the term "voyage," whose full meaning takes shape by giving rise to subtle relations of inclusion and exclusion between the various signifieds. But, by the power of words, it also opens a window onto intertwining values, the ambiguities of both the term and the person who makes the voyage, who is transported and transposed into an elsewhere. Finally, it means the possibility of seeing the voyager as someone who, by taking distance from a physical, intellectual, or spiritual environment, becomes engulfed by this elsewhere.

On his return, because he has glimpsed another world, the voyager generally considers himself able to competently develop and transmit an original discourse about this world. In the majority of cases, this discourse is presented by its author as knowledge, and is received as such by the non-voyagers, those who stayed at home. From Herodotus to Father Huc, from Goethe to contemporary travel narratives, it is clear that

Christianity: A Question of Life? 43

voyagers' accounts and reminiscences are explicitly intended to present knowledge in the mode of revelation, the revelation of a remarkable world or experience.

I will be told that "mission" does not necessarily imply "voyage," and will be shown facile counterexamples: thus, for example, Thérèse de Lisieux, a Carmelite nun who never left her native Normandy, became a "patroness" of missions. I hold to the original value of the term, which is also the word's etymological meaning: *missio* derives from *mitto*, which signifies "let go, let leave, release, throw."

The voyage, or at least the symbolism of the initial voyage, signifies all the preceding ruptures. It seems to give the missionary the right to "incarnate" the truth that he speaks and is planning to carry to distant lands. As witness to a "kingdom," he assumes its exigencies, and he explains it in his preaching, as in his works, in the light of his "Faith." But in reality, speech as testimony of the missionary's life is regulated by reference to reflectors that are external to the "Faith." These reflectors are "models," discreet but imperative. At times they may coincide with the constitutive elements of the norm that Wundt defined through three fundamental classes: logical thought (the idea of truth), voluntary activity (the idea of the good), and free representation or sentiment (the idea of beauty).

Witness to "the truth," the missionary approaches "the mission field" as a "guide": his project is, at once, to reflect a message, "the" message, and to lead the pagans to knowledge of the one truth. The paths he points out, with the aid of sacred books and the teachings of the magisterium, are signaled by effects that refer explicitly to Christian ethics and aesthetics – that is, to serial ideas that are indefinitely renewed by the ways that Western culture lives the propositions of the Gospels.

The missionary, any missionary, thus

> carries a heavy load. He profits from the work of many centuries. His knowledge of the Faith is inscribed in the tradition within which, at length, the language that he will take up in turn has been elaborated. His very sensibility was formed and flourished within a familial and cultural environment. He wants to transmit universal truth, but can do so only by way of his particular experience; and this experience makes him, in the country to which he travels, a stranger.[3]

Paradoxical notions, then, the mission and the missionary who actualizes it: they are comprehensible only at a distance marked by departure and rupture, but they are thinkable only by reference to the original milieu that made them possible. They authorize the transfer of a spiritual project that is considered "universal," but in reality they account for and can only account for archaeological configurations of the cultural space that supports them. Perhaps this is the source of the mission's fundamental ambiguity: it is the reduction of the "pagan." Or at any rate, concretely, it is the formulation of relations of comparison between the "elaborated and coherent" dogma of Christianity and the "disordered" beliefs of the pagan, in the light of "exemplary" Christian morality opposed to the "aberrations" of pagan behaviors, etc. By fixing the boundaries of difference, these relations explain the effectiveness of this reduction – that is to say, of this violence that is the passage from the "pagan universe" to the "Christian universe." In its classic and traditional form, the mission is also expressed through definitions of the relation to the other, the pagan who is to be "conquered" or "led to baptism."

One could thus say, with a play on words, that the "missionary complex" lies fundamentally in this: the ruptures that it presupposes, like the relations that it establishes, lead and can only lead to the reconstitution and reproduction in foreign lands of the cultural preconditions that are its foundation. From here, the problem is to know what the missionary "can" say, and what, exactly, the Faith he thinks he is proclaiming means.

* * *

The missionary speaks. He speaks and writes a great deal. On one side are testimonials and relations of his sojourn in a distant land, autobiographical narratives, reflections on the foundation or aim of the mission, and explanations of how the mission can move forward according to the spirit of directives from the Propaganda Fide, and, at times, instructions from his "superiors." On the other are sermons, religious instruction, interpretations of Scripture, catechismal research and adaptation, and summary works of introduction to "Western Christian culture." These are addressed primarily to the edification of the "Christianized" and the possible interest of the "Christianizable" in the country of the mission.

Subject of a singular speech, the missionary sovereignly defines the space of his own speech. He acknowledges – or more exactly, he recognizes – a double duty: first, to ward off all challenges in a foreign land by clearly establishing grids of orthodoxy for his actions; from which his program *ad extra*. Then, second, to articulate among the "savages," as profoundly as he can, the sense of the "Catholic mission" and to demonstrate, with proofs at hand, the scope of "Christian generosity"; from which his program *ad intra*.[4]

In the program *ad extra* the missionary, while trying scrupulously fulfill the rule of obedience to the primacy of "Saint Peter," regulates himself at the same time according to other instances: an "Order," a "homeland," and even on occasion a "social class." All of these are useful in animating the "charity" of the people of the old Christendoms of the West, to the advantage of his program *ad intra*. This latter program is above all a human enterprise of conquest, the complexities of whose determinations quite often align, in scholarly coherence, with a plethora of evangelical pretexts circumstantial to the interests of appropriating goods and expanding capital, according to the basic formulas of the capitalist mode of production. But one of his speeches does assume this economic risk: one that paraphrases the Gospels in the light of Western history; that recites the epic of Jesus Christ through the readings and strategic interpretations hallucinated by the cultures of the West ever since the Constantinization of Catholicism – that is, ever since the strange de facto fusion of the symbols of Christianity and the signs of empire.

When he speaks of "his Faith," of course, the missionary is not always conscious of giving a cultural recital. In good faith, he believes he is truthfully conveying the object of scriptural norms. But his speech is there: and if it is attentively followed it will appear that, just as the ceremonials of liturgy have for some time reenacted medieval rites and duties in honor of the emperor or prince, the missionary's speech doubles another, silent, discourse. This is the discourse that still today organizes the meaning of those "units" of Christian life piously conserved in museums (at Saint Peter's, the Vatican, the Vatican Library, the Via dei Cerchi in Rome, the Doge's Palace in Venice, etc.) and ancient churches (such as the great Roman basilicas), or presented on the doors of churches (think of the series of discourses that unfurl along the doors of Saint Peter's, San Lorenzo in Lucina, Santa Maria in Trastevere, Santa Cecilia, etc.) and in cloisters and diverse other constructions: crypts, grottos, cemeteries, monuments, etc.

In this speech, which claims to speak the Gospels, the message thus tends to be obscured by the history of a "Christian culture." The missionary is a prisoner of a complex of enunciations that are always already given – institutional texts, dogmatic propositions, doctrinal ensembles, groups of aesthetic relations, a history of ideas, etc. By his ethnic origin, culture, and training, he is enclosed within the space of an archaeological field that has "digested" the word of Jesus Christ. He can therefore *say nothing* to the "gentiles": what he speaks of is not an original Jesus Christ, but an "encultured" one. What he believes that he has heard and wants to communicate is not the Word of Christ, but a cultural and historical reading of the Gospels. The Christ who constitutes the object of his monologue to the pagan exists and could only have existed, for him, through a relay of indefinite, contradictory formulations in an intellectual and spiritual genealogy formed within permanent and distinct commentary on a particular historical period and geographical territory. The Message has been "colonized" – that is to say, arranged, formed, assumed, and very rigorously governed – by a particular history to the point that it has melted into the fluidity and cadence of its breathing. This is the site from which the missionary speaks, and the statements he offers report only on the site that made them possible.

Given all this, what, in truth, does the missionary say? The Faith he brandishes regularly is neither a philosophical category nor an interpretation that can be shared: it is personal, and not at all communicable. There thus remains nothing but "Christianity," that is to say "the system": the synchronic pyramid with its spirit, its exterior signs, its laws, its instruments of human and spiritual advancement; or the tradition and history of the monumental body called the Church, with its conflicts and misfortunes. To bear witness to this, it is thought, is a way to perpetuate the truth that came from Israel. And thus the mission *ad intra*, incapable of living a dialogue it could undertake only by destroying itself, makes itself explicit in a politics of expanding an ideological structure, Christianity. No doubt the remarkable importance the mission places on its works (schools, hospitals, orphanages, printing presses, etc.) derives from here.

These become the primary means of enunciating a *savoir-être*, a way of living, and a model of knowledge that have all been conceived, or so it is said, in the light of "Christian experience." It is thought that these works will guide others to the Faith; and the historic example of the Christian West and its most vivid representations will assure the permanence of the "spirit" of Christianity, if it can be successfully inscribed in the pagan tunic.

A critical testimonial from 1960:

> The mission is no longer the humble dwelling-cum-chapel where the first missionary spent so much time in work and prayer. It now has a fine church, recalling amid the tropical storms the Gothic architecture of the missionary's native land. It possesses huge buildings for the accommodation of men and stores. It is surrounded by gardens and plantations which bring in quite a good income. It has its own garage and workshops. It will almost certainly have a dispensary, or even a hospital, complete with dental surgery. The sound of children's voices will be heard, for every mission has its school. A whole world revolves round the tower of the church: the mission, half monastery, half parish. It might even fulfil only too well the theocratic dream in which few missionaries swear that they have never indulged, if only for a moment: the old dream of happiness on earth while we wait for happiness in heaven. It is the happiness of a people sheltering in the folds of an ecclesiastical robe, a robe as soft and clean as a mother's dress; happiness in the homely surroundings of the nearby sanctuary, under the authority of the ever-present priest. Shades of Paraguay![5]

How can it be said that this is still a matter of witnessing Jesus Christ? While what is haphazardly set in place – strongly reinforced by biblical citations, references to pontifical documents, and humanitarian appeals, but also by truly exemplary injections of finance – seems instead to display, on the one hand, the most skillful techniques of psychological conditioning, and on the other, a restructuring and Africanization of something that the West has already lived.

Above and below the vicissitudes of the mission itself, the program *ad extra* most visibly maintains the coherence of the missionary project. The complex play of ideology, right, and meaning that characterizes the missionary enterprise is assembled and organized, according to precise rules, on two major and highly interdependent levels. The first is explication, articulated in constant dealings with civil or ecclesiastical authorities in the metropole, and in the "relations" or reports on the life and progress of "the mission" commissioned by the Sacred Congregation of the Propaganda Fide. In general, this fantastic body of texts responds to the missionary's apparently simple questions: what have I been doing in this distant country? What has been the aim of my actions? To what extent have my speech and action contributed to "expanding" the "kingdom"? These questions, as we have seen, also reflect the difficulty experienced by thousands of missionaries in reconciling their "apostolic" project and a "civilizing" aim. But on the level we are discussing here, these questions are merely addresses presented to the princes or to the magistrate. They obey an imperative: the demand to give account.

In parallel, through the mediation of metropolitan support organizations, the missionary "maintains" a whole literature meant to make its readers feel admiration for "his gesture," compassion for his difficulties, and pity for "the pagan and miserable people" he must evangelize. This "propaganda" literature already troubled Benedict XV, who saw it as scandalously affirming the interests of nations to the detriment of the universal vocation of Catholicism.[6] But it is a flourishing literature, which, in addition to ensuring additional support and financing, propagates and diffuses a certain image of the mission, the missionary, and the evangelized.

Two brief illustrations will show that, from the past up to today, both the "relation" presented to the prince and the review article offered to the curiosity of European Christians are cultural codes. They establish and found the mission through an endlessly renewed performance of Western culture and ideological presuppositions unduly attached to biblical texts.

First: the *Relations* of the Italian Capuchin Fathers, missionaries in the Congo between 1645 and 1700,[7] set to work two principal thematics, one biblical and one cultural. The essential motifs of the first are "the vine," "the construction of the kingdom," and the norms of "the life, the truth, and the way." The untamed forest is a vineyard, worked by laborers from across the seas. Few in number, confronted with the immensity of their task and the maleficence of nature – intensified by the malignity of an Enemy who arrived before them – they claim to incarnate the way toward the light. For an audience in Rome, they transcribe the dignity of their presence in this "savage," "cruel," "insalubrious" universe, inhabited by Blacks in "strange costumes," with "Satanic" morals and a "blocked" intelligence that makes them close to "animals." The cultural thematic grasps onto these biblical motifs: how can they "open the eyes" of the pagans and lead them to the light? The pagan world, in the missionaries' estimation, is a sick universe to which "health" must be brought; a world "in disorder," "mad," "furious," subjected to "rage," to "diabolical illusions," a world in which they must establish the "eternal" order, measure, and norms of truth and morality. It is also a "primitive" universe that must be transformed: led from "bestiality" to "humanity," from "barbarism" and "savagery" to "urbanity," from the "lies of sorcery and fetishism" to the lights of "reason" and "the Faith."

Here is, quite neatly, "a code": the production of a specific cultural and spiritual community which, under the guise of promoting an abandoned humanity, contributes very concretely to "the illustration of a culture."[8] In reality, the discourses under discussion do not define any new field; although they speak of a "savage" context, they merely actualize an ancient symbolism by reciting the traditional discursive practices of the missionary West.

Second: nineteenth- and twentieth-century missionary periodicals celebrate the extension of a cultural system by narrating the myth of the gap between "the White Christian" and the "pagan man of color," between "the civilized" and the "savage." The missionary, as liaison between the two universes, is considered "the champion of the good," "the herald of the faith amongst barbarous populations," "the father" of the people who are to be Christianized. Paternalism, we might say; this is an attitude "conditioned by a society that favours relations of a vertical type" and reflects "an ambient paternalism, product of faith in the educational vocation of Europe."[9]

Faced with the stranger, the pagan, the missionary's speech can mean nothing else. It is offered as the sign of a cultural limit, but it wrongly imposes itself as the expression of a truth. God, Jesus Christ, the Church, and even the Faith of the missionary all derive from a culture, and this culture is what the speech testifies to. The "despair" of a Tempels or the temptations of a Dournes find their meaning here, in the objective impossibility of dialogue: in reality, the missionary has strictly nothing to communicate, has no revelation to unveil that would not essentially belong to the order of his own accumulated human experience.[10]

God, Jesus Christ, and the Gospels thus seem to be no more than pre-texts for a speech enmired in the circulation of a few cultural myths, those of one civilization. So then, as de Certeau writes, if "the pagans are to believe in a God preached by a messenger from somewhere else, the missionary must make himself docile before the presence signified to him by a people among whom he is out of place."[11] Or, no doubt more precisely, among whom he ought to make himself "out of place," by relying on silence. But no, he speaks – depending on the circumstance, he offers a firm and assured voice or chains of tautological propositions. On occasion, to prove his sincerity, he invokes – the supreme argument – his fellow brothers' death or his own death in ultimate sacrifice for the "mission." I will repeat what I have said elsewhere: "We have the right not to believe these 'witnesses' who have gotten themselves slaughtered (however ignominious the killers may be: there are too many of them, and of all sorts). By dying, they prove their courage, not the truth of what they affirm."[12]

* * *

The mission is a multivalent field. Instigated by the West, it is not surprising that its central elements and ordinating codes would lead back to this space. The problem, if there is one, lies in its transplantation. We could therefore distinguish two groups of questions. There are questions about "the mission's" project, which is to overflow beyond its initial space. The meaning and foundation of these will generally be found in Scripture. Then there are circumstantial questions that result from the actualization of the mission in African territory. In theory, both refer to the program of promoting a "new form" of salvation; but they can be measured most clearly in declarations of the conquering dynamism of Western civilization. Together, the two groups of questions account for the ways in which "evangelization" is effectively exercised. On the one hand, older African traditions are erased by being repressed or covered up. On the other, processes are established to integrate Christianity and colonization. These questions also define or determine the strange fields where new ideological ways of speaking the Westernization of Africa take shape.

The hierarchy of Christian churches in Africa has been very largely Africanized. The philosophy of "the mission" has attempted to update itself, and has produced new concepts (Africanization, indigenization, "toothing stones,"[13] etc.) that, with unequal success and by replacing earlier languages, have animated and are now attempting to organize the founding discourse of the project of "tropicalizing" Christianity. The liturgy has been opened up to accommodate African gravities and forms of living, and in often patently artificial structures it combines Western scenography and Black antecedents. The urgency of adaptation has encountered the imperatives of alterity, and current studies – sometimes questionable – proclaim in harmonious agreement that it is useful to respect different traditions and collective identities. But I am not at all sure that these quests can all be explained by the same discursive principle. I would rather be inclined to agree with Michel Foucault, who said – thinking of the foundational discourses of the principle of evolution – that "identity is not a criterion even when it is exhausted; even less so when it is partial, when words are used each time in the same sense, or when the same nucleus of meaning is apprehended through different words."[14] Thus, to paraphrase Foucault, beneath the phrasings of theological or pastoral writings on indigenization, adaptation, toothing stones, Africanization, etc., only the analogy is an effect of the discursive field in which they are found.

Whatever the case, the currently ongoing program of "tropicalizing" Christianity – which is the work of African theologians – prompts me to note two important problems facing the "interior" mission of African Christianity. The first has to do with the principle of "tropicalization" itself, and the second with the policies that have been set in motion to actualize this tropicalization.

If we agree to dissociate "Christianity" and "Faith in Jesus Christ," and admit that the order of Christianity, in its themes as in its historical trajectory, does not necessarily coincide with those of the axioms of the Faith, then what reasons are there to shake off the systematicities and distortions of "Western Christianity"? In theory, it would be enough to return directly to the texts and sources of the Revelation to establish the guiding principles of the Message. At the same time, again in theory and in complementary fashion, new attention to African traditions would open up different expanses, where the truth of God might be – why not? – the explosion of Jesus Christ. The Gospels could be read with increased visibility and independence, autonomous from the commentaries of the Church Fathers and equally indifferent to the strategic directives of the Latin Church. At the same time, it would be acknowledged that African peoples have had uninterrupted states of religious maturity which, in their own unique archaeological derivations, bear witness to a unique and universal God. In this perspective, at one moment or another the essential question would need to be broached: why do we need the relay or mediation of the Nazarene, if the God who gives himself to be recognized and lived in African thought is the True, Unique, Universal God, Creator of heaven and earth, Master of life, death, and the universe?

On the contrary, we could refuse to dissociate "Christianity" and "Faith in Jesus Christ," and conceive of them instead in a dialectical unity, seeing their coexistence in the discursive formulations exercised in the Western tradition as a cultural sign. They would be separated only "theoretically," and only for the purposes of conceptual analysis – whether to take the measure of one or the other, to determine their modes of coherence or enunciation, to understand their applications within a determined field, or their regular coincidences with other orders, types of explication, programs of thought or action, etc. But in this case, the "tropicalization" of Christianity would be a non-sense. That is, unless we understand it in the sense of a prescription, an opportunistic adaptation – indeed, automobiles, radio and television stations, medical packaging, etc., are "tropicalized" in the goal of maintaining profitability. Some of their structures are conditioned to "adapt" them to the climate and ambiance of the Tropics – but they are not fundamentally modified.

The religious projects of indigenization, Africanization, adaptation, toothing stones, etc., do indeed seem like such exercises in tropicalization. They cling to the application of codes – liturgical languages, catechismal processes, etc. – that might match the particular sensibilities and approaches of African intelligences. Despite its violent consonance when applied to evangelization, the concept of "tropicalization" describes reality well. This is the very same reality that was promoted by the great missionary encyclicals, such as – if we restrict ourselves to the twentieth century – Benedict XV's *Maximum illud* (November 1919), Pius XI's *Rerum ecclesiae* (February 1926), Pius XII's *Evangelii praecones* (June 1951) and *Fidei donum* (April 1957), and John XXIII's *Princeps pastorum* (November 1959). The openness to non-Western humanisms in these fundamental texts signifies, as John XXIII said clearly at the Second Congress of Black Artists and Writers in 1959, the possibility of registering and integrating non-European cultural values into the centuries-old Western patrimony:

> The Church, with a youthfulness that is constantly renewed by the breath of the Holy Spirit, remains willing to recognise, welcome and even to serve as the inspiration of everything that seeks to honour the intelligence and the human heart. And it is willing to do so on shores of the world other than this Mediterranean basin which was the providential cradle of Christianity.[15]

But it does not seem to me that this openness signifies – even if, by force of circumstance, it marks the possibility of – a liberation of "the doctrine and common tradition" of the Church. What it involves, in sum, is an exercise of liberties in terms of cultural differences. Each culture can actualize its capacity to integrate "the common deposit" into its own economy, in a specific and original form, while watching to ensure that its essential contents are neither altered nor transformed in any major way. And these contents are an infinite and inexhaustible providence, indexed carnally and spiritually to the fundamental and vital experience of the West, by which it has been channeled, determined in its essence, and objectified.[16]

I can thus understand what expressions such as "African liturgy" or "African catechism" might mean. But I admit that I can understand "African theology" only in a metaphorical mode. As a science that interrogates sacred texts that bear witness to a revelation integrated into a particular series of questions, it is unthinkable if it is meant to be in a relation of coexistence with a non-African theology or theologies. The expressions "Greek theology," "Latin theology," or "other theologies" are only simple images: they do not explain their differences, and, moreover, they cannot do so pertinently without risk of becoming "heretical." Haven't the sites they need to occupy in order to be

Catholic and theological already been invested by the essence of "Western" Catholic tradition and theological thought? In this precise sense, we can understand how the task traditionally given to theology runs fatally up against the Western acculturation of Jesus Christ and the complex determinations of the Church – which have been made, adjusted, and completed in time with the same rhythm that has carried along the history of the West.

* * *

The missionary, as I said, has strictly nothing to say to the pagan. I do not see, either, what the African theologian or priest has to say to me. I affirm my irreducibility in the face of their existence, and would like them to do the same. Difference, an essential difference, situates me and poses me as an existence before the missionary, but equally before my racial brothers who are preachers or Christians: we have nothing to communicate to each other apart from the weight and confusion of the silence that condemns us to withdraw into ourselves.

And this experience, as de Certeau notes, has a meaning that the Gospels reveal, and that theology ceaselessly explains: access to meaning is a permanent conversion of the letter.

II.
ANALYSES AND TENDENCIES

1
Society, Education, Creativity

Before quickly noting several relations that connect these three terms, it would be interesting to try to "define" what we mean by creativity. To do this, it will be helpful to draw out the link between a particular social structure that tends to engender a determinate form of socialization – and thus, eventually, a type of education like that found in the West – and what that society understands as creativity. Put differently: although I do not think it would be easy to begin by defining creativity "in itself," it seems legitimate and methodologically advantageous to want to bring to light certain types of creativity that are linked to modes of socialization, which in turn are specific expressions of a given society.

Starting from and following the particular exigencies of its history, the modern West has produced what is likely one of the most rigid and elitist modes of socialization, which it calls "education." We can ask ourselves whether the secular and democratic ideology of this "generalized" education – that is to say: education that is accessible, in principle and by law, to children of all social classes, with, in theory, initially equal opportunities – really manages to exorcise two of its most rigorous and, no doubt, most constant characteristics. The first is uniformization; that is to say, the production of citizens shaped by the discipline of a system and so, in a certain way, "cast in the same mold." The second is the advancement of those subjects who prove themselves the most "scholarly," the best adapted to the system, intellectually and spiritually. These two characteristics seem to be the goal of all education; and the primary means of attaining them – but also the most inconspicuous, and multiform – is discipline.

Uniformization? At first there are many diverse features, noisily or silently at work, which appear in different colorings from one country to another. The structure of the academic system functions quasi-mechanically in the obligatory progression from one "class" to another, from one "cycle" to another. Set curricula are established by official "decrees" or "guidelines" that are applied either faithfully, with the same regulations across a whole territory, or freely, but in such a way that students are still guided on a set time line to the levels indicated by regional or national plans. There are also pedagogical prescriptions, normative paths of thought and research that, despite the extreme variety of their aims, are explicitly or implicitly meant to introduce students to a determinate form and particular practice of knowledge. There is as well each nation's framing, at once precise and imprecise, which is relayed by the political authorities and gives educators and schools their missions and duties. For instance, looking carefully at primary education under the Third Republic in France, we might ask today whether one of its central tasks was not in fact to reinforce the one and indivisible Republic, especially by working to efface regional differences – particularly those involving local traditions and languages.

Selective advancement? The Napoleonic system, whose basic philosophy seems alive and well today, is defined by the decree of 17 March 1808 as a body charged exclusively with teaching and public education across the empire. It is a normalizing system, a stern, constraining, and paramilitary organization, whose great virtues are of the order of discipline. It reprises the "disciplinary grammar" that was one of the great problems of the eighteenth century, as Michel Foucault has recently shown: "The first of the great operations of discipline is, therefore, the constitution of '*tableaux vivants*,' which transform the confused, useless or dangerous multitudes into ordered multiplicities."[1] Inspecting men, noting their presence or absence and constituting a general and permanent register of the armed forces; dividing patients, separating them from each other, carefully dividing the space of the hospital and making a systematic classification of illnesses:

these are so many paired operations in which the two constituent elements – distribution and analysis, control and intelligibility – function in solidarity. The table, in the eighteenth century, is at once a technique of power and a procedure of knowledge. It is a matter of organizing the multiple, of providing an instrument to survey and master it; of giving it an "order."

To order is then to discipline a space in which precise norms and hierarchy can be established. Thus discipline, as Foucault puts it, "produces subjected and practised bodies,"

> increases the forces of the body (in economic terms of utility) and diminishes these same forces (in political terms of obedience). In short, it dissociates power from the body; on the one hand, it turns it into an "aptitude," a "capacity," which it seeks to increase; on the other hand, it reverses the course of energy, the power that might result from it, and turns it into a relation of strict subjection.[2]

A "new political anatomy" is thus established, rigorously organizing and structuring the space of the school, hospital, barracks, etc.

Must not one consequence of this "disciplining" of the individual be the "disciplining" of speaking and dreaming? Can the procedures of control and of limiting freedom set in motion to promote "docile bodies" be reconciled with the notion of "Enlightenment progress," also inherent in the cultural ideology of the West?

François Duyckaerts defined creativity as an "aptitude to orient oneself in a given objective world,"[3] and thus to adapt without knocking against the corners of those great orders that Durkheim defined: the biological, the cultural, and the institutional. According to Duyckaerts, "as long as institutions truly bring individuals together, they are positive and creative. It is up to the individual to ensure that they serve this goal." More precisely, he believes, situating himself in relation to Freud, that

> whether we begin from adaptation to the other or adaptation to cultural values, we are always led to the central notion of creativity. It is by being a creator that the individual surpasses the conflict between submission and revolt. On the level of social relations, he surmounts the contradictions of instinctive attachment by accessing a world of values, principles of inter-individual unity and cooperation. On the level of his relations with cultural tradition, he manages to

avoid the choice between conformism and anti-conformism, while relying on the support of tradition to intensify his social life. In short, he unites with the other in order to create values, and recreates traditional values in order to draw closer to the other.

In sum, working with this model of creativity will allow us to derive the concepts of active and passive sociality as understood by Georges Gurvitch[4] – the first characterized by the communal projects that it proposes, while the second does not propose such projects.

Do these theoretical landmarks not suggest, as well as a style of knowledge, modes of normalizing and "disciplining" thought and freedom? From an extreme point of view, we could say that if creativity is a function of an aptitude for adaptation, and if sociability can only be either active or passive, it will then be normal for creativity to lead on occasion to the production of "disciplined errors"; or, more bluntly, that Galileo would have been mistaken. This "discipline" that seems to regulate creativity in the Western tradition is in fact supported by a will to truth. Foucault puts it marvelously: "I believe that this will to truth – leaning in this way on a support and an institutional distribution – tends to exert a sort of pressure and something like a power of constraint."[5] This will is articulated in a complex of norms and duties of scientific practice, and is in more or less direct relation with the principle of discipline, the guarantor of truth, which in a given space and by function of rules and a theoretical horizon creates "the possibility of formulating new propositions, ad infinitum."[6]

Thus if, as Foucault proposes, the great scientific mutations can also be read as the appearance of new forms within the will to truth, they can equally be understood as moments in which "heresies" are assumed; that is to say, where "wild" practices are inserted into a space submitted to the control of a "police."

It would be instructive to determine, in the history of the West, different generations of the "discursive police" assumed by the Christian Faith, Science, and Society. Not only has each of these themes been an ideal in itself, but the three of them constitute, together and separately, notable expressions of a will to truth, expressed in a complex and scholarly deployment of networks of surveillance and control of action, thought, and speech. Thus, like Science and Society, the Faith can only be an absolute that by its very nature excludes any proposition that does not derive from the order it at once incarnates and guarantees. To paraphrase St. Thomas Aquinas: does not any individual reality, whatever it may be – thing, person, nation, etc. – derive from the idea of God who is the creator, father, and master of the universe, and the study of whom, according to St. Bonaventure, is the only conceivable science?

The West thus had to combat all "heresies"; that is to say, non-disciplined discourses bearing on the Faith, Science, and Society. In the European Middle Ages, as we know, to attack one was to attack all three at once. Beginning in the sixteenth century, the growing space of a freely wild exteriority gave rise to discourses undisciplined by the three institutions. But despite this, it was perhaps the partial victory of heretical reforms that led gradually, among many other factors, to the reactivation of discarded discourses and the removal of the seal of monstrosity they had carried. Up until these reforms, banishment, massacre, the stake, or calamities like the plague had reduced the brilliance or violence of heresies, while the discourse of official science had subjected any non-orthodox knowledge to ridicule or forced it into clandestinity. But once heresy against the Faith became concordant with heresy against the temporal power of the Church, the power of "disciplining" passed bit by bit from the Church to the state. The latter then reworked it, attentively revising and restructuring certain systems, including the army and the school. At the same time, the revision of the role of the sacred within the major and institutionalized orthodoxies seems to have the consequence of allowing creativity to manifest in a more or less free exteriority, and not only in the arts, where it had taken refuge up until then. Thinking and speaking "otherwise," at least within certain limits, no longer necessarily led to "excommunication."

But the West was cultivating another Faith, the one transmitted and inculcated by education: Faith in Science, Scientificity, Reason; Faith in the methods said to be scientific and logical – that is to say, in the use of techniques that offer mastery of what is required in order to "speak" science. Thus, for example, as Foucault writes:

> A discipline is not the sum of all that can be truthfully said about something; it is not even the set of all that can be accepted about the

same data in virtue of some principle of coherence or systematicity. Medicine is not constituted by the total of what can be truthfully said about illness; botany cannot be defined by the sum of all the truths concerning plants. There are two reasons for this: first of all, botany and medicine are made up of errors as well as truths, like any other discipline – errors which are not residues or foreign bodies but which have positive functions, a historical efficacity, and a role that is often indissociable from that of the truths.[7]

Simply put, a hypothesis or proposition belongs to a scientific discipline when it forms part of a horizon, when it strictly obeys given conditions, and when it uses, as Foucault shows, well-defined conceptual or technical instruments.

"Disciplining," therefore, of scientific creativity: a normalization that casts non-conforming practices into the exterior of science. Galileo and Mendel, of course; but also any practice that cannot be assumed by "Western scientific reason."

But what if creativity – rather than being this faculty of adaptation I have been speaking of – was "also," in the sciences as in life, the faculty of being able, when faced with the contradictions a culture poses, to accept shock and collision outside of civilized spaces? What if it was the capacity of inventing, from within deviance – in other words, outside of habitual framing procedures – radically new pathways?

It is true that this type of creativity is totally absent in our system of education. More: the procedures of excluding unschooled individuals function with a rigor that speaks, in exemplary fashion, to the enduring consistency of a spirit of orthodoxy. Examples can be found *ad absurdum*. For instance, when faithfully transplanted into sub-Saharan Africa, the European model of education often engenders frustration and alienation, because the socialization it pursues is a function of Western society, not of African society. There is a double negation of creativity here that encourages all sorts of neuroses: the educational function of the traditional African model of training is de facto denied, while a system of education is established that is a particular mode of intellectual, moral, spiritual, and socioeconomic "disciplining." Yet we tell ourselves that it is among the graduates of this school that Africa will find the creators of its future society, the promoters of its new destiny. There is more than one paradox here. We could ask ourselves: in the West, and wherever the West has imposed its model and consequently that eminent mode of socialization that education is, has creativity not taken refuge among those who escaped schooling, or those who despite schooling remained able to detach themselves from the principles of discipline – those who were not "converted" to scientific ideology and are not "slaves" of the rule of technology? This essential creativity, from a place of wild exteriority, is the power of freely "creating" the radically new while undoing the rules of normalization of science and society.

In any case, in our contemporary world we could enumerate other models, other modes of socialization: for example, the Qur'anic school in the Muslim world, close in form to the school of the European Middle Ages; or the initiatory pedagogy of traditional Africa, based on a vision of the world and the human very different from that of the West. In this pedagogy "disciplining" is not a goal, and education does not exactly consist of making a person an object of power, but rather a subject of freedom.

The problem has been posed: how, today, in spite of education, can we fully liberate creativity, rediscover the right to difference, become able to take up madness?

2
Cultural Cooperation and Dialogue

The proposed title, "cultural cooperation and dialogue," seems to me too ambitious not to call for a principle of economy – or rather, to avoid the contradictory meanings of economy as concept and reality, a principle of parsimony. Sidestepping the title's technical complexity, and at less expense, we will see if we can note a few working or partial hypotheses that might explain, within the current context of relations of international cooperation, why it is pertinent to question those relations.[1]

Whatever route we take, this approach may at first glance seem useless; to specialists in cooperation it may seem utterly annoying. Wouldn't the everyday experience of cooperation make my questions seem more like sentimental effusion than anything critical? And at any rate, given political imperatives and the need for international cooperative programs, wouldn't they be utterly ineffective? In reply, I would say that to me these responses do not seem very satisfying. They tell me nothing, fundamentally, about what cooperation means today. They do not tell me the how and why of cooperation, and still less about how, in practice, specialists and aid workers resolve the complex and ambiguous problems of contact with culturally different regions. Finally, it might be useful today for us to say where exactly the demand for cooperation comes from.

One of the major contradictions of the human and social sciences as they are practiced in our African universities will help me to clarify the paradox of cooperation, particularly of the vertical type, between Euro-America and the so-called underdeveloped countries.

There is a constant and remarkable silence in the human and social sciences as they are practiced in Africa. This silence can be explained neither by methodological prudence, nor even by the norms of science. It shamefully covers over the gaps, the tedious blanks that Africans will one day need to fill by starting from the concrete modalities of their existence and the perspectives opened up by their questions about the world and life. This silence rises up whenever it is a question of knowing who is speaking, from where, and why. Nonetheless, it is obvious that the human and social sciences do not everywhere speak a "same," like the one produced by mathematical models. These sciences, in their aims and their applications, contain and assume the discretion and efficacity of a particular epistemological field. Only by this, it seems, are they offered norms and categories, themes and values, which are as much ethical and philosophical as they are scientific.

We can find a magnificent illustration in structuralist ideology and method, which have taught us in particular how to think and bring forth the structures of a whole, a totality – that is to say, how to privilege one synchronic level among many others and congeal it through analysis into tables whose formulas and rules can be formulated according to the norms of a given intelligibility – and how, on the basis of abstract models, to establish relations between mind and reality.

Three things seem troubling to me in this approach, which despite requiems recently pronounced for it appears more confident today than ever. In any case, it reigns royally over the human and social sciences, and even exercises influence in the exact sciences. For instance, it is current practice in biology to speak in terms of coding, encoding, and decoding, after the linguistic model, or to speak of a cellular category by using terms taken from sociology.

These three things are: first, the implicit philosophical project that presides over the technical play of decomposing a whole into its constituent parts, analyzing interdependencies, and interpreting the structures exposed in the process. "Kantianism without a transcendental subject," as Paul Ricoeur said to Lévi-Strauss! And hasn't it often been pointed out – most recently by Luc de Heusch – that this "metaphysics" is indispensable neither for the logic of *Mythologiques* nor for its comprehension. For my part, I have previously noted that nothing in this apparently highly elaborated system presents me with anything other than the measure and derivations of one epistemological universe, the Western – the same one that, by the subtle accidents and fulgurations of an essential order, also some years ago made possible neo-Thomism and neo-Marxism, existentialism and personalism, and, in general, the energy and renewed vigor of voluntarist, vitalist, and subjective philosophies.[2]

As an African, then, why can I not live and think the rift between this "metaphysics" and the ideologies that recently ruled over the human sciences as at once a frustration and an expression of fantasies proper to Western culture – expressions named, conveyed, and justified by a particular moment in the history of Western culture?

That it has been possible, concerning structuralism, to speak of a "de-Westernization of scientific knowledge" – particularly to oppose the liberality of certain concepts like the "savage mind" – is a sign. But, in my opinion, this sign is meaningful only when situated and understood in a sort of Western heritage: Kant's Copernican revolution, to use Jules Vuillemin's nice phrase. Kant left behind an unfortunately reassuring and utterly encumbering paradox, making any subsequent theodicy indefensible. As we know, his enterprise was a great failure: the difficulty (impossibility?) of any thematization of the sacred after Kant condemns us today, with unhealthy modesty, to manipulate dissimulations of a sacred whose name must almost always be silenced.

To this first inconvenience is added a second; less strong, no doubt, but logical. From the moment we accept that the complex play of homologies between thought and reality contains something a bit excessive, and that there is a playfulness in the rules of structuralist reading, these homologies return us – by what channels? – to the sterility of a certain scholarly philosophy, the same one that led Claude Lévi-Strauss to flee the discipline. An example of this play of analogies: as part of a competition, I once had to write a thesis on the differences between the notion of structure and the structure of the notion. This gave me the idea, two years ago, of proposing two "amusing" assignments to my students: I asked them to note the correspondences and relations between, in the first case, "the commercialization of the pocket mirror and the extension of subjective philosophies," and in the second between "the progress of European women and the hardening of colonial policy in sub-Saharan Africa during the first quarter of the twentieth century."

You will tell me that I am not being serious. I reply: perhaps; but, ideologically, is any such exercise really neutral? I know only that the "classical" models of certain logics (in the plural) are open to this type of freedom, and so they too can lead to the exhilaration of applying logical operations to meaningless propositions. I also know that, at their extreme limit, such operations of thought belong more to mathematics than to philosophy. But, at any rate, it is not the method that is the problem. As professional epistemologists will tell us, the foundation and meaning of the approach are what merit "explication."

And structuralism, we are told, "explicates" and "founds."

Here is the question. It leads me to my third point of reticence with regard to the pre-meditation that claims to "uncover" structures. Taken as a norm, the concept of structure implies that every structuralist practice involves the constant exercise of a materialism that can be qualified, in the language of the Schools, as either vulgar or scientific. In any case, it signifies the preeminence of a single concept, the affirmation of a single concept: the philosophical concept of matter, a concept which is precise but covers an extremely vast field, because it includes everything that was, is, and will come as a product of nature.

Thenceforth, to postulate eventual homologies between mind and reality in structural terms is to accept this essential concept of philosophy. Although speaking of something completely different and in a fictional context, S. Allen puts it nicely: "What to do then, but to transform the scybalum into an image, a metaphor, and to make it pass before the mirror like any old reflection of coquetry?"[3]

But something other than coquetry is at play here. Foucault, establishing his approach in *The Order of Things*, offers a sentence that puts an end to Allen's novelistic ambiguities: "The image should stand out of the frame."[4] This is spoken by a Spanish master initiating his disciple into the art of painting.

By historical coincidence these methodologies, which put forward particular techniques of self-exhibition and arrogantly assume the unity of an ancient knowledge that is complete but remains also always to come, carry in themselves contradictions that concern Africa. This should, at the least, encourage us to look more closely at the sociocultural tendencies that made them possible. Two examples: first, the old cry that arose from the European nineteenth century, "God is dead," seems to Foucault to be merely a simple accident, mentioned in passing during his archaeological analysis of the types and process of knowledge in the European tradition. He insists, instead, on the disappearance of man from the field of knowledge. Second, it is worth thinking about the success experienced by the republication of a 1714 treatise by Mandeville on the proper use of vice in society. One of the text's major principles is this: private vice makes public good by creating dependency and solidarity between evildoers and honest people; both are thus indispensable for society. Its central thesis claims, astonishingly: morality is the greatest of hoaxes.

These two examples help illustrate what I mean when I say that Africa is affected by, and almost constrained to live with, methodologies or ideologies from the West. One of the concrete questions prompted by these examples might be: should the African response set out from within the categories proposed by these frameworks, or spring from elsewhere? What elsewhere would this be? What meaning would it have? How would it be different from the environment and frameworks inherited from Western history and our contacts with it?

Elsewhere, I have posed this question in terms of possible inheritance between cultures, thinking particularly of the Western heritage. In practical terms, I thought it was necessary to begin by clarifying my reasons for this approach; and in this vein, I ended up presenting a utopia reduced to an act of speaking. I now wonder if it would have been better to take as my starting point "signs of the times." The first step would then be to rigorously identify which of these are the real trends of our societies, and the most concrete expressions of our contradictions as people situated in a given time and space.

Cooperative programs generally avoid these questions, and retain from them only the need to determine "styles" of "contact." Would it be so indecent, then, to coldly analyze how these programs, and the "styles" they assume, are both a collection of ideological hypotheses and cultural prescriptions whose essential meaning lies in the fact that they are merely concrete, precise, and present formulations of another discourse, another order?

In my opinion, it is certainly useful work to reflect on and outline the broad strokes of a scientific, academic, or administrative program of cooperation. But such work tends to ignore or to surreptitiously falsify the major articulation found throughout every social formation: the dialectic between nature and culture. Indeed, as Michel de Certeau writes of historians,

> They modify space in the manner of the urban designer who integrates fields into the town's network of transportation, of the architect who regulates the lake with dams, of Pierre Henry, who changes a squeaking door into a musical motif, or of the poet who completely transforms the relations between "noise" and a "message." Historians metamorphose the environment through a series of transformations which change the boundaries and the internal topography of culture. They "civilize" nature – which has always meant that they "colonize" and change it.[5]

The approach of Euro-American specialists in cooperation is thus fundamentally "colonizing" (in the precise sense just mentioned). They are no different from researchers and teachers in the African university who, consciously or unconsciously, actualize reductive practices of knowledge. The other is always simultaneously perceived as a reflection of the self and as a distance from what one is; and this is the foundation from which programs for its "advancement" are elaborated. And I tell myself, adapting Foucault's comments on ethnology to fit my argument: obviously, this is not to say that the colonial situation is indispensable for cooperation – neither hypnosis nor the patient's alienation in the phantasmal figure of the doctor is constitutive of psychoanalysis. But just as the latter can be deployed only within the calm violence of a singular relation and the transference it induces, in the same way cooperation only takes on its proper dimensions within the historical sovereignty – always restrained but always actual – of European thought and of the relations that confront it with all other cultures as with itself.[6]

* * *

But aren't these remarks, with their insistence on the usefulness of respecting differences, in contradiction with the evolution of our world? Specialists in futurology point to the existence, clearly indicated by current trends, of dominant centripetal forces working toward the unification and homogenization of culture and civilizations.

This is an important argument, and I would like to pause on it at length in order to reach a balanced conclusion. A methodology based on the principle that all knowledge of a future situation implies a comprehension of the real present or the immediate past, and vice versa, allows us to apprehend our societies' current tendencies with relative precision. As an example of the demonstrations, definitions, illustrations, and general conclusions of this methodology I take the work of a team of researchers at the Hudson Institute in New York. I draw in particular from two collective volumes published under the direction of Herman Kahn: *The Year 2000* (henceforth cited as Y2), and *Things to Come* (henceforth cited as TC).[7]

One of the basic tools of the method is "surprise-free projection," in which "the most surprising thing that can happen ... is that there will be no surprises."[8] It is supported, in particular, by the *Delphi method* and the method of *envelope forecasting*. The first is a type of expert opinion polling: specialists are given questionnaires based on current trends, and their responses are systematized to produce predictions. Using this method, "juries" of historians, biologists, economists, or even theologians can be constituted to predict and describe, in a theoretical space, ongoing trends or mutations and the likely results of their continuation. Envelope forecasting, a more elaborate methodology, uses curves calculated according to precise techniques and approaches. It is applied especially to the field of technology, to flag probable rates of innovation – for example, the effects and consequences of changes caused by new inventions.

Using these methods and others, particularly biological analogies, the Hudson Institute team traced the macro-historical outlines of what was called, in the 1960s, the "multifold trend" of the 1970s and 1980s. Their model of reference is the Euro-American context. It is striking to me that we can reflect today on the relevance and accuracy of their projections. Attentive analysis will help us live the tensions of our present in a no doubt more calculated way, and allow us act on the future, if only to prevent unnecessary dramas.

The long-term multifold trend has, according to Kahn's team, fifteen salient points. I would like to highlight two of the points they emphasize:

- "The continuance, or 'forward movement,' of the multifold trend does not necessarily suggest that this trend is beneficial in the way that nineteenth century writers assumed that progress was always desirable. This is just the way the world seems to be going in the long terms, like it or not." (TC, p. 9)
- "The multifold trend is conceived of as a long-term base line which may include within it certain short-term fluctuations, some of which may temporarily reverse" the trend and slow the general movement over the next fifteen years (TC, p. 9).

The salient points of this trend are as follows:[9]

1. An increasingly *sensate* culture: empirical, humanist, pragmatic, explicitly rational, utilitarian, contractual, Epicurean, hedonistic, etc.: "Apparently we today are viewing pronounced tendencies toward a *late sensate* culture, particularly in the culture area of Northwestern Europe."
2. A very marked tendency toward the constitution of "bourgeois, bureaucratic, and meritocratic elites has been almost universal. In the last five or ten years there has, of course, come into being a rather spectacular revolt against middle-class bourgeois values." It seems this trend can be considered largely established in the sociopolitical structure of countries outside of Euro-America: power "has been largely transferred to a centralized government bureaucracy. Of particular importance in the embourgeoisement of the Westernistic countries is the existence of a Westernized military which in every country offers an alternative government to the status quo."
3. A marked trend toward the centralization and concentration of economic and political power: "Since World War II, the number of sovereign states in the world has increased threefold and while there are a few possible states which could still be established and whose liberation or attempted liberation could create severe international crises, the number of such states is limited." Nevertheless, based on current structures, it is very likely that between now and

1980, "on the economic level … [there will be] increasing government control over economic activities in almost every nation of the world. Laissez-faire is just about dead and there is little prospect for its revival."
4. A net process tending toward a greater and more complete accumulation of scientific and technical knowledge: "This trend should go on unchecked even though its velocity and impact may be slowed down as a result of attacks by its critics"; "In consumer technology … important new development is almost certain."
5. A very likely institutionalization of technological change and new developments, notably in terms of policies concerning research, development, diffusion, etc. There is only one likely problem: hesitation on the part of scientists. Nonetheless, even if "individual scientists may now drop out of institutional environments because of opposition to bureaucracy or to 'immoral' research, such men will usually find it difficult to work successfully because of need for comradeship, critiques, and research equipment and aid."
6. The continuous progression of modernization and industrialization, and a very likely expansion of Western values that will tend toward the development of mass culture, aided and maintained by the acquisition of technology: "The actual trend towards … industrialization should not only continue, but will probably accelerate through the entire 1975–85 decade. The decline in direct Western political rule over the rest of the world has been accompanied by an acceleration" of a critical process of integrating Western values. "Not only the government, but the people [in non-Euro-American societies] … show their preference for modern commercial culture by flocking into the growing cities." It is very likely that "in 1985 the people of the world will be more culturally similar than they have been at any time in the history of mankind." (Here one could say: the reality of one economy, one culture, one global society.) "This 'global metropolis' … will be a mass culture, mechanized, pragmatic, and cheerfully anarchistic; fundamentally philistine by highbrow cultural standards; and irreverent by traditional social standards."
7. A very likely expansion and extension of affluence and leisure, particularly in the Euro-American world, as a result of economic tendencies that are already visible: the growth

rate of annual GNP per capita, increase in disposable funds, investments, etc. In any case, it should be noted that "if society is to move towards a generally more liberated life style, the most pressing problem that it faces is how to rectify its economic needs with the more liberated values."
8. It seems likely that current trends of population growth will also be largely maintained. Overall, while noting both the increase in birth rates in non-Euro-American zones due to medical progress, and these countries' movement in the direction already traveled by the West, "population growth is not accelerating, but slowing down and may even be topping out, although probably not before 1985."
9. Another major trend that will mark the world over the next years, particularly the industrialized countries, is urbanization, suburbanization, and the growth of giant cities: "In the industrialized world, urbanization takes a somewhat different form, which may herald the eventual development of the underdeveloped world ... people abandon the farms and hamlets, and even smaller towns and cities, for great cities."
10. Another continuing trend: "Decreasing importance of primary and (recently) secondary and tertiary occupations; increasing importance of tertiary and (recently) quaternary occupations." The commentary explains the scope of this tendency in more detail: "Most of the world is currently trying to industrialize and increase secondary industries ... however, some countries, already industrialized, have moved on beyond secondary (manufacturing) to service occupations and industries. In the most advanced industrialized countries, particularly in North America, there is a shift to a different kind of service industry. We distinguish between *tertiary* industries, which are services to primary and secondary industries, and quaternary industries, which are service done for their own sake, or services to such services, and are oriented toward ultimate consumption rather than toward production."
11. A growing and uninterrupted increase in literacy and education in general is also a salient point of the decades to come: "There is a continuing educational boom, and ... more and more people spend more and more of their time attending formal courses of education. The quality of this

education varies considerably and its very purpose is under dispute; but, despite the qualms held by both the intellectuals and the masses, it seems that the educational system fills certain basic needs in our society which will not be abandoned in our time." This general observation supports another, which flows from it and also belongs to a tradition found in many countries today: the function of intellectuals, who, whatever the particularities of their training and production, are defined and situated in relation to a particular type of knowledge. Nonetheless, it must be recognized that, as has always been the case, "intellectuals, or at least highly intellectual people, are necessary to running the world. Unfortunately, the intellectual does not necessarily have other equally useful attributes such as courage, decisiveness, steadfast loyalty, and common sense."

12. A very clear inclination can also be noted in the contemporary world toward the establishment of social planning. This functions according to a rhythm marked, perhaps, by a kind of "ritualistic rationality"; that is, "rationality increasingly applied to social, political, cultural, and economic worlds as well as to shaping and exploiting the natural world." In simple terms, this is the more and more generalized trend toward innovative and manipulative social engineering.

13. Alas, it should also be noted that, around the world, there is no reason to hope that military capability will diminish: "The long-term trend toward *increasing military capacity* is likely to continue despite attempts at arms limitations."

14. The last two constants are complimentary to each other, and summarize the other differences. Both involve the "Increasing universality of the multifold trend": "The last two items in the multifold trend are almost self-explanatory and should impact very strongly until 1985. The *increasing universality of the multifold trend* can be seen in its spread throughout the world and throughout all the classes of the societies of the world, although by 1985 this trend may begin to top out, if only because the universality will have become nearly universal. And overall *the increasing tempo of change* of the items of the multifold trend is clear enough, with the few short-run exceptions we discussed above."

* * *

What is there to say about this perspective, which is presented as a likely vision of our near future and claims to take its bearings from our present?

First, there is the problem of how credible such a firmly "ethnocentric" vision can be. Does it really concern Africa? Yes, certainly; to the extent, for example, that it also concerns communist China, whose own short-, medium-, and long-term projections and analyses are, due to ideological differences, different from those presented here. I noted earlier the impact of ideology on practices of knowledge. The limits I described there also apply in this case, where the West is established as quasi-absolute reference for humanity's present and future.

Perhaps this extreme limit can help us understand the "why" of certain rules of economic dependence and interdependence, which schematically guarantee the "good sense" and "appropriateness" of the increasing universality (though varying by country and climate) of the long-term multifold trend described by the Hudson team.

Then, in a more global sense, there are methodological questions that could relativize the conclusions, supporting or undermining the model that Kahn and his team use. These are not among my concerns; and at any rate, other scholars have already praised and judged the research. The name of the science that produces this type of study, futurology, has and continues to produce hare-brained associations, particularly with poetry or novels describing the future. Whatever the field's scientific validity may be, all this "noise" seems to have been a disservice to the project and its audience. Finally, disagreements between different schools, often technical – think of the "horrors" evoked by the Club of Rome or the author of *Future Shock* – naturally instill a skepticism and a certain relativism.

But to me what is essential is not the brutality or finesse of plausible or implausible arguments; it is not even the truthfulness of the possible transformations predicted from the trends. It is rather the attitude of thought taken toward these hypotheses, and toward the ethnocentric meaning of a thesis that lends itself admirably to explaining the many dependencies arising from the establishment and extension of a mode of production.

* * *

These theses and hypotheses clearly show the context in which reflections on the promotion of the Third World are developed, and the unequal relations that, prior to any consultation, establish the working rules of collaboration. As we have seen, comments on ideology, the practice of knowledge, and cooperation open directly onto philosophical and ethical questions. The determination of modern social trends as sketched by the Hudson Institute team also poses important philosophical and moral problems. In both cases, confronted with the ethnocentric violence of Euro-American culture, we can ask ourselves how Africa might advance itself while remaining culturally and spiritually original. But we are also permitted, within our own spheres of competence, to ask ourselves what practical modalities should be privileged if we are to ensure that projects explicitly designed to promote humanity and its culture do not, once again, become instances of dispossession.

As specialists in political economy have demonstrated, the general movement of our modern societies can perhaps be explained in terms of the multiple and varied interactions and combinations of a few fixed themes. These include the nature and type of relations between the production process and social relations of production; the nature and type of relations between the organization of production, the organization of power, and the discourses that interpret them; the nature and type of relations between ideological signaling and speculative practices; and finally, whether viewed in terms of dominance or merely of reciprocal influence, the nature and type of relations between infrastructures and superstructures.

In this optic, Dr. Kahn's work has particular value insofar as, despite its ideological presuppositions, it allows us to estimate, concretely, the gaps and differences that separate the countries of the Old World and the young nations. These gaps point to the living and working conditions in each country; and it is in terms of them that a "politics" of cooperation might be faithfully (or, to be sure, unfaithfully) elaborated.

While political independence in Africa seemed to guarantee the assertion of difference, it would be useful to ask just how real the "claiming of power and speech" attributed to Africa and African culture actually is. Does it not seem instead that, in the imperial Euro-American perspective, culture occupies the same place as the "folklore" of this or that Euro-American minority?

That is to say, it is at best a survivance of the past: a "serious spectacle" for ethnologists, "amusing" and "interesting" for vacationers at Club Med.

Unfortunately, things will stay like this as long as African culture is understood and defined in reference to the African past, to African tradition. They will stay like this until this culture is explicitly defined as a project encompassing Africa's present and future; that is, until it is the speech of contemporary Africa and its social movement, the living and solid expression of its becoming. From this perspective, precisely, language is of the order of a short-term tactic. In my opinion, it is interesting but not essential to know in what language the true African cultural discourse will be made – because even a national language could very well be a vehicle and instrument of alienation. The essential lies in what African culture truly is: an art of reuniting, without tension, work and life, existence and death, the sacred and the profane, play and passion, into a harmonious synthesis. Confronted with this promise of equilibrium I think, like Michel de Certeau, that:

> The need to find a space, to be resituated in relation to institutions of private life (family, marriage, household, locality), to list the forms of achievement on the basis of risk, to explore other *styles of life*: this is a source of debates, research, and reactions that are now composing a cultural expression.[10]

The problem in Africa is posed in terms somewhat similar to those of the Western world (the society of the spectacle, the negation of the cultural creativity of a "people" now become a "public"), and here the stakes seem important. Indeed, on both sides the deculturation visible in the sort of autophagy that is the "consumption" of culture goes hand in hand with the pretense of being able to isolate a properly cultural domain or dimension.

While cultures are different, just as people and countries are different, the function of each culture is nonetheless everywhere the same: to promote freedom (which should be understood in all its connotations) and affirm a right to existence in the full political sense of the term. Here resides the essence of any debate on "the dialogue of cultures."

It is hard, then, to see the use of trying define "the specificity" of African culture. For my part, I see that what the West calls its culture is nothing other than a system of values supported by an ideology; and one of the aspects of this system is precisely the pretense of culture as a specific and differentiated domain.

Initially, at any rate, the problem of a dialogue of cultures and the cooperation that this dialogue might engage thus hangs on how the other, whether present or not, is approached, seen, and spoken of. What Sartre said in his "Response to Lefort" about the "gaze" that places us face to face with the other applies, in an exemplary manner, to my argument: "The Other is there, immediately accessible if not decipherable, and his experience is there; it is completed in my experience, or else mine ends in his. All the imperfect, poorly closed, interrupted meanings that constitute our real knowledge here reach completion in the other, who perhaps knows the answers." And also, "at any rate, these values and points of view, which are not our own even though they are mixed up with ours, give themselves up to us as systems of comprehensible relations; but they keep forever their irreducibility. Forever other, forever foreign, immediately present and unassimilable."[11]

Obviously, every encounter is always violent. How could it not be? But how can we think and understand this violence if we do not know the old truth that the members of the Club Jean Moulin, among many others, remind us of: "Every form of action is implicitly or explicitly guided by a prospective idea of society, of the modes of human relations of production and exchange."[12]

From this angle, a dialogue of cultures could only be tragic; and all cooperative projects will be similarly tragic. This is because efficiency, which is generally one of their goals, is often possible only to the detriment of the "irreducibility" of one of the partners, of its culture and history.

3
Universities: What Future?

In its enthusiasm for cooperative projects, the contemporary university – an enterprise that belongs to the state, totally or partially, or at any rate is submitted to its control – runs up against the state's political imperatives. At the same time, directly or indirectly, it is dependent on them. These imperatives vary between countries and between universities, but are principally of three types.

First is the demand to improve the country's economic presence within the international community. Thus an "economic" or "commercial" contract often precedes and makes possible the establishment of "cultural" cooperation. The "type" of cooperation pursued also seems to depend on economic imperatives: pharmacy and medicine, software and hardware, etc.

Second is the "imperial" and ideological vocation of the countries of the Old World. To take a now-classic example, Mr. Sabourin, a member of the parliamentary committee set up by Pierre Abelin in 1974, remarked in a synthesis report submitted to the Minister of Cooperation that "France is seen (in francophone Africa) as a privileged cultural partner – by reason of language, and also of administrative and commercial customs – but as one that to date has not shown enough interest in African cultures, and too often passes off its cultural models as universally valid."[1]

In general terms, we could also take the example of two connected issues. First, the "monolingual" proposal made by a certain conception of *la francophonie* is opposed to the linguistic claims of the "former colonies." The justification for this proposal seems to derive from a concrete and precise articulation between culture (Western), science (normative), and language (of culture). The dangers of such a universalist schema are easy to see, and in a cooperative program could only be a source of alienation, acculturation, and deculturation. This contradiction then follows: Jacobin political centralism "adapts" to the primarily sociopsychological demands of the new style of cooperation, but the problem is redoubled by the culturally and linguistically centralized model of the "mother" universities. What results is the objective negation of equal exchange, and thus the rejection of any true cooperation between Euro-America and Africa.

Third, another severe condition, especially in Africa, is the demand that programs and structures be profitable. The criterion of profitability may be established by an administration that is a simple transposition of the colonial administration. Or, following guidelines for the scientific organization of work, the criterion may be postulated normatively by means of precise rules for maximizing productivity in any correctly functioning enterprise. Here we see the impact of the mode of production on the university as a "business."

These three imperatives can be found in the various theoretical models that have been proposed for the university. The existence or creation of a given university in a given country proceeds from one or another of these models, or a combination.

The university as productive enterprise (model A): an organization (bureaucratic, administrative, more professional than scientific) whose activities and functions all contribute rationally to the formation and production of cadres for administration and industry. Profitability is established as dogma; and research, especially fundamental research, is often discarded.

The university as a site of ongoing education (model B): a "socialist" university par excellence, with unfixed structures; a "popular university" meant to continuously engage social movement and questioning. One of its projects is to run ahead of and orient this same social movement.

The university as ivory tower of culture and research (model C): an eminently elitist and bourgeois model, where the university finds its justification in itself. It is the site of reproduction of an "initiatory" knowledge, and also of dominant ideology; it is characterized by rigid structures and an extreme hierarchization of its members' merits, rights, and obligations.

Clearly, none of these models is perfectly applied anywhere, but we can find examples of their combinations.

A and B: the rapid evolution of technical knowledge and of knowledge in general restricts the university to a permanent "recycling" of cadres, and thus reintroduces into model A the need for research.

A and C: as the model C is older (e.g., the European university of the nineteenth century), socioeconomic exigencies have permitted the combination of A and C. For instance, the creation of short-term programs at technical universities, and the orientation of selection criteria toward production (cadres) or research (university professors, etc.).

B and C: this is a difficult combination, since at least in their theoretical purity B and C are in principle mutually exclusive. Certain "new" universities (Vincennes?) have attempted to break the frame of C in an attempt to realize B. The serious objective difficulties they encounter suggest a de facto incompatibility between B and C.

A and B and C: this combination seems to illustrate the reality of most contemporary universities. Starting with C, there is first the combination A and C, then A and C and B. This combination also reveals the origin of the sometimes insurmountable contradictions that arise in the "old" universities. The supporters of each of the three models are in competition, but the evolution of modern society (and particularly of economic demands) constrains them to an unrestricted application of A plus institutionalized recycling. "Socialist" and "leftist" demands propose the creation or promotion of universities according to model B, or at any case refuse to be restricted to A. Where rare examples of C are still to be found, they can likely be explained by a "theory of residues."

Building on these remarks, even a cursory analysis of African universities will show that they are copies, although with sometimes important modifications, of Western "mother-universities":

- despite a few differences, their structures serve the same purposes;

- they illustrate the same conception of the human and, in one way or another, participate in the demarcation of social groups within society and the creation of certain myths (scientificity, technicity, etc.) needed for any university to function.

African universities have inherited the three models presented above, their combinations, and the contradictions inherent in them. In a first phase, the Western model is fully and faithfully applied. However, this model comes more and more to be seen as "Westernized," precisely to the extent that model A seems to dominate. It is then acknowledged that "adaptations to African reality" are needed to guarantee the profitability that is the very principle of that model. Programs are restructured, materials are "Africanized," selection criteria are revised, and quotas are distributed according to faculty with (naturally!) a priority for the sciences.

We might ask whether these tactical and circumstantial transformations really contribute to the development of a truly African university. For my part, I agree with the Belgian sociologist Benoît Verhaegen that

> The African university is not first of all a university located in Africa, directed by Africans, teaching material said to be African, using a pedagogy adapted to African students. These are all clearly secondary requirements. A university is African when it contributes as much as possible to understanding and resolving the contradictions of African societies, and takes part in the creation of new social forms in an Africa that is facing the challenge of development and adapting to the modern world. One that does not is certainly not African, even if it were to be composed exclusively, from top to bottom, of Africans. In this case, we might even ask if it could be a real university, rather than a simple enclave of Western cultural influence made up of Europeans with black skin, whom the surrounding society would despise as intruders.[2]

What can be done, if we refuse "the Western model" and are critical of "Westernized" approaches in African universities? What could cooperation between Euro-American and African universities mean? The answer is simple: in my opinion, what matters is that African universities find their own path. This path should respond to the needs of the evolution (I prefer "evolution" to "development," because of the latter's economico-rational implications; evolution implies only change, whatever it may be) and the authenticity (in the original sense of the term) of African societies. True interuniversity cooperation can occur only within this framework, and has three principal requirements: creativity, an enduring spirit, and rigor.

Creativity – but starting from the fundamental basis of African culture. As Joseph Ki-Zerbo puts it: "Culture is the most immediate and most important dimension of independence ... There is no conscious nation without national culture ... In the end, the African soul will dissolve if the elites of the continent continue to refuse their past, to fear immersion into the masses and preach cultural exodus."[3] For my part, I have no doubt: if African culture and history were to become the order and site according to which the present and future were thought in African universities, we would be able to substitute values that are more attentive to the real flourishing of humanity for the eminently castrating norm of immediate profitability at all costs, which so violently marks universities in Africa.

Enduring spirit – this is at once faith in the social, scientific, and spiritual mission of the university ("I will live; even if I must die, I will continue on") and, through it, a critical openness to all possibilities. In sum, every university must think itself and its future in terms of its social and political possibilities, beginning with its essential mission – which is, as is sometimes forgotten, to train and produce true men and women of science.

Finally, rigor – a scientific rigor that is a serious exercise of "freedom," a refusal of paths traced once and for all, a permanent questioning of what has been learned, and a dialectical overcoming of knowledge. But also a political rigor that is both a calm analysis of the social and economic structures that "condition" the university as a social organization, and a fervent but critical attention to its hopes and needs.

Based on these three requirements, any operational model of interuniversity cooperation between Africa and Euro-America should answer at least to the following conditions:

- In all fields affected by cooperation, the offer must respond and correspond to the demand. Up until today, as we know all too well, the demand has been conditioned by the offer, in

keeping with the simple formula of difficult times: we settle for fish, because there is no more meat.
- Scientific and cultural demands must take priority over economic imperatives. This means the impact of "political tactics" on the material chosen for cooperation must be limited as much as possible.
- Reciprocity must be the norm. In other words, there must really be cooperation: that is to say, exchange on all levels rather than "assistance," technical or otherwise.

4
Western Cultural Power and Christianity

When it is approached, the question of Western cultural power in Africa is usually discussed from the perspective of the West. For many people, we might suspect, the question does not simply boil down to whether to live with or without the West. A useful preparatory step might be to inquire about the conditions and meaning of contacts between the West and Africa, and then to examine the modes and procedures by which cultural power is exercised and manifested. After having done this, and only then, the question would be how to (eventually) think a break or rupture, and under what conditions and for what goal such a break could be lived.

One of the major problems facing Africa today may be simply the reconciliation of two major but different programs, often seen as opposed. On the one hand is the establishment of norms and rules to govern the factual priority of the economic sphere; on the other is the definition of concrete means of promoting African culture that are genuinely faithful to Africa's history and present environment. In principle, the two programs are complementary, and factually each should implicate the other. But in practice they raise difficult questions, which we could sum up as a sort of quarrel over words: priority of the economic and primacy of the cultural; or primacy of the economic and priority of the cultural?

This is not merely a question of vocabulary. Or more precisely: doesn't this issue of vocabulary bring us back to the tensions and unsteady approaches that characterize the organization of power, structure of production, and ideological postulates of economic development plans in our African countries? To speak of organization and production in contemporary Africa means to once again encounter – differently, of course, but very concretely – the issue of African dependency on the Euro-American metropoles. It thus means returning to questions that have been trivialized out of laziness: under what conditions can African economic space be restructured? And, on the basis of this new order, how can we envision a genuine development of African cultures?

In the period after African independence, these questions led to the condemnation of a whole cultural universe. In particular, criticizing and rejecting colonization seemed to entail setting foreign culture and languages aside, as key instruments of Euro-American imperialism. It is true that this culture, and the languages that express it, carried out questionable projects in Africa, including ventures of economic dispossession and disfiguring local cultures. So it was normal that Africa, taking its destiny in hand, would try to redefine the status of existing cultures and to establish a new form of cultural contact.

This quest, which is also a sort of program of action, is usually supported by three principal demands:[1] a historical demand, a political demand, and an epistemological demand.[2]

The discipline of history is an excellent mirror: the experiences of the past illuminate, and often explain, current relations between cultures. It is sometimes forgotten that Western cultures were present in Africa – or more exactly, were in contact with African cultures – well before the nineteenth century. This contact was driven by the commercial imperatives that, beginning in the fifteenth century, led Europeans to open up to the rest of the world in search of the goods of the Far East. Barely one century was enough for, as Raymond Mauny writes, "an exploit unique in the annals of humanity: the discovery of the African coastlines, the Americas, and the circumnavigation of the globe."[3] Many textual sources on this period exist, but they are often little known and for the most part still unedited or poorly edited. They tell of the troubles and misfortunes of different civilizations experiencing difficulties in development, and seeking complementary goods that today we cannot always easily identify with objectivity. In Mauny's description:

The state of Africa between the seventeenth and nineteenth century could be compared to large segments of Europe in the eleventh century during the age of the great invasions and feudal wars, to the Middle East during the Mongol invasions, or to China in the twentieth century before the communist revolution. It would be a mere game for the imperialist powers to seize countries that had been ruined and morally exhausted by centuries of fratricidal struggle. Another degrading effect of this era affected Europe: a growing contempt for Africa and for Blacks, which culminated in the end of the nineteenth century at the moment of conquest.[4]

At the least, these contacts, contaminated by the triumphalism of Western culture and civilization, testify to an unhappy and denied fraternity between the White European and the Black African. Paradoxically, however, from the end of the fifteenth century this same fraternity provided a basis for "missionary projects of evangelization." From this moment on, the mission managed to escape questioning about its goals and actions. African practices and expressions were purely and simply erased as irrelevant, and the mission tried to convert the new universe to its own basic facts: the law of civilization and the glory of Christianity, two complementary terms of political and economic conquest. This privilege was supported by the papacy, beginning with the fifteenth-century bulls *Sane clarissimis* (1418) by Martin V, *Inter coetera* (1456) by Callixtus III, and *Aeterni regis clementia* (1481) by Sixtus IV.

It is worth noting that, in spite of everything, these initial and thoroughly ambiguous contacts inspired dissenting texts. In them, the century of Enlightenment declared its objection to the idea that Western culture was superior to all others. A notable example is Pigafetta's "reading" of the Kingdom of Kongo in the sixteenth century, based on information provided to him by the navigator Duarte Lopes.

The historical demand that animates African questions is not always, as is often thought, concerned with redefining History and its methods. It is perfectly appropriate to leave that problem to historical "professionals." It seems to me, insofar as contacts between cultures are involved, that the demand insists on the acceptance of a basic fact: today as in the past, the practice of history is condemned to look continuously for norms that can make its conquests and results a bit less subjective. This conception makes it possible to exorcise certain European works that contain impressive accounts of Africa. The demand can also be highly useful in relativizing the facile enthusiasms promoted by triumphant nationalisms on the African continent.

A critical reading of history as it is practiced confirms several important points. In particular: on the one hand, the originality and relative autonomy of each culture; and on the other, the de facto complementarity between cultures. This means that every culture is always foreign to every other, even when there are genetic links between them. It also means that every culture has its own personality – because it expresses and sums up the logic of a singular historical experience – and a sensibility and respiration unlike that of any other culture. Anglo-Saxon experience may well derive from Indo-European culture in the same way that French culture does, but it is none the less singular. French, like Italian, Romanian, Portuguese, and Spanish, all derive from Latin, which in turn – if one cares for genealogies – is historically related to Russian, Sanskrit, and Hittite. But it is still the case that each of these cultures was molded by the particular history it has carried and been marked by, and that it reflects today. Over the centuries, each culture has been progressively transformed through contact with a particular environment, and as a function of a particular people and their needs.

How, then, can we understand why Africa, with all of its nations and cultures, is still today commonly reduced to a sort of uniform region? Of course, this unanimist prejudice might signify something else: that no culture is an island. Indeed, a culture's personality is also in large measure made and solidified through contact. This does not mean that no culture is truly self-sufficient, but only that, due to history, diverse human communities regularly intersect and influence each other through lived exchanges and influences. By the way, on this point the famous Sapir–Whorf hypothesis on linguistic relativism can be slightly stretched: if every culture can perfectly give an account of its sociohistorical universe and respond adequately to all the needs of the members of its community, this is also, importantly, because every culture is at once the mirror and the product of history. By this, it reflects not only the norms of its rooting in one place, but also processes and consequences of multiple uprootings, aggressions, and marriages. What is true of culture as a totality is a fortiori true of cultural subsystems such as religions and philosophies.

Christianity is a magnificent example. It is a site of very diverse contributions. Even the story of the existence of Jesus Christ is not neutral: it calls on or recalls earlier myths from different cultures. The nativity can be read with interest in relation to the Greek birth of Dionysos, just as it can be read alongside the birth of the Buddha, who was born to the Virgin Maya and praised by an army that came from heaven. The Virgin Mary's flight into Egypt to protect Jesus from Herod's hatred can be compared to the Egyptian legend of the goddess Isis, who was obliged to hide herself and her son Horus to escape from the god Seth. The transfiguration of Christ can be compared to that of Buddha, his death with the crucifixion of Mithras or of Attis, and his resurrection with that of Osiris.[5] Examining these representations confirms the fact that artists actualize the divine in the light of the ordering codes of their own culture. The traits of God the Father are substituted for those of Zeus the Master; the Virgin Mary with her child is incarnated first in the heavy dignity of Roman matrons, as seen in pre-Christian Madonnas, before taking on the physique of the ladies of the European courts. This integration is often only the final moment of a process of indigenizing values borrowed from other cultures. For example, this is very likely the case with icons showing Christ with three faces, which seem predicated on older representations of a three-faced Shiva in the Indian tradition.

The existence of exchanges between cultures introduces a dimension of universality. They show us that, whether meetings between peoples are correct or incorrect from an ethical point of view, or peaceful or violent from a political point of view, they are in total signs and expressions of a complementarity.

We can note here that the political demand, voiced so forcefully today, to "reread" history and reorganize the present in terms of Africa's own interests is directed at the signification of needs and objective inclinations to complementarity. In general, this demand grasps and analyzes contacts between cultures in terms of relations of violence. It often launches projects in the superstructural realm – particularly the organization of power and production – whose impact would sometimes be greater if they were first aimed at the principles and functional rules of economic space.

With hearts racing, the political demand often has the feel of voluntarism. It is drawn to inflexible models of action, and generally sets out theoretical programs to disseminate particular articulations of ideological objectives among members of the national community. Its goal is to defend and illustrate a nation or state – or, at any rate, a culture and, sometimes, a difference. The political demand has two precise and concrete objectives: to fulfill the community's aspirations and to organize the national space. In the process, it sometimes ends up asking important questions about the right to historical and cultural difference.

Here the epistemological demand intervenes. Africa's violent contact with the West in the nineteenth century provoked a rupture in modes of being, thinking, and living whose full importance is still poorly understood. In particular, this contact brought Africa into a radically new space. Despite the discreet maintenance of older modes, the practice of knowledge has been lived since then as an opening to something else. This dispossession, with its hallucinatory character, has the feeling of a process of initiatic purification. Thus, for example: a five-year-old African who enters school has, in many cases, been baptized into a Christian religion, which is Western in origin. Her family, and sometimes the school environment, initiate her into the truths of that religion, and two or three years after she enters elementary school she will receive a particular education that structures and completes the training she has already received, to prepare her first for communion and then for confirmation. Meanwhile, the school will gradually introduce the child to categories, to concepts, to schemes of thinking, to a way of living and understanding the world and the universe derived in a straight line from an epistemological field and order that, at least geographically, are foreign to Africa. The young African will learn a foreign language that will allow her to commune, following intellectually consecrated norms, with the values of a tradition and a culture which, while they may be impressive, are foreign. And when one day, after graduating from high school, she begins to wonder about her own history and the past of her environment, it will be with a strongly marked gaze, and most likely in a foreign language, that she will read about her people's past destiny, her own condition in the present, and the future prospects of her land and culture. As this example shows, a rupture that is lived should be able to be thought: what does it mean, and what does it really open onto?

It is clear that these three demands intervene every time there is contact between cultures. If we bracket the aberrations and scandals that can be found, always and everywhere, each time different civilizations intersect, we see that these demands converge to argue for a particular task. In contemporary Africa, they take shape especially in ideologies of action and the questioning of political practices, and posit a will to the transformation or overturning of the cultural relations that connect Africa and Europe.

* * *

Christianity in Africa is certainly among the systems that most clearly and explicitly pose the question of cultural change. Both today and in the past, this change has involved tensions in the attempt to establish complementarity between the new norms introduced by the colonizer and the essence of African tradition. This collective conflict is also taken up on an individual level, raising questions about how to formulate typologies and modalities for the adaptation of Western values.

As in the case of the Arab world, although more violently,

> Experiential change becomes an inner imperative; adoption of new human attributes which enable and require the ameliorative transformation of the milieu becomes a matter of self-esteem; reform of education, of the state, of the social order becomes a sign of having proved one's mettle, of fruitful assimilation to an ideal of life – originally acknowledged to be heterogenetic but now thought to be orthogenetic – characterized by infinite, invigorating breadth of experience and action. Nevertheless, the foreign origin of the ideal is not forgotten and remains as knowledge which troubles the spirit, threatens self-confidence, and serves as a weapon for those who are not receptive to the new life and are neither capable nor desirous of going beyond the traditional bounds of experience. For change not only enriches life, it blocks access to trusted spheres of experience, especially in the religious sphere.[6]

Because of this orientation, no doubt, the African is extremely sensitive toward Western languages, profane or religious. We have recently seen African states make major policy shifts, with unprecedented speed, in response to a European newspaper article. Even the counter-discourse that emerges in the human sciences is comprehensible only in relation to the Western discourse whose negative reflection it is. In the Churches, many openings or adaptations to the African context are fundamentally, in spirit and in reality, merely reprises of practices earlier opposed by colonial missionaries.

Missionary languages, as sites where profane projects of colonization meet the evangelical goals of European religious orders, are expressions of a particular power – and as a result often serve as excellent foils to provoke African counter-languages.

Jean Pirotte recently published an important work on *Périodiques missionaires belges d'expression français:. reflets de cinquante années d'évolution d'une mentalité, 1889–1940* [Belgian Missionary Periodicals in French: Reflections of Fifty Years of the Evolution of a Mentality, 1889–1940].[7] This exemplary project describes the particular experience of Belgian Catholic missions in Africa and in the Far East. This case study provides us a means to draw out a spirit – the spirit that, uniformly, animated all Catholic missions.

How did the missionaries make sense of their encounter with Africans?[8]

Between 1892 and 1940, the Jesuits recognized these positive characteristics of Blacks:

(a) physical characteristics: vital power, resistive force, skill in swimming;
(b) one sole talent: a gift for languages;
(c) psychological characteristics: good humor, a cult of authority, respect for legitimate chiefs, sociability;
(d) three moral characteristics: indifference to the refined sensuality of civilized peoples, the preservation of rich virtues, the fact that "their heart is only sleeping" and so the possibility of a more elevated civilization;
(e) the Black child is a fine, penetrating, sweet, docile, trusting spirit.

As for faults and imperfections, they note:

(a) psychological traits: peoples in childhood, child-people, primitive spirit, thoughtless joys, wild joys, inconsistency, recklessness, improvidence bordering on foolishness, secretive, performers;

(b) moral traits: poor and inspiring pity, disinherited, unfortunate populations, with all the vices of the uncivilized Black races, profoundly debased race, brute beings, dull in spirit and heart, weak in spirit and heart, a barely human heart, savage, great barbarity, ferocious in tribal wars, lazy, native laziness, liars and accustomed to lying, whose lies are almost presented as virtues, perfidious, thieves, hustlers, greedy for others' goods, not scrupulous in conscience, egoism, polygamists.

The Jesuits also observed traits that they could not decide whether to consider qualities or faults: the Black is close to nature, emotive; he always laughs, is quick to joy, and has short-lasting sadness; finally, he adopts the friendships and enmities of his family, village, tribe, and race.

Although less elaborated, the Scheutist missionaries' judgments of Blacks, Africans, and Congolese are massive:

(c) as positive traits they note: on the intellectual level, ingenuity and, as a practical talent, prodigious ability for carrying objects on the head; lastly, a physical characteristic: agility;
(d) the negative traits noted are: intellectually, the Blacks are natural idiots; psychologically, large children, versatile, fanciful, impatient, barely meditative, even less contemplative, simpletons, made, like a fearful dog, to serve a higher power; morally poor in the sense that they inspire pity, unfortunate, depraved, abject, savages with brute instincts, cruel, lazy, seldom compassionate, malleable natures.

Pirotte writes, drawing conclusions from these tables:

> Missionary action apparently rests on a fundamental belief in the equality and perfectibility of men. What surfaces in the reviews is rather a diffuse sense of superiority; a sentiment, shared by many Europeans of the era, of needing to take charge of other peoples in order to guide them to their fulfilment ... A second element reinforces this sentiment of superiority, and contributes to the not always flattering image of the native: does not the missionary tend to insist on the pagan population's state of degradation in order to show the utility and efficacy of his own work? The focus is on the distance travelled by the convert: the scope of this task is meant to inspire new workers to enroll, while the compassion of the masses will ensure material and spiritual aid.[9]

There you have it. But the language that conveys the missionary's gaze and judgment is not exclusively used to name or designate real or imagined infirmities. This function is balanced by the mission's explicit projects: to spread the Gospel and expand Christian society. In the periodicals, the terms and expressions that convey this include:[10]

(a) the Gospel:
- preach, carry, announce the Gospel;
- take up the light of the Gospel, lead to the knowledge of the Gospel, plant the first markers of the Gospel, sow the seed of the Gospel;
- evangelize, evangelization, evangelical penetration, preaching and spreading the Gospel;
- preaching the word of God, giving the Holy Scriptures.

(b) expansion of Christian society:
1. the Church
   - establish, expand, and organize the Church;
   - installation of the Church;
   - growth of the people of God.
2. Christianization
   - Christianize, Christianization;
   - cause the Christian ideal to penetrate, to triumph.
3. faith and Catholic religion
   - preach the faith, prepare the way of the faith, propagation of the faith;
   - rooting, implantation, penetration of the Catholic religion, of Catholicism.
4. conversion
   - conversion, conversion of pagans, of souls.
5. the rule of God
   - extend, expand, establish the rule of God, found the rule of God here below;
   - universal establishment of the rule of God.
6. the rule of Christ
   - extend the rule of Christ, of the Sacred Heart;
   - conquer, win souls for Christ; conquest of souls to Christ.

(c) the salvation of souls
1. salvation of souls
   - salvation, saving;

- salvation, searching, rescue of souls;
        - saving, fishing for souls.
     2. seizing souls from the empire of Satan
        - seizing souls, poor pagans, from the yoke, the slavery, the empire of the demon, of Satan.
(d) moral regeneration and civilization
     1. regeneration
        - moral and social regeneration, recovery, moral advancement and elevation of a people.
     2. civilization
        - civilization, Christian civilization, civilizing mission;
        - civilize, obtain true civilization, instruct.

In truth, these themes are the soul of a language, the heart of missionary discourse, and pretexts for exalting the missionaries' actions. This language is not a totality that reveals or expresses the religious message; it is rather a social fact that must be put in relation with the objective conditions that make it possible. By all accounts, these are the same conditions that enabled colonization: processes of European economic expansion and the explicit project of the universal extension of a particular version of the will to truth. At the turn of the twentieth century, these processes made possible the gradual transformation of African space. A whole cultural a priori found itself invested in the mission of reviving Blacks and enrolling them into Western culture. With the support of classical schemes and metaphors, missionary language systematically opposes the immobility of African culture and Western dynamism, the mysterious and little-known destinies of African religions and the profile of Christianity with its vigorous historical conquests.

Violently interwoven into the fantasies of primitivism that this language projects are a discourse in praise of the West and an invocation of the Gospel that is saturated with prejudices and cultural and theological postulates. These derive in particular from the multiple discourses of the Catholic Church. As we know:

> The revealed message, the magisterial documents that define dogmas and practices, the discourses of Popes' and Bishops' letters, the writings of theologians, pastors' homilies, catechismal productions, positions taken by secular representatives of movements mandated

by Catholic Action, editorials in Catholic journals, etc., are so many languages that emanate from different levels in the hierarchy and are endowed with varying coefficients of legitimacy. This shows to what extent their legitimacy or index of credibility are dependent on the hierarchical system of the Church.[11]

Missionary languages are not theological languages. They are systems, whose most constant themes and motifs involve the practice of Christian proselytism, the illustration of a culture, and – with varying degrees of systematicity – the discreet or explicit support of colonial politics. They are languages, in the proper sense of the term, and actualizations of the "language of propaganda" that disturbed Pope Benedict XV, leading him to write in 1919 in the encyclic *Maximum illud*: "We have been deeply saddened by some recent accounts of missionary life, accounts which displayed more zeal for the profit of some particular nation than for the growth of the kingdom of God."[12]

It would be a poor description of the ambiguities of the Church's actions in Africa to say that it supported colonization and the colonizing program. The Church was within colonization; it took up the principles of the conquests meant to disaggregate "savagery"; it was integrated into the program of colonization that the European metropoles established in the name of civilization. While the principles of universality and catholicity may have functioned according to the wishes of the papacy, they never truly suppressed national motivations.

Missionary language is thus lodged within the colonizing action. Starting from an avowed will to convert African peoples to Jesus Christ, it leads by way of the defense of a European country's interests to an exaltation of the virtues and norms of Western civilization. Its practice is illuminated by ideological presuppositions: Pirotte mentions the impotence of human nature without divine grace; the theological adage "No salvation outside of the Church"; the fight against the city of Satan; and, finally, the "toothing stones"[13] of the faith said to exist in African traditions.

Remarkably, the exercise of this violence that is conversion to the West or to Christianity did not begin with the onset of colonization. It can be found in identical form in older experiences, such as those of the Italian Capuchins, missionaries in

Central Africa during the second half of the seventeenth century.[14] They employed practically identical normative phrases defining the rules for passage from Satanic obscurity to the light of the Gospel, and the requirements for transformation from primitive to civilized society. The missionaries wrote long *Relations*, on Rome's order, which describe the "gestures" of a civilization, of "the" civilization, and trace the thread of the conflicts that arose from the implantation of the "Truth" among savages. Biblical themes – the vine and the harvest, the construction of the Kingdom and the light and life – intertwine with cultural themes: leading the Africans to the common denominator of the West, bringing them out of the periphery of civilization. Imagistic forms and metaphors open the way: Christianization is the guarantor of passage from Africa's physical and moral sickness to a state of health, from bestial lives and morals to humanity, from fetishism to faith in Jesus Christ.

There is no fundamental discrepancy between the language of the Capuchins in the seventeenth century and that of the missionaries who went to conquer Africa at the end of the nineteenth century. They share the same continuous background, despite minor divergences arising from differences between eras and the conquerors' mindsets. This essential murmur unites the Gospel and the civilizing crusade of the West, and the plans that both have for the status of African souls. Throughout, it is articulated and expressed in terms of the political, economic, and cultural interests of European countries.

* * *

We have discussed the historical, political, and epistemological demands raised against the privileges the West claimed for itself by discovering and colonizing Africa. These same demands are raised against Christianity to the extent that, in a relatively recent past, it was one of the finest expressions of Western imperialism in Africa and the most notable symbol of its cultural power. When independence came, at least politically, the new Africa of Nations attempted with unequal success to find the measure of a new sovereignty in a world of extreme interdependency. But "the mission" persisted. While it abandoned its earlier exoticism and softened its presuppositions to the point of deracializing them, the networks that founded it remained in place and invariable, supported by biblical themes Westernized by centuries of European culture.

Thrown abruptly and almost despite itself into the modernity of a global history, Africa today works to connect its past and history to the still-unclear demands of an economic dependence that links it to the former colonizers. It is chained by ideologies of development to foreign models, whose application is guided by grids that take account of neither its specific contradictions nor its real problems.

In the discussions and debates that argue for increased independence from the metropoles, the most distinct themes seem to involve a will to cultural autonomy. I will note only a few of its most vivid expressions: a call to outline an original African thought (or thoughts) that will eventually lead to a fertilization of the present; an enthusiasm for African languages as means of communication and tools of expression; and an explicit desire for books and museums where traces of past experience are carefully preserved to serve Africa's ideological interests. The substance of African sciences was born from these conversations – particularly African philosophy and theology, which try to understand their own derivation from the West and reflect on themselves as new disciplines emerging from an African physical and spiritual setting.

In a recent book, the Reverend Father Hebga, a Cameroonian Jesuit, tries to draw concrete conclusions and sketch out a program of African Christianity for the post-missionary era:

> Christianity is not a Western religion, but an Eastern religion monopolized by the West, which imprinted on it the indelible seal of its philosophy, law, and culture, and then presented it as such to the other peoples of the world. It is up to us, in turn, to imprint our own indelible seal on the same religion. We must no longer put on the same level as divine revelation Aristotelian-Thomist philosophy, German or Anglo-Saxon Protestant thought, or the Gaulish, Greco-Roman, Lusitanian, Spanish, and German practices and customs that have been "Christianized," if not deified, by Europe.[15]

So, then, it is no longer enough to establish one or another common denominator, or even to accept Christianity solely for the virtues of its humanitarian vocation. Instead, it is necessary to define and understand, drawing on African demands, how Christianity can be profoundly Africanized. This is why this project of decolonizing Christianity seems dedicated to refuting missionary practice, language, and spiritual imperialism:

> Suppose that one day Christianity were no longer the patrimony of the West (which, of course, denies this); that its supreme leaders were not exclusively white; that its theologies were no longer exclusively European and American, the dogmas of its faith defined only by whites according to European or Byzantine philosophical formulations, its law and its ecclesiastic discipline established unilaterally by whites, its liturgy and cult emanating, essentially, from Western or Eastern cultures; and that people of color were allowed to contribute to it more than a bit of musical and choreographic folklore for the European tourists, who love new sensations.

The division that is announced and outlined here does not seem to me to signify a refusal of revealed truths. Rather, it is a desire to integrate them into a new relation between African man and his world and culture.

The hypothesis of the "revealed God" is saved; fidelity to Rome is explicitly affirmed; the snares of syncretism are avoided by a pure and simple rejection of the myths of animist religions. And the new methodological discourse that Father Hebga fervently wishes for will find its home within faith in Jesus Christ: "We want Jesus Christ as our unique supreme reference."[16]

Perhaps action plans for the post-missionary era could see the animist religions earlier opposed by the mission in the name of the Faith as something other than myths. These religions still invest lives and events as more than empty symbols: for many Africans they are a fundamental mode of being, a knowledge and history by which positive knowledge is organized, modified, harmonized. In my opinion, if post-missionary Catholicism is to root itself in Africa, it will need to pose and position these religions in harmony with itself. This is no different from what happened in the West: the Westernization of Christianity is one measure of its visible and invisible harmony with earlier local animisms.

Syncretism, then?

We can reflect on Jean-Émile Charon's hypothesis:

> I would like to emphasize the great underlying unity that exists behind different faiths; and also to show how, sooner or later, a convergence of these different religions must occur: not, as is often

suggested, through a syncretism of existing religions, which would mean making a sort of "jam" out of existing beliefs. Modelled after convergence between different scientific disciplines, I believe that the religious convergence will conserve the entire originality of each existing religion.[17]

The argument proceeds by analogy. Charon describes the difference between particle and wave theories of matter, which appeared irreducible at the start of the twentieth century:

> Matter had to be at once particle (that is, discontinuous) and wave (that is, continuous). Evidently, the same matter cannot be simultaneously continuous and discontinuous. To resolve this grave problem it was necessary to become aware that, *absolutely*, matter was neither one nor the other; that, in fact, we do not know what matter "really" is. But certain "languages" could be constructed to speak of it; and like all languages, these were based on postulates. If everything was described in terms of what could be *observed*, this led to the discontinuous particle, which is "clipped" out of the continuous by the limits of human meaning and understanding whenever an observation is made. On the contrary, if phenomena were described as evolving *between observations*, this new postulate led to a wave-like and thus continuous matter.

The irreconcilability therefore does not reside in the things, since they remain as they are; instead, it is in our representations of them and in the languages of particle and wave.

> What then do physicists do? They must avoid the pitfall of seeking to make a "compromise" [a jam!] between particle and wave, which of course cannot be reconciled in the *same* language, but which have equally validity in *one or the other* of the two languages of the observable and the inter-observable. The solution was to make a sort of "retreat" from the two preceding languages, and to construct a new language capable of containing, *without deforming*, the two opposed points of view: particle and wave.

It was precisely in this way that Einstein reunited the two tridimensional concepts of particle and wave in the four-dimensional frame of space-time.

Religions, as both interior individual exigencies and social systems, are expressed in different and even contradictory languages. These languages try to symbolically render the

Absolute, but they are not themselves the Absolute. As a result, every theological language is only an approximation and an attempt to express the Inexpressible. Strictly speaking, it cannot be affirmed that any single theological language is absolutely true. Charon maintains:

> There thus is no place for discussion of whether such and such a language is the true language, or is to be preferred to such and such another. All these languages are destined only to permit *each* man to translate the universal archetype of Religion into symbols that his conscious ego can assimilate ... The dogmas of different religions are only the postulates of various languages, and in no way can these languages pretend to describe the Absolute, not even when it comes to fundamental issues like monotheism or polytheism.

An individual's insertion into the universe that one of these languages describes and presents allows that individual, as a singular being, to live a particular relation with Being by means of symbols. This experience is fundamentally personal, and individualized to such a degree that it could be metaphorically said that every person has their own personal religion. But, as a general rule, this singular actualization of the symbols in a system can take place only because of the existence of social Religion. This is a mass phenomenon that produces images and symbols, and guarantees the continuity and permanence of the essential language through which it is interpreted. The diversity and number of religions, and thus of languages, divides humanity. But, as Charon writes, this division derives not from the phenomenon itself – of which we cannot express anything in an *absolute* fashion – but from the postulates that form the basis of each of the religious languages in question. And these postulates, because in every case they have been proposed by people, are not irreconcilable. Or rather – they would not be irreconcilable within a larger language, one that would recognize the full value, and even the full complementarity, of each religious language, while remaining conscious of their relativity and diverse symbolism.

Antagonisms between religions – which are, in reality, antagonisms between competing modes of cultural and spiritual power in Africa – could thus be undone. The problem of the Africanization of Christianity and the problem of the integration of African religions into modernity are isomorphic. At present, they are posed in terms of how cultural units can best be organized to promote Africa's real interests. But perhaps we should begin to examine, in depth, the real space within which yesterday's differences are resolved, transformed, or affirmed, to discover new calls that will connect us to a world more vast than ever.

III.
QUESTIONS AND OPENINGS

1
"*Niam M'Paya*": At the Sources of an African Thinking

There are many ways of reading "*Niam M'Paya*," Alioune Diop's discreet preface to the Reverend Father Tempels's *Bantu Philosophy*.

We might see in it no more than prudently selected words and phrases to frame what was, for a young African publisher in Paris, a choice find: a little book first published in Flemish in Elisabethville – today Lubumbashi – at the peak of Belgian colonization, by a dissenting Franciscan who cried out to anyone who would listen that "the Bantu have a philosophy." By the good offices of Antoine Rubbens, a Belgian lawyer also based in Elisabethville, it received a French translation and an international audience – to the great displeasure of a few leaders of the Holy Roman Church and a good number of gentlemen of the colonial power.

A matter of philosophy, then, even of ontology; but also a matter of politics. After all, in the last chapter, deliciously titled "Bantu Philosophy and Our Mission to Civilize," Tempels writes: "Are we to conclude that the Bantu are incapable of attaining civilization? For anyone who holds that view there can be but one piece of advice: it is that *he should systematically liquidate the Bantu*; or more wisely, that he should pack his bags and return to Europe!"[1] The book is addressed to "colonials of good will," and for them it sketches a previously unknown field of knowledge. It shows a possible future for the expansion of

Western civilization through the medium of indigenous cultures, and an original path toward profound Christianization:

> The proof has been given of the impotence of our economic civilization, our "philosophy of wealth" to civilize the Bantu, to produce *évolués*[2] in the fine sense of the word. On the other hand, it has not been proved – the attempt has not been made – that the philosophy and wisdom of the Bantu are incapable of serving as the foundations upon which to raise a Bantu civilization. There are serious indications which allow the conclusion that the attempt would be worth trying.[3]

As for the integration of Christianity:

> Christianity – and especially Christianity in its highest and most spiritual form – is the only possible consummation of the Bantu ideal. But it is essential to set out this perennial doctrine in terms of Bantu thought and to present the Christian life that we offer them as a vital strengthening and a vital uplifting. Bantu civilization will be Christian or it will not be.[4]

This "political" project has a slow and subterranean movement. Présence Africaine allowed it, in broad daylight, to describe a possible order of cultural encounters on the pretext of doing philosophy. Alioune Diop welcomed the book and celebrated it as the secret code of a new syntax: "Of all the books I have read about Africa, this little book is the most important: so my own concerns encourage me to hope." Among his silent wishes, it responded to one hope in particular: it clearly presented proposals that, in a new and different way, could serve to denounce European practices and reflections that target Africa.

Perhaps it is from this angle that we should reread "*Niam M'Paya*," which, to coney the central meaning of Tempels's *Bantu Philosophy*, insistently excavates the misery of the Black – negated, reduced to silence and the night:

> What is there, then, more gripping than the spectacle of distress: an abandoned being, stripped of all social guarantees, reduced to its proper naked liberty, its original powerlessness, and delivered over to the terror of Fate? The authentic grandeur that breaks free of such a spectacle does not, all the same, characterize misery in Europe.[5]

Here is the ideal tableau of the Black, from the sixteenth century to the turn of the twentieth, from the era of the crumbling of the Sudanese empires, through the decadence of the Niger Valley civilizations and the great crises south of the tropics, to the establishment of the colonial powers. New political and cultural configurations contributed to transform Blacks into "docile bodies"; but these were "negative" and "servile" bodies in comparison to the ones that Europe had categorized within its own territories beginning in the seventeenth century, as it progressively established a new economy of social organization. The latter were, in effect, individualities endowed with four types of characteristics: cellular (through the play of spatial distribution), organic (through the coding of activities), genetic (through the accumulation of time), and combinatory (through the composition of forces).[6]

Closed within a space of surveillance, European docile bodies were, if we accept Foucault's hypothesis, blocked in by two walls:

> At one extreme, the discipline-blockage, the enclosed institution, established on the edges of society, turned inwards towards negative functions: arresting evil, breaking communications, suspending time. At the other extreme, with panopticism, is the discipline-mechanism: a functional mechanism that must improve the exercise of power by making it lighter, more rapid, more effective, a design of subtle coercion for a society to come.[7]

Could the solidifying and narrowing of norms and rules that emerged from the gradual concretization of discipline as an exemplary value and reference in Western culture have led to the "carceral city" the Reformers dreamed of – as the last pages of *Discipline and Punish* suggest? In any case, Foucault tells us, as he pauses before beginning an interrogation of "the power of normalization and the formation of knowledge in modern society" in the West, that

> ultimately what presides over all these [disciplinary] mechanisms is not the unitary functioning of an apparatus or an institution, but the necessity of combat and the rules of strategy. That, consequently, the notions of institutions of repression, rejection, exclusion, marginalization, are not adequate to describe, at the very centre of the carceral city, the formation of the insidious leniencies, unavowable petty

cruelties, small acts of cunning, calculated methods, techniques, "sciences" that permit the fabrication of the disciplinary individual.[8]

The "Black" misery Diop speaks of, a misery "flagrant to the point of pure tragedy," was no doubt primarily and principally the result of an encounter. On one side was an internally shattered Africa, broken and undone by itself.[9] And on the other, a "disciplinizing" Europe in the process of elaborating its future, by attempting to master whatever could not be derived from the application of its new order as it came out of the Renaissance, and defining the status of anything that was not itself. The consequences of the encounter (treaty, pillage, colonization) came afterwards. From the start, Europe lived the encounter by attempting to reduce African difference: on the one hand, by the erasure of individualities and collective identities in favor of a continental body invented by Europe – an obscure, unnamable, and unnamed monster (*hic sunt leones*) that it gave itself the task of reducing, dismembering, and naming – and on the other, by the annulment of African memory to the advantage of its own rhetoric and history.

What Europe tried to "discipline," therefore, following precise arrangements and values it had brought with it, was neither beings, nor ethnic groups, nor nations.[10] It was instead a monumental and savage object, crawling with "entities" about which Pacheco Pereira, in the sixteenth century, was uncertain whether they "belonged to the descendance of Adam." What explorers and missionaries describe in their accounts is thus at best a larva. They often call for Western action to lead this larva to the chrysalid stage and, over an indefinite period of time, to complete its evolution and transform it into a butterfly. In these projects of conversion and promotion a separate status is usually given to Arab Africa, Abyssinia, and Nubia. The usual practice is to cast a glance over their history, noting their decline and sometimes taking the opportunity to express contempt.[11] After this, depending on the needs of the cause, they can be assimilated to the Blacks of the continent or distinguished from them.

The disciplining of the continent was assured by three principal means: the invention of savagery, the trial of meaning, and the conceptual grid. Set in motion, these worked efficiently to create objects submitted "to surveillance and to normalizing sanction."

From the sixteenth century on, the historical a priori – the demand to classify species and cultures – parceled out the space in which discourses on non-Westerners were expressed. Montaigne proclaimed the non-barbarism of the "savages of America,"[12] and compared what he considered to be virtues (the profound philosophy implied in a song sung by prisoners; their courage in dying; polygamy) to his own culture's ways of living. In the process he described, by criticizing, the profile of the ethnocentrism already in force in his day. The evolutionism of Bonnet's, Buffon's, and Pallas's natural history intersected with the theological conception of a hierarchy within humanity, feeding the first ethnological writings. Following Charles Bonnet's model, "evolution" here is nothing other than the "interdependent and general displacement of the whole scale from the first of its elements to the last."[13] The forward motion of Western humanity and the (absolute) delay of the savage thus took on the status of scientific notions, and very rapidly became operative in the description and comprehension of cultures. The savage was born; and colonization would then, paradoxically, discover it and confirm its savagery using the same a priori arguments by which it was produced.

The trial of meaning also appears from the start: it is the walling-in of any space through which "consciousnesses" might escape while on their way to confinement. Blocked in, immobilized, the Black discovers that evil is not exterior to him. He incarnates vice and irrationality more perfectly than anyone else in the world: he is lack in relation to fullness, illness in relation to health, obscurity in relation to light, nonsense in relation to meaning. The gaze and discourse of the West, whether offered or imposed, purely and simply dissolve him. But in parallel, the process by which he is tamed – progressive integration, under surveillance, into the space of a new society – forces him to actualize his modes of being and acting within a rigorously demarcated field. There is no objectively possible recourse outside of this space, which is animated by precise reflections of concepts. Negated by and in the speech of the other, he survives only in the violence brandished against him, which extends out into rigorous procedures of controlling and limiting freedom. And all of this was present from the first encounters between Africa and Europe.

"Misery," Diop writes,

of the intellectual, engaged in the labyrinth of values, where the false is hard to distinguish from the true ... of the artist, the thinker who does not have enough resources to evaluate, on his own, the creations in relation to which he situates his own ... misery of a people, alas, victims at times of passion, exploding in just but imprecise anger – more often of a learned propaganda, always the same and never suspected, which devours their most secret intimacy, their essential equilibrium and lucidity.

Misery of Africa – but also

misery of Europe, encumbered with means and having lost the taste for happiness to the extent that it sacrifices it to those means ... Europe does not always realize this, because for centuries now – has it not? – it has seen its reflection only in the mirror of its own consciousness. It has condemned itself to incomplete knowledge of itself and of life, because it deprives others – less out of hate than from a sickly prudishness – of the Gaze and Speech that would allow them to grasp and reveal the Destiny of humanity.[14]

Europe extended its desire and its normalizing destiny to Africa. Brutally but surely, and with unbelievable violence, in less than a century – between the last quarter of the nineteenth and the first quarter of the twentieth – it destroyed or perverted the original impulses of Black lives and civilizations. The docile body of the continent became, despite itself, a vast field that masterbuilders organized into parks, mines, gardens, etc. Carcerality was institutionalized: scholarly and constraining apparatuses of surveillance presided over the Westernization of Blacks and the exploitation of territories and goods. "No one," Jean Chesnaux stated during a conference at Royaumont in 1961 on the ideals and criteria of social progress,

would deny that, in the structure of the colonial regime, there was a real evolution in relation to the feudal, tribal, or sometimes even more backwards regimes that the colonized countries had previously known. Railways appeared, along with modern mines. Taxes in money were introduced by the new administrations, where before only taxes in goods had been known. The colonial state was also able to define its borders much more rigorously than the political formations it replaced. Modern science has spread, as well as a certain number of modern political theories (though to quite a small degree, due to very low rates of education); modern vaccination has begun to be practiced on a large scale, etc. But do these *innovations* have the character of progress?[15]

These innovations, Chesnaux thinks, "far from constituting progress, are an integral part of a regime that is incompatible with the harmonious development of the economy and the society." Real progress can only occur once "political independence" is posed as a prerequisite.

Writing in 1947, Alioune Diop prudently identified the West's "blindness, fruit of alienation, misery, and fear," and announced Black alienation, even if he did not himself live its values as presented in Father Tempels's book. He also says clearly: "We know only that neither the European nor the African can prevent the latter from entering into the cycle of modernity and, by this, losing the virginal freshness of his traditional characteristics."[16] Chesnaux would explain this same line of thought several years later, but from a Marxist point of view: "The demands of the age of the cosmos will only accelerate the march towards a unification of human cultures – which, I believe, goes hand in hand with the birth of a socialist world."[17]

The moment that "Africa" is so much as breathed, it is immediately condemned to modernity and its stipulations. Stunningly and abruptly, the extravagance of the trial of meaning wipes it clean of everything that had earlier been condemned or cast into the fire of disdain. By beatifying the ancestors it proposes eulogistic ways of reading and deciphering a culture that was earlier reduced to a chaos of primitivity. But it was not this new trial that Alioune Diop was celebrating as he introduced Tempels's work at the end of the second European war. What was in play was something altogether different. On the one hand, for Africans in exile in Europe, there was the hope of a cultural re-rooting. The extent of their insertion and progress within a foreign Western culture had shown them the blatant limits of its mystifying civilization, and led them to wonder about the pertinence and relevance of African culture, of their culture. On the other hand, there were the records of failure established by faithful servants of the West overseas, who understood that the norms of discipline and normalization, particularly the trial of meaning and the conceptual grid – despite punishments, and perhaps even thanks to them – in the long run played against Europe's presence in Africa.

Thus, then; on one side, Alioune Diop, and on the other, Tempels. On the one side, a dynamic conception of a history to come and the role that Blacks might play in it:

> Daniel Halévy has recently published an elegant and seductive little book, *Essai sur l'accélération de l'histoire* [Essay on the Acceleration of History]. We have the right not to espouse its thesis, which is inspired by Leibniz. But it may still be that the destiny of man is to refrain more and more from rest, from stability, and thus from the nourishment that has sustained him until now, and gave him an equilibrium that evokes a serene and living eternity – and to give himself over to the freedom that is anxiety, combative activity, instable equilibrium, and history.

On the other side, Father Tempels's project, articulated on the basis of anti-modernist systems of thought, elucidates and unfolds the text of an implicit philosophy in order to contribute to the establishment of an African civilization more permeable to Christianity:

> Industrialization, however, the introduction of a European economy, permanent raising of production – all that is not necessarily a measure of civilization. On the contrary, it may lead to the destruction of civilization ... We have the heavy responsibility of examining, assessing and judging this primitive philosophy and of not failing to discover that kernel of truth which must needs be found in so complete and universal a system, constituting the common possession of a host of primitive and semi-primitive peoples. We must proceed with the Bantu towards its sources to the point at which "the evolution of primitive peoples" was led into a false path by false deductions; and, taking this as our point of departure, help the Blacks to build their own Bantu civilization, a stable and noble one of their own.[18]

The equivocation is clear; it signifies an epoch and the viewpoints that could be held at the time by an African and a European infatuated with Africa. It reminds us of an even more remarkable case: the ambiguous relations that link Senghor to the ethnologists, Leo Frobenius in particular. Their writings bring him back to Africa – but this is a mythical Africa that he contemplates with new eyes. He believes he is reading the site where the speech of his father, his ancestors, and the nature of his childhood are preserved, when what he is offered is a scholarly construction. He also finds them moving for other reasons, notably the curious affair of affinities between the "Ethiopian" – that is to say, Negro-African – and the German soul.[19] No doubt, to fully understand these equivocations we would need a better understanding of the real atmosphere in postwar Europe when it came to Africa. Ethnology seemed to renew itself: a pared-down methodology, a lighter and more flexible tone, and a new outlook all gave it the feel of a reprise, a new beginning. The tableaux it unfolded were seductive, especially to Africans, who no longer saw the heavy outlines of racist orthodoxy. Instead, they were stories, complex narrations or descriptions of African cultures that seemed to confer a noble status. The *libido sciendi* of the West thus recuperated a vice[20] and gave Africa a new image of itself. But this renewed science did not, in fact, exist. As we know, "The idea of a 'psychoanalytic anthropology,' and the idea of a 'human nature' reconstituted by ethnology, are no more than pious wishes. Not only are they able to do without the concept of man, they are also unable to pass through it, for they always address themselves to that which constitutes his outer limits."[21]

Previously negative and absurd traits were washed white and became relevant; bent or broken norms were reconstituted, traditions and oral literatures that had been deformed – or at any rate ignored and doomed to perish – were celebrated, collected, and even studied with the goal of reinjecting them into society. Today, these inoffensive games advocate brilliantly for the majesty of African cultures and civilizations. But in reality these cultures are moving ever further down the path to folklorization, thanks to the efficiency of Euro-American economic rationality and power.

But between 1945 and 1947? Alioune Diop was witnessing an agony: "The genius of our civilization, so respectful of the autonomy of beings, of the freedom of the other, lent itself marvelously to the yoke of the will to power."[22] Tempels's book gave him material for dreams: "It uncovers the actual meaning of the Black man's adventure in the European bush."[23] Critical and conciliatory, making no excessive claims, he notes:

> Europe had the fundamental experience that man cannot find himself by knowing only himself ... What we hope for is to arrange a meeting with Europe in the country of the Universal ... our own road will have been harder. But because it is called the pathway of Faith in Man, we have not hesitated to take it.[24]

With bold strokes, Alioune Diop traces a possible heading for a critical adventure. This comes at the start of a book that aimed to restore an ethnological framework for Africa, to allow for cultural and religious syncretism. Perhaps this is where we can find the central question that provokes hallucinations today in every study of African philosophy.

2
On African Literature

There is an image of the African – the *Nègre*, as is commonly said after Césaire, Damas, and Senghor. The *Nègre* is not only the negation of the European; he is also, and principally, the primary sign and symbol of the caprices of Nature. Man of the unknown forests, living in torrid climates, he is presented in turn – and sometimes simultaneously – as the eternal child, the good or naughty savage, or the incarnation of dereliction in its pure state.

And the West sings the praises of its sons – explorers, merchants, missionaries, etc. – who since the fifteenth century have worked to discipline African space. Through the violence of weapons, or the quieter violence of conventions, these emissaries of the West submitted beings and things to the discourse of measurable quantities. They transformed the contexts of free African life into spaces of production in order to establish, by natural right, a new model for exploiting riches and a code for advancing – in fact, for "taming" – the African natives. It was said – is it really no longer said today? – that

> humanity cannot be condemned to suffer that the carelessness, laziness, or merely the incapacity and ignorance of primitive peoples will let sleep indefinitely riches that God has put on earth for the benefit of all. If there exist lethargic regions and riches that are managed poorly or not at all by their original holders, to the

disadvantage of universal needs, then Man, as a party wronged by this incompetent administration, has the right to take the place of these incompetent managers and to exploit, for the profit of all, these riches, some of which humanity has only recently learned to harvest. Accordingly, a society or a people which possesses the intellectual and material means to exploit these goods in time with human needs has the right to substitute themselves for this incompetent primitive people. In other words, the bequest of the goods of this world to humanity as a whole is legitimate, and so *a priori* is colonization ... The right of colonization cannot be negated without attacking the very basis of Natural Right: man and his nature.[1]

These fine ways of rationalizing present us with desires and drives that might explain the dilation of Western space. But they cannot hide the strangeness of their ways, or silence the risks and violence of the projects in which they were worked out in detail.

There was also a particular model for the conquest of African space. This concrete reference, the Roman, had been used to justify the establishment of grids on European soil and society at the start of the sixteenth century. Reference to Rome, Michel Foucault notes, had a double index: "Citizens and legionaries, law and manoeuvres. While jurists or philosophers were seeking in the pact a primal model for the construction or reconstruction of the social body, the soldiers and with them the technicians of discipline were elaborating procedures for the individual and collective coercion of bodies."[2]

A mastery of space, then, whose refinements and styles – haven't we heard, endlessly, of English, Belgian, or French models of colonization? – signify both the Western-style arrangement of African territory through various disciplinary exercises, and the convergence of colonizing projects around one central objective: the reduction of opposites. It became clear that the West was trying to establish itself in the memory of Humanity, and to make its own time line into the time of history. Hegel, traversing a hazardous terrain of facts and words, made the course of Spirit coincide with the archaeological current of a land and its culture. The presuppositions of this trajectory were the same ones that, not long before, had hallucinated the bloody trajectory of the conquistadores. Later on, these presuppositions would support the arrogance of colonial troops. On another level, they would make anthropology "possible" and "thinkable"

– a discipline that might instead have been the place to reply to Kant's question: *Was ist der Mensch?* Within this trajectory, anthropology was and could only be the "glorious" discipline that studied "our ancestors, the contemporary savages": providentially conserved links of a chain testifying to the passage from primitivity to civilization, as had been "proven" by theories of the stages of humanity (Lewis Henry Morgan), the phases of evolution of civilization (Eduard Hahn), or the hierarchy of peoples (Ernst Grosse).

These fantastical bodies might tempt us to enjoy Rousseau's quip in his *Social Contract*: it is, in a sense, by force of our study of man that we are put out of a condition to know him. But in this shameless exhibition of force – because that is also and perhaps principally what is involved – we can find an allegory. In book 24 of the *Iliad*, Achilles is moved by Priam's defeat to draw a tragic moral from an epic: he assigns responsibility to the gods for the curious destinies of mortals. But the West, victorious by its weapons?

This process is what the "fathers of négritude" taught. Aimé Césaire, Léon-Gontran Damas, Jacques Rabemananjara, and Léopold Sédar Senghor took their arguments from the mortuary spectacles that the West paraded endlessly around the world, in the name of civilization – and then were shocked to find themselves attending suicides. They tried to understand the mythic discourses of the "civilizing god" who makes History – and then were surprised to find empty statements that, when they speak of Black people, run counter to their own norms. This history is well known and does not need to be repeated here; it has been adequately described in sympathetic terms by Lilyan Kesteloot, and more haphazardly by Janheinz Jahn.

Here I will note merely that the négritude movement, in its project and in its meaning, was and still is a vibrant and paradoxical form of the culture it rose up against. Its creators are Black, as has often been repeated. But they are also French, by nationality and by education. Certainly, their writings contain many traces of their own upbringing and of Black life, tremulous memories that stubbornly persist in innumerable registers and sometimes explode provocatively into remarkable cries of counterviolence, such as Damas's *Pigments* or Césaire's *Cahier d'un retour au pays natal*. In these memories the cry is sometimes conveyed literally, obliging the authors to double another text. For example, Senghor's appeals to the space of his childhood are illuminated by the writings of the ethnologists who helped him to discover it. The barriers that Damas sets up between the obscenity of European civilization and the rapture of Black life are, from his earliest poems, inscribed in the social text of Western bourgeois normality, transplanted to the "Islands." And as Sartre showed in "Black Orpheus," the cry is specific to the extent that it wills and defines itself as an echo of the being-in-the-world-of-*Nègres*, an explicit will to take on the misery of a race and the chance movements of its history, defying the psychological and cultural unity that the West has tried to impose on it in the name of its own historical experience.

The possibility of thematizing this "I am different" in the mode of négritude was an offshoot from a Western, and particularly French, trajectory. Between the two last European wars, there was a singular shift toward relativity and individual destiny, the idea of the unhappy consciousness and the force of the unconscious, the value of intuition and the demand for freedom. In particular, and decisively, it asked how we had believed for so long in the omnipotence of the goddess Reason, and had thought it possible, in truth and in science, to regulate life, thought, and action by the myth of an ego that speaks in logical formulas. Négritude, like surrealism or existentialism, finds its original meaning in this shift: subversion is both offered and accepted within a culture that questions its own norms and the operations that police its discourse.

It is significant that it was Jean-Paul Sartre who Senghor asked to thematize négritude by writing the introduction to his *Anthologie de la nouvelle poésie nègre et malgache de langue française*. The existentialist philosopher's approach looked for new values, and gave a philosophical coherence to allegories and poetic metaphors tinged by surrealism. Négritude thus became a project and a theme of combat, at once consciousness and exercise of the freedom to be Black. As the foundation of Black Orpheus's insurrection, it is what allows him to return from a reading of his own history to invade the present and to stun it with his hallucinatory difference. As the explanation for his neurosis, it lets him to work toward liberating his long-suppressed energies.

Sartre's intervention in the development of this thought is important. It gave philosophical credentials to a current that was seething in a chaos of words, while at the same time its ambiguity marked the precise limits to the emergence and flight of the Black cry. Sartre, as "Black philosopher" [*philosophe nègre*], shows how négritude is dialectically made to destroy itself: it is an antithetical moment that will necessarily be followed by some new dazzling thing. But Sartre's text is also, and remarkably, an antithesis: "Black Orpheus" displaces the goal of the rebellion by "young French university students with black skin." Indeed, his text changes the scale of their initial protests, sets principles for interpreting their writings, names the rules that direct their actions, and, finally, gives a form to the claims of the Black race and proposes a universal strategy.

The cult of the antipodes and the themes of suspicion and disgust at the West, like the celebration of difference affirmed in African writings starting from the end of the second European war, portrayed the scandal of the Black condition with a rare generosity, and worked effectively to prepare the call for African political independence. But within the same constellations of "Black Orpheus" where these categories were named, they were also definitively cancelled out. It can thus be understood why critics of African literature spoke of a "crisis" at the dawn of African independence. In that moment works of literature, like lives, tended to be made available for other tasks; they did not necessarily respond to either the pathetic suffering or the exhibitory violence that critics were conscientiously searching for, following the prescriptions of Sartre's antithesis. Other readings had also helpfully focused matters: for example, Frantz Fanon, who wrote in *Black Skin, White Masks*:

> I do not want to be the *victim* of the Ruse of a black world. My life must not be devoted to making an assessment of black values. There is no white world; there is no white ethic – any more than there is a white intelligence. There are from one end of the world to the other men who are *searching*.[3]

* * *

Today it is agreed that African literature has a particular function and role. At present it is even for the best to integrate it into the frame of the myth called "the development of Africa" – a myth which, on analysis, seems to signify underdeveloped

Africa's aspiration to reach the point of equilibrium currently incarnated by the rich countries of Europe and North America. What literature can do within such a project is something of a problem, so as long as we prudently and reservedly agree with Jean-Pierre Richard that literature is the very pure result of an act by which the writer, transmuting his objects into thought, causes everything but this thought to vanish.[4]

Perhaps it is time for us to look, even if only rapidly, at the real status of texts in Africa, and then to propose one more way of defining the literatures of Africa.

In common practice, African literature refers to any text whose author is African. What determines whether or not a text belongs to the field of African literature is thus the author's racial characteristics.[5] So, to take an extreme example, the work of a European missionary who has lived his whole life in Africa would not be African literature, even if he writes in an African language, while the work of an African who has lived his whole life in Europe would. This racial criterion is a problem in itself. But we can also note that it often works in support of a unanimist prejudice. One of the finest expressions of this is the reduction of all of Africa to a single cultural nation, whose "literary" productions – despite their diversity and differences in style and function – can without major difficulty be gathered under the label of "African literature."

At least two questions can help us better perceive the limits of this unanimist prejudice. The first is about the diversity of African texts and the irreducibility of certain genres, and the second is about African cultural nationalities.

The concept of African literature covers three fields, which differ in both geography and meaning.

The first is so-called oral literature. It has still not been seriously asked whether, and in what way, this can be considered literature – in the sense that the concept and term are understood in the Western tradition. In any case, even a quick survey of traditionalists will show that the terms and labels used to describe material offered to sub-Saharan African listeners in the form of song or story hardly correspond to the category of African literature. As for the subsets of this literature, a systematic comparative study of genres of expression and their function in several African cultures would surely invalidate the familiar classifications based on categories like myth, epic, riddle, etc. Despite surface similarities, it is clear that the *mvett* is not the *kasala*, just as the *nshinga* of the Luba tradition is called a "riddle" only for convenience in translation. Rigorous research would show how complex and mutually imbricated types of stories can be, and from one cultural region to the next would clearly confirm the singularity of different genres and the specificity of each tradition.

Next, another field, obscured by the lazy concept of oral literature: written literature. Perhaps it is still necessary to announce, loud and clear, that in Africa today there exists – and in a number of countries has existed for many years – a vibrant and important literature written in African languages. This literature is relatively recent, generally dating from Africa's first contacts with the Arabic or European alphabet, and is without doubt the least well known of African literatures. Its borders are also the most difficult to define. For example, the Reverend Father Kagamé wrote remarkable translations of the Holy Scriptures into Kinyarwanda. His work surely belongs to literature in the same way that, for example, the *Versio Antiqua Gallica* of the Psalms[6] is part of French literature. But the genre also encompasses the works by South African authors that the late Janheinz Jahn collected, and the poems, stories, and essays that writers in the former Belgian Africa began to publish in the 1920s in small missionary journals like *Nkuruse*.

This field would also include contemporary African musicians, such as many bandleaders on the continent, who write their lyrics in African languages before setting them to music. But would the work of the "Mwondo Theatre" – a young theatre troupe in Lubumbashi whose very modern problematics and techniques (spontaneous creation, integration of spectators into the play) are "brought to life" in African languages (and accidentally also in French) – belong to this group, or to so-called oral literature?

This literature is poorly known, little commented on by African intellectuals, and barely studied. It receives little support from the state, outside of rare countries like Tanzania, which has a rigorous program to promote it. Nonetheless, it is among the most total of African literatures: in its own way, it takes up the encounter of tradition and modernity, and its judge and accomplice are the people – this faceless, immense people who are excluded from the spiritual and intellectual consumer goods expressed in foreign languages.

Finally, a third field: literature in foreign languages. This literature is surely the best-known internationally, and at least in francophone African countries it receives the most social approval. This literature, produced by Africans trained in Western schools – university and/or simply the harsh experience of European life – draws its force and power from what Pierre van den Berghe sees as the essential reasons for the persistence of foreign languages in Africa:

- the linguistic diversity of Sub-Saharan Africa;
- the centrifugal forces that arise from this diversity;
- the practical advantages to using foreign languages; and
- the relative absence of linguistic nationalism in Africa.[7]

To these four reasons, I would add a fifth, the most important: the economic constraints that forcefully determine the modes of African dependence in relation to the international metropoles.

In reality, these three literatures constitute only two fields: literature in African languages and French (or other) literature in Africa, what is called literature "*d'expression française* (or x)."

There are, then, two African literatures, both of which we should know better. In terms of literature in African languages, we will need to revisit the concept and reality of oral literature. We will especially need to examine the real but poorly understood implications of philological transcription, which despite all methodological precautions is always re-creation and interpretation. Transcription is at once the moment and site of a singular rupture: it leads to the production of a text that is new but also has a particular fixed status. This text belongs to the same space as literature written in African languages, and the two share a number of characteristics – in particular, language, integration with an environment and a tradition, and their resonance with African people.

African literature in French, for its part, is the product of a particular period. Born and developed in large part from the contradictions of colonization, it was for a long time a literature of protest and revolt. It was intended as violence, and became so through the constant theme of the murder of the father – incarnated by the colonizer and the metropolitan power. Close attention to recent publications suggests the emergence of a new thematics; or, no doubt more precisely, a clear diversification of themes. African literary productions, like all literature, tend to move into new spaces and so to become particularized by their authors' ideological and literary tendencies – and also, to a certain extent, by nationality.

It may be objected that the concept of nationality is new to Africa and has little meaning, and that ethnic structures show the superficiality of the new national borders. Fair enough. But an attentive rereading of recently published texts shows divergences that we can explain by the different sociopolitical environments and relations of social production that have been gradually established since independence. The father to be killed or celebrated, when he appears, is not the same in Senegal, in Congo, or in Madagascar. The social context that provides writers with material is not identical in the Central African "Empire," in Rwanda, or in Zaire. These facts condition current literary production to the point that we might ask whether national tendencies are already beginning to be sketched out.

Whatever the case, it seems more than likely that the fervor with which many writers of the present generation are interrogating the real context of their lives and traditions is leading to a differentiation of sensibilities and writing styles. It is thus possible to see each creation, in Richard's words, as a positive and creative activity within which particular beings manage to coincide fully with themselves.

3
Sorcery: A Language and a Theory

The exemplary rigor and ambitious project of *L'Impensé du discours: "kindoki" et "nkisi" en pays Kongo du Zaïre* [The Unthought of Discourse: "Kindoki" and "Nkisi" in the Kongo Region of Zaire][1] will irritate the beautiful spirits of the anthropology currently in fashion. It will also worry those Africanist ideologists who, following the late Janheinz Jahn, believe that by an impressive but random arrangement of certain dazzling presentations of African culture they have been able to definitively identify "Africanity." This is because Buakasa's book, with an apparently innocent manner and a scrupulous respect for the codes that regulate scientific discourse (is there an ironic gap here, or respectful distance from the "masters" who imprudently agreed to endorse his research?), wants to speak the truth of an "apparent irrational": the polyvalent chains of what is customarily called, for convenience, "sorcery" or "magic."

Benoît Verhaegen wrote the preface to the book, because he felt Buakasa's scientific approach was similar to his own. Nonetheless, he thought it useful to clearly separate himself from the project. No doubt this is done with a smile, but by that very fact it sets up a gap that cannot be erased afterwards without serious consequences for the quality of the research and the totality under study. "By what right," Verhaegen writes, can a European, who has been educated in respect for reason and science and whose profession is the diffusion of this knowledge, write the preface to – which is to say, understand and appreciate – a work dedicated to phenomena of sorcery and traditional practices? Furthermore, I believe in mathematics, and in Marx's historical materialism. So what common denominator do I have with Buakasa's discourse?[2]

A logic of friendship? In the preface, these propositions are preceded by a significant measure of distance. Verhaegen begins by declaring:

> In my own eyes at least, I am neither sorcerer nor fetish priest. I do not cast evil spells, even though sometimes when listening to my colleagues I regret that inability ... I possess neither medications nor magic therapies ... I was not born in a Kongo village. My mother never accused her uncle of having caused my father's death, no more than she ever blamed her brother, my maternal uncle, for the death of my brother! And although I have no faith in doctors, I do not, for all that, turn to priests to heal me.

There is a problem, then; but what is it really about, in the end? This suite of remarks is followed by an introduction to Buakasa's "scientific" method – existential, structural, and hermeneutical. But the initial humor marks the presentation throughout, leaving the reader to suspect this preface involves more than one "affair of sorcery," and at least one unsaid. Buakasa claims to have reconstructed "the temple of Solomon"; Verhaegen responds that the giraffe dies in its skin.

* * *

To me, the notable traits of this "discourse on sorcery" are its modest approach, its forceful – and nicely provocative – hypotheses, and its supple and fine writing. In the introduction Buakasa shows the scope of the project when he writes that

> for the Kongo, kindoki is presented as a "theory" that simultaneously explains, in its own way, its own existence, and indicates how it is to be understood. It allows individuals to explain certain facts of their existence ... finally, it prescribes a set of rules for behavior. As for nkisi, it is grasped as the product of work, the object of a

necessary relationship with a simbi ("genie") that animates it; in the hands of men, particularly the ngaga ("healers"), it is a magical instrument that protects or harms.[3]

Buakasa shows his cards from the start: his discourse is neither commentary, arrangement, nor even explication of "practices" scattered throughout Kongo tradition, but instead the construction of another discourse. Concretely, it is a kind of montage, an interpretation of the subject of kindoki. What he offers is a discourse on a discourse. Notably, this implies that reflexive and scientific discourse, in Western fashion, is not the only norm of intelligibility for an organization like sorcery in Kongo territory. Indeed, the Kongo discourse, which is the pretext for this new interpretation, is already itself a theory, or better still a complete ideology. It cuts across the whole of the space of representations; it presents all the operations that arise within this space, defines their necessary interconnections, and rigorously names the rules of their de-structuration. It would thus be a "science"; and Buakasa, breaking with the methods of the White Man's School, attempts to "speak" this first discourse differently: "We have tried," he writes, "to construct our own discourse."

The project of this second discourse is twofold: on the one hand, to "grasp the mode of formation and functioning of kindoki and nkisi as 'realities' at the heart of a society," and on the other to "put a finger on ... the theoretical status of kindoki and nkisi."

The work is divided into three main sections, successively presenting the discourse of "sorcery," the nkisi, and an interpretive essay.

In the first part, the author sets out to describe the real horizon and concrete regime of kindoki by analyzing, in minute detail, first a case of a persecution fantasy, then the exercises of transcendence used by a kindoki lineage. Finally, he offers a reconstruction of what kindoki is.

These developments begin with an important postulate: "'Sorcery' or kindoki signifies, *grosso modo*, a knowledge (ngangu) and a power (lendo) by which the man who possesses them can 'eat' (suppress or cause to die) another man." This framing is extremely important; it shows the type of gaze Buakasa has chosen: to look, listen, and read – critically, of course, but also positively – the discourse of "sorcery" so as to "contribute to providing theoretical elements that will help to understand, and so to organize, social life."[4]

This perspective refuses to understand "sorcery" according to the lessons of Western tradition, which almost always considers it a major crime of "divine lèse-majesté."[5] By its clarity and orientation it also rejects the timidity of ethnological currents, including recent ones, that make use of hypotheses like the ones R. F. Fortune developed concerning the Dobu Islanders in the Pacific.[6] These hypotheses start from the disorder that sorcery and magic supposedly become when confronted with order as understood in the light of Western codes. They then lead to claims along these lines: "It cannot be affirmed that in this society social behavior emanates from the system of magic, nor that the system of magic emanates from social behavior. Nonetheless, in all of this an internal coherence can be made to appear: jealousy is the cultural dominant."[7] Although with different inspiration, missionaries and administrators working in the name of civilization and Christianity perceived "sorcery" as an "evil" and set to work to eradicate it so that new languages and values could be established. "Their enterprises," Buakasa writes, "contributed to destroying what remained of the former African social formations, so that African populations could be prepared to submit to a different social system and a different way of life."[8] In his view, many African intellectuals merely took over from the missionaries and colonial administrators, and now "combat 'sorcery' while placing themselves on the level of the ideologies of European societies."[9]

Buakasa's aim becomes clearer: he gives no credit to any gaze that sees and locates "sorcery" in reference to codes that are foreign to African discourse.

The detailed case analysis of a persecution fantasy that follows demonstrates a research program whose singular rationality could only derive from lived experience of kindoki Kongo. The case presented is exemplary: Lord Kimputu is 55 years old, of the Mata ma Kongo lineage; primary studies at l'École Normale de Tumba, subsequently a teacher, merchant, and farmer. "Spirits" alter all his activities, leaving him with only one plausible explanation: he is being pursued, and his persecutors' project is to bring about his death. In a montage, the persecutee names one of the principal reasons he is persecuted: "They are jealous of me because of my intelligence. Ziami took this one from me and gave her to his brother Ndombele."[10] In the mirror of Buakasa's text, this case is "thought" starting from its field, situation, or history – the site from which a phenomenon is constructed.[11] His appeal to the real setting and its truth avoids possible arbitrary approaches. To solidify his interpretive technique, it gives rise almost naturally – I will return to these too-happy coincidences – to a perspective that is visible or invisible, depending on where it is viewed from: the lineage-based social form of the recent past, the context of current modernity, and the effects of this double articulation on the subject. In sum, according to Buakasa, "the scene" of disorder and agitation that surrounds Kimputu becomes clearer through analogy with another "scene." This scene, although at first glance external to the subject, animates Kimputu as the plaything of a persecution fantasy. It is "an ideological site – the way that Kumputu lives his relations to his conditions of existence – in which he becomes conscious of what goes on in his society. He is thus not there for himself, but as an ideological modality that insidiously manifests a tension, against the backdrop of an ideological 'already there.'"[12]

The "Kimputu case" is nicely rounded out by Buakasa's analysis of a kindoki lineage[13] and his critical presentation of recent issues involving sorcery in Kongo society.[14] These allow Buakasa to reassert his hypothesis: sorcery can explain disequilibrium, unreason, and disorder because it is the essential meaning of an ideological site. This means that, from another angle, when a Kongo person establishes a relation of necessity between a behavioral disorder and "potential eaters of men" this does not belong to nosology, but rather to the "truth" of a social formation and its contradictions. Buakasa's theory asserts: "Kindoki presents itself as a theory that simultaneously explains, in its own way, its own existence, and by explaining how it is to be understood allows those concerned to explain certain facts of their existence, while prescribing a set of rules for behavior."[15]

Thus, to understand "sorcery" is not, as one might think, to decipher in it the limits of rationality. Instead, it is to recognize the order of a particular logic, the arrangement of a "negativity" unfolded in a fundamental language which is itself the expression

of a field rigorously delimited in time and space. This negativity, like madness but incomparably more so, to paraphrase Foucault, "[offers] itself in a plenitude of phenomena, part of the well-ordered riches in the garden of species."[16]
The second part of the book aims to identify and analyze the concept of nkisi. Through an exegesis of different informants' speech, and an attentive reading of field notes, it manages to extricate the figures and reality of nkisi from the usual confusion. In the precise sense of "an object of civilization, lived and presented as a receptacle of forces with ambivalent action," nkisi, or fetishes, are privileged links between two levels of reality, the visible and the invisible. This eminent role of liaison clarifies the "being" and "ambivalence" of the nkisi – which incarnate particular forces (in their proper names and specialized functions, and the structural relations between them) – and their relations with genies (*nkulu* – ancestors; *matebo* – ghosts; *kadia-mpemba* – demonic agents; *simbi* – genies *stricto sensu*): "A nkisi is always connected to another 'reality'; and as one term of a necessary relation, it is thus seen as a representative of that other 'reality.' It is its materialization and support, and so its substitute. This has caused many anthropologists to say that nkisi refer to natural forces."[17]

There is also a problem of power: a nkisi is always the property of an individual, generally a nganga or a ndoki. The simbi can animate the nkisi only through human action. Here a whole original economy of the power over life and death is described, expressed concretely in speech or gesture: manipulation, poisoning, etc.

While discussing this economy, Buakasa contests that "the institution" of nkisi, sustained by dominant belief, is a site of speech:

> We know – this is a banal fact, but useful to remember – that the social structure is chronologically prior to each individual who arrives in society. From the contributions of psychoanalysis and linguistics, we now know that ontologically it is through language, which surpasses and conserves all other symbolic relations, that social reality or the social structure as such is represented to new arrivals. Language enters into them and constitutes their subjectivity, which will in turn have no objective social existence except by being represented in language, by being exteriorized in it.[18]

The third part of the work presents a general interpretation of the "languages" of "sorcery" and "fetishes."

The author distinguishes three levels within the process through which the facts of kindoki are formed and organized. The first is the level of the event, or the manifest scene in which an accident (sickness, setback, death, etc.) arises. This leads to a discussion of the meaning of what arrives. The second level is a general system of indetermination, a background that "gives events a meaning: it helps to 'see,' to 'read' what is assumed to be found beyond the events." Finally, the third level is that of revelation: "The scene is found to be a 'substitute' resting on a substrate of real social relations. For instance: 'Ndombele caught pneumonia'? One says: 'they' have struck him with pneumonia."

To explain the formation and organization of nkisi, Buakasa presents a sociohistorical hypothesis according to which the time of nkisi mirrors the history of Kongo society. In an initial period, the simbi, (wild) genies, were linked to villages: "The existence of the simbi is thus based on the history of the occupation of territory and the founding of villages by men." As for the order of the nkulu, the ancestors, "as we know, they are linked to lineages"; "The nkulu are in effect the founders of the lineages within which men live."[19] And the "gardens" of the kindoki, where the nkisi were elaborated and then rigorously put into practice, are sites of conciliation between the universe of the dead (which kindoki is outside of but comes into contact with) and that of the living, for whom kindoki is theory and practice. A second period, corresponding to the simbi's entry into "civilization," is metaphorically expressed by the construction of the nkisi: "The nkisi object is a mechanism and mode of domesticating, caging, or, better, of capturing the simbi in a material object that is at once representation and double."[20]

In other words: the formation and organization of nkisi corresponds to a doubly encoded language. A first reading leads necessarily to another, more secret, reading.

First reading: the nkulu, ancestors of the Kongo, occupy foreign lands and crush the indigenous populations. Seized by remorse, the Kongo give the subjected former inhabitants the status of simbi in order to gain their sympathy:

> This solicitation assigned them a new function: having ceased to be masters of their homes and thought to nourish sentiments of hatred

and hostility, the former proprietors are incited to become calm and benevolent. They are also invited to become the protectors of the new society, as if it was their own. They are offered worship to persuade them to take on this new function.[21]

Second reading: in order to survive, the new Kongo society with its "protective genies" is careful to ensure that the simbi remain "benevolent prisoners" forever. This explains the principal mission of the nganga, and the counter-mission of the ndoki:

> Nkisi constitute an institution which ... contributes to maintaining and reproducing social relations ... The therapeutic techniques [of the nganga] ... are a means of communicating with the simbi and, by so doing, of commanding them or using their transcendence to serve society. In other words, it is a matter of setting to work, by means of nkisi, a mechanism aimed at warding off an eventual rupture with the simbi, so that they will remain at the service of society to combat the ndoki.[22]

The general interpretive essay that closes the work begins with a quote from Freud, which sums up the lessons Buakasa draws from his study: "There is no truth that is not historical, that is to say constructed."

* * *

Buakasa seems to have two principal reflectors: Marx and Freud. He situates them with impressive freedom and precise art, but their complementarity is sometimes unclear. Once could easily imagine, for example, the reluctance of a follower of kindoki who would be required, even silently, to cite Marx or Freud at every turn. But the half-silences that follow from this raise questions whose answers, even if they can often be found in the text, are ambiguous. For example: if it seems to me that in his "analysis" of the "Kimputu case" Buakasa is trying to bring together dialectical thought and psychoanalysis and, in so doing, to "in the first place ... offer a view of mental life as an interplay of urging and repressing forces, with conflict as a central dynamic factor,"[23] I am likely expressing the author's own conviction. But in the context of the "Kimputu case," shouldn't this logically lead to an attempt to delimit the rationality of the ego and the irrationality of the id, or to a reading of "enchantment" in terms of the transformations (displacements, sublimations, reactionary formations) of the irrationality of the id? This would certainly pervert the norms and codes of kindoki, but would its interpretation be any different from Buakasa's?

This example requires us to take up in theoretical terms a problematic that Buakasa addresses concretely, while leaving certain things unsaid. The debate concerns one of his most important hypotheses. Beyond the issues noted above, Buakasa twice, almost in passing, invokes a Kongo refrain: "Monkey, are you hiding? But your tail sticks out and gives you away."[24] This is notable as a sign and symbol of an invisible presence that gives itself away or expresses itself by traces within the visible. Sorcery, a particular code, reveals itself only by accidental traits; these make it possible, on the level of a discourse like Buakasa's, to construct "the truth."

Writing from a Marxist viewpoint, Louis Althusser recently offered a demonstration that psychoanalysis is a "reactionary ideology."[25] Althusser's suggestion, for and against psychoanalysis, is stimulating:

> Since Marx, we have known that the human subject ... is not the "center" of history – we have even known, against the philosophers of the Enlightenment and against Hegel, that history has no "center" but possesses a structure that has a necessary "center" solely in ideological misprision. Freud in turn reveals to us that the real subject, the individual in his singular essence, does not have the form of a self centered in an "ego," "consciousness," or "existence" ... that the human subject is decentered, constituted by a structure that, too, has a "center" solely in the imaginary misprision of the "ego," that is, in the ideological formations in which it "recognizes" itself.[26]

Taken to its logical end, from a materialist point of view, this suggestion leads to the preeminence of historical materialism as "the principal explanatory role for human phenomena." In effect, Lucien Sève shows, materialism "without doubt includes the position that psychoanalysis proposes to occupy scientifically, but in a doubly subordinate position, because it cannot be accessed except through knowledge of social relations, which are themselves derived from fundamental relations."[27]

Buakasa seems to adhere to the demands of this optic, and indicates this several times. To cite only three cases drawn at random: first, in the working hypotheses: "Kindoki and nkisi are only an ideological discourse for another reality. This other reality is the set of social relations. In other words, the phenomenon that kindoki and nkisi are concerned with could be seen as an argument in defense of the social relations at the heart of a given social formation." Second, in the conclusion to his analysis of Kimputu's persecution fantasy: "The analysis of social 'reality' seems to us the only way to construct the theoretical support of such a case. This analysis participates in constructing operative concepts that can, in the last instance, account for this case – which, to continue speaking in these terms, reveals itself to be a participant in the field of ideology of the social formation under consideration."[28] Finally, in the interpretation that closes the book: "The conflicts and tensions that occur at the level of social relations are realized differently on the level of kindoki and nkisi, understood as practices and discourses. They are thus displaced, or cathected, in favor of events occurring in the society."[29]

This system and its implicit norms clarify the complicity between the writer of the preface and the author, beyond or beneath sorcery and all its pomp. But curiously, sorcery as power is also an object of desire for both accomplices: Verhaegen regrets not knowing the secrets that would allow him to strike down his colleagues, while Buakasa describes at length his admiration for kindoki. But, to return to our problem, this master-system could surely have offered more solid support for the architecture of the demonstration. Verhaegen says this elegantly when he notes, in the preface, that "kindoki and nkisi should equally be studied in terms of supply and demand, exchange and use values, and unequal economic relations."[30]

Well then, I can "dream" up a concern. Buakasa's discourse offers us up a theory that is already given. But, to interpret this first structure, he erects markers and limits that cover so much ground that they may miss "the truth" of the first organization of kindoki. As we can see, a gap is established between the two superimposed discourses, and their interaction can then only be a sort of conceptual game. It is a bit as if, wanting to express the language of an ancient college of priestesses, I took as my methodological guide contemporary outlines for the treatment of nervous conditions among the anxious in highly industrialized societies.

I know this is a somewhat impudent remark. But as a "dream" of anxiety or concern addressed to Buakasa, who as a scholar and as an African tries to reconcile us with our "archaeological milieu," it could at least be an encouragement to pay more attention to the perversity of the great explanatory systems of the social that we have inherited from the School of the West. Or again: from this dream, we could move toward a "game," one more easily and regularly inserted into "scenarios" inherited from African tradition. Buakasa says:

> Kindoki and nkisi are a "social game," an "organized scenario." We know well in saying this that the people who find themselves in this "game" are not lying. Because society – or better, its unthought – is not transparent to the subjects who "play," it functions to render them unconscious of the conditions of their existence, and thus the real reason for their "play" in kindoki and nkisi.[31]

To revise the norms of the second game – that of second-degree interpretations, of "scientific readings" – would mean, among other things, to set our gaze in harmony with the gradients of our cultures, so that scholarly works like Buakasa's could be conducted within the singular originality of the real field that gives them meaning. Buakasa tries to attack the "real" – that which, as Serge Leclaire puts it, "resists, insists, exists irreducibly, and gives itself only by concealing itself as jouissance, anguish, death, or castration."[32] Like the psychoanalyst, his work, and its extensions, "should not consist merely ... in being caught up in the literal (signifying) game, but rather in making visible the lack that is its motor, and, in a certain sense, its 'absolute cause'."[33]

But then, is there anything that couldn't be drawn from the lessons and experiences of "Geistesgeschichte"?[34] Karl Vossler believes that it is possible to mark and access the personality, like the genius, of a people by starting from the study of language. Sorcery, a coded language [*langage*], is integrated into a particular tongue [*langue*], which – as is not understood often enough – is a collective spiritual activity. No doubt sociolinguistic analysis would testify to the rich complexity of a culture that, by putting forward a particular language – that of kindoki – is an expression both of this language and of the tongue or language system in which the language takes its place with particular social functions.

Buakasa's remarkable book is both a brilliant and a challenging promise. We can quibble with the author over details or even his subject's lack of clarity. But what importance do these reservations have in the face of the project's significance, and the quality of his work? For my part, in this striking book I see a symbol: a sign of the future. And I think of Lacan, who noted prudently in his seminar on 5 February 1964:

> The ancients recognized all kinds of things in dreams, including, on occasion, messages from the gods ... What concerns us is the tissue that envelops these messages, the network in which, on occasion, something is caught. Perhaps the voice of the gods makes itself heard, but it is a long time since men last lent their ears to them in their original state – it is well known that the ears are made not to hear with.[35]

4
And What Will God Become?

Dieu dans le Vaudou haïtien [God in Haitian Voodoo] is a doctoral thesis that was defended in Paris by Laënnec Hurbon, a Haitian scholar living in exile.[1]

Geneviève Calame-Griaule, in her preface to the published version of the thesis, clearly presents the meaning of Hurbon's project. "This book," she writes,

> first of all appears to be an act of courage: political courage, of course, but also religious courage. It is easy to see how uncomfortable it would be for a Haitian Catholic priest to take a stand against the Church in his country, and to turn a lucid and objective gaze on Voodoo, which the Church denounces as a mass of diabolical superstitions. This gaze, although not lacking in human warmth, is as much an ethnologist's or philosopher's gaze as a theologian's. The book offers a new interpretation of Voodoo: it presents it as an original vision of the world and a people's effort of self-affirmation in the face of the dramatic conditions of their history, which has gone from slavery and foreign domination to underdevelopment and political dictatorship. This interpretation, despite the scientific rigor with which it is supported – or rather, because of it – constitutes a very eloquent cry of revolt and plea in favor of the oppressed people with and toward whom Laënnec Hurbon feels himself in solidarity and, one might say, responsible.

Calame-Griaule's note shows the complexity and richness of the book. It belongs as much to theology as to philosophy;

as much to ethnology and sociology as to an original form of political engagement.

The central theme – which in a sense is also a pretext – is Voodoo. Hurbon analyzes it using three types of gaze, which he calls "approaches": a phenomenological gaze, a structural gaze, and a hermeneutic gaze. An introductory chapter dedicated to methodology explains and justifies the shape and meaning of these approaches.

This explanation and justification help us to grasp what Hurbon's project means. In a certain way, they hang on a refusal to work within the "tradition" inaugurated by Tempels's *Bantu Philosophy*.[2] In Hurbon's view, in that book the Franciscan missionary offered "a certificate of humanity to peoples previously described as plunged in fetishism, idolatry, and magic," by demonstrating that Black people had "a philosophy" and were "monotheists." More precisely, "the notion of God served as guarantee and criterion of humanity, and the God of the Blacks could without difficulty be ascribed all the attributes of God as found in Aristotle and St. Thomas."[3] This approach was ambiguous, although at the time it seemed fertile to many scholars, such as Kagamé, Mulago, and others. It also seemed to rely on a "theological interpretation traditionally given in the missions in support of the First Vatican Council's position on the possibility of knowing God through reason." Whatever the case, one of its key concepts, vital force, was seen at the time as "the Black Grail par excellence," the key to all Black civilizations, and was used even in Haiti, particularly by Achille Aristide.

Following Eboussi Boulaga, Hurbon contests the validity of this generalization, and he does not find Tempels's approach relevant. Dumézil's point of view when discussing another generalization – the concept of mana, previously applied to diverse religions to make them uniform – gives Hurbon reason to think that Tempels's work, despite its merits, was only one moment in the search to understand Black culture, and that another approach is required today. He conceives of this new approach as total and totalizing:

> It must take seriously the whole cultural and religious field of the society in question, and the mode of articulation of elements within this field. In addition, it should not be purely descriptive. It must be a way of approaching this cultural field without the pretense that we

can abolish our presuppositions and our prejudgments, but at the same time without prejudice as to the originality of the situation of Voodoo.

Hurbon tells us that he will try to understand a single object, Voodoo, using three complementary methods. The phenomenological approach, as he sees it, postulates a bracketing of a priori categories that have to do with God – explications of the religious by cause or origin – in order to grasp the religious phenomenon "as a meaningfully organized unity, an ensemble or structure."[4] He attempts to place Voodoo in its "vital milieu": a history, an economic framework, and a social context. A historical retrospective drawn principally from the classic works of Bastide, Herskovits, and Moreau de Saint-Méry allows Hurbon to sketch out the history of Voodoo in broad strokes: the transplantation of the structures of African religions (particularly those of the Fon and Yoruba) during the era of slavery; the extraordinarily complex role Voodoo plays in the daily life of Haitians, despite Catholic prohibitions; and, at times, the important repercussions of its activity in political life, such as at the island's independence (at the start of the nineteenth century) or during American colonization (1915–34). Hurbon also tries to show that on the social level Voodoo – a culture and religion of disadvantaged strata – is an expression of class relations and, to use Bastide's expression, represents a veritable "dialecticalization" of the social – in the sense that it is language that allows the Voodoo practitioner not only to live and sense situations as objective givens, but also to give them meaning. Thus, Hurbon, following Bastide, comes to treat the religious as a "metaphor of the social."

The chapter on Voodoo as a personal and family cult is a synthetic arrangement of information taken from ethnological works, particularly those of Jean Price-Mars and Alfred Métraux. This chapter introduces the question of whether Voodoo is a syncretic religion. Hurbon answers in the affirmative, and he runs through different manifestations of syncretism (on the levels of ecology, rites, and collective representations) before critically taking up, in turn, Herskovits's and Bastide's interpretations. At this point, the most important question arises: the Christian God, or a God specific to Voodoo? But Hurbon tells us that "we cannot enter into understanding the God of the practitioner of

And What Will God Become?

Voodoo while remaining below the level of the articulation of the total system in which it moves."[5]

From here, the two following parts of the thesis – the structural and hermeneutic approaches – attempt to introduce the notion of God by showing how the universe of Voodo is articulated. The theme and pretexts of the structural approach are, on the one hand, the dialectic of life and death surrounding the symbol of the tree, and, on the other, the world of spirits seen as an "articulated" language. The principal conclusion that emerges from these analyses is that, thanks to an original and rational structuration of the imaginary, there is no place for the absurd. Order and disorder, good and evil, life and death find their foundation and are integrated into a field of meaning. The third and final section of the book complements the two preceding ones by engaging the theme of God in more depth. The author notes that

> in the universe of the loa and in the symbolism of trees, in the interpretations of good and evil, of order and disorder, the place left for God [seems] quite thin. Nonetheless, the name of God is on all lips in Haiti, it is invoked in all circumstance. We could, working from stories about God, proverbs, songs, everyday invocations, and formulas of politeness, draw up the characteristics of God in Haitian Voodoo. But it is not enough to know all of God's characteristics and attributes. For a veritable understanding, the totality of verbal expressions must be integrated into the field of the total system.[6]

The position he takes here involves an extremely subtle form of polemic: it is at once a refusal to condition his analysis of the conception of God according to the norms of "civilized peoples," and a hesitation concerning easy declarations, even scholarly ones, of God as a "common good of all humanity." The headings he uses speak loudly and provocatively: "God outside the system"; "God and the interpretations of evil"; "God and the horizon of the clash of cultures." They lead to vigorous conclusions, in particular that "the best safeguard is still to put God at a distance, outside of the human field of man," and that "every recourse Christianity makes to the theodicy found in a traditional society like that of Voodoo is in itself an obstacle to effective conversion to Jesus Christ."[7]

This poses an important question. If in an earlier time it had seemed that a particular form of ethnocentrism justified, explained, and even in a certain way founded the systematic denial of conceptions of God other than that of the Christian West, recent valorizations of Voodoo or of African religious universes also seem to share a particular orientation. Here Hurbon is severe. He takes a stand against "the 'toothing stones' approach"[8] and insists strongly on the limits of any speech "about" God. He judges that "one can only dare speak of what God means to someone or to a people if one is well anchored in one's own culture. Indeed, no one speaks from nowhere."[9] But to assume one's own culture also means to accept confrontation. Hurbon confidently describes the profound meaning of this henceforth indispensable confrontation, which is:

> First of all, to make appear the truth of the situation as it has been lived up to the present: by this, Christianity will be called on to acknowledge and recognize, on the one hand, the particularity of its language, which in any case is tied to a culture, in this case that of the West; and on the other, its history of violence in Haitian society. This cannot be done in a theoretical and abstract fashion; it implies a real rupture with the structure of domination and subordination through which Christianity has lived its relation to Voodoo.[10]

I will not address the theological implications of these theses. But there are two things that seem important to me in these affirmations, which neatly situate God as something to be thought and lived at the intersection of cultural confrontations. These are, first, the reduction of the fact of Christianity to an ideological phenomenon; and, second, Hurbon's main methodological choices, which in a certain way explain some of his deductions, while allowing other things to be inferred without demonstration.

It is clear that the study of conceptions of God might, under certain conditions, require us to bracket the mystery of the act of faith. We may also admit, with Louis Althusser, that what people express in every expression of religion is not their relations to their conditions of existence, but the way in which they live their relations to their real conditions of existence. In this case, we are justified in asking about the deeper meaning of some of Hurbon's choices, and of what we might call a sort of modesty. He believes that any theologian who turns to study Voodoo today will be viewed as particularly problematic. This is because, "from the start, he will be suspected of trying to devise a strategy to once again ensnare the Voodoo practitioner, or to save a Catholic tradition whose bankruptcy in Haiti has been well established, and which is more and more losing credibility." So be it. But for Hurbon, this choice justifies his criticism of theological language (language with abstract categories, obsolete language with an ideological character, etc.), and leads to an obvious fact: "a theological approach to Haitian Voodoo is not ... a priori innocent."[11]

Of course, we might ask whether any approach in our human and social sciences could be a priori innocent. But it is remarkable to note that Hurbon's positions lead him to agree with materialist theses. Think of Marx, for example, who wrote in *The German Ideology* that

> "Liberation" is an historical and not a mental act, and it is brought about by historical conditions, the development of industry, commerce, agriculture ... The nonsense of substance, subject, self-consciousness, and pure criticism, as well as religious and theological nonsense ... these mental developments, these glorified and ineffective trivialities, naturally serve as a substitute for the lack of historical development, and they take root and have to be combatted.[12]

Or of Althusser's more recent affirmation: "The decadence of theological thought is evident and irremediable: no theologies of 'revolution' or 'violence' could restore a moribund theological thought to truth."[13] This last comment turns paradoxically against Hurbon's project, which claims that the return of God's universality, confiscated by the West, can take place only through confrontation.

From a sociological point of view, in my opinion, this book's fundamental ambiguity lies in its use of the concept and reality of ideology. This would be inconsequential if it were not the foundation of both Hurbon's discrediting of Christianity and his valorization of the conception of God in Voodoo.

If Hurbon is correct, then given that Christianity is an ideology – according to Althusser, a system that possesses its own logic and rigor of representation and plays a historical role at the heart of a given society – it should go without saying that Voodoo is equally an ideology. That is, like Christianity, it is in its own way an essential structure of the historical life of a society. Consequently, since, as Hurbon admits, "the question of human meaning itself cannot be found outside of the cultural and political field," we might wonder what specifically scientific reasons justify the use of certain contingencies and aberrations of Christianity to describe the sacred in Voodoo.

I wonder, then, if the most important thing Hurbon has to offer us may lie in the anguished and anguishing hesitations of a theologian who, when doing ethnological work, no longer knows what exact status to give the truth of the religions he studies. These hesitations display, and in a remarkable way take up, the methodological tensions involved in research on traditional religious beliefs in the countries of the Third World over the last fifty years or so: how can their approaches to God be scientifically understood and spoken of? How can the essential meaning of these beliefs be defined and grasped? And, for the theologian, how can these beliefs be situated in relation to the revelation of Jesus Christ? Hurbon is skeptical of the "toothing stones" approach: it seems to him too marked by the "exterior," by norms that emanate from "outside." But his appeal to approaches currently in vogue – the phenomenological gaze, the structural approach, and the hermeneutical perspective – also leads him, in the name of the singularity and richness of every sociohistorical experience, to a curious impasse concerning the sacred in Voodoo ideology. Hence this plea:

> If a whole current of modern theology and even of modern anthropology has wanted to celebrate the death of God and the death of man in present civilization, in truth it has been a question only of the death of the White God and the White man of the Western world, in their pretention to universality. Instead, the voices of the other cultures of the Third World are beginning to rise up ... The task of Western Christianity is to open itself to the lessons of syncretism: the Haitian masses who practice Voodoo must and can find the path to their liberation for themselves, without becoming exiles in a Western culture which the Church, by force of imposition, has passed off as the site of human universality.[14]

Here we touch the root of the problem. What interests me is the project's meaning, rather than the importance of its conclusions. This project is today almost a rule of scientific practice for many Africans, for example those working in the human and social sciences. The demand – sometimes the pretext – of respecting a sociocultural setting regularly produces discourses that invite us to abandon every universalist project. If it is well founded to believe that universality is thinkable only to the extent that the particular exists – that a universalist project has no meaning unless those who promote it are justified, in one way or another, by the "archaeological milieu" of their own culture and their own individuality – then what could be the meaning of a project according to which the "truth" resides only in difference? If we take this route frankly, logically, and to its extreme limit, must we doubt the truth and good faith of any project that tries to "construct" a discourse about any community whatsoever, Black or otherwise? Must we invoke for each individual only the right to "speak" for themselves, and so not to "construct" any theology, sociology, or psychology other than individual and personal? Then none of our human and social sciences would have any meaning, and the cults of difference and singularity would extend, finally, royally, without domination but also without barrier. But in promise of what?

On finishing Hurbon's book, which is remarkable in many ways, I asked myself: what is God becoming?

5

Interdisciplinarity and Educational Science

Interdisciplinarity! The term is in vogue; it figures regularly in scientific projects and discourses that aim to undo the compartmentalization of research. It is likely that the term, and the thing it signifies, would seem less fragile and more precise if it had emerged at some other time. In the present moment, all of us know and manage to name, in each of our different disciplines, the violence of factual limitations. These alternate, I believe, between two boundaries. On one side, the most common and constant, is the fact of incomplete information as a result of the role language plays in transmission (if one can read English, German, and French, there remain immense gaps, particularly works in Arabic, Chinese, Portuguese, and Russian). On the other side are objective lacunae that can be explained by each scholar's technical and ideological inclinations. For example, a specialist in performance assessment may, without major scandal, cultivate only a few basic concepts of psychotechnics in his professional practice. No one would take him to task for not having an up-to-date bibliography or documentation in a neighboring discipline like psychophysics, reflexology, or social psychology. If on occasion he refers to concepts or methods borrowed from linguistics or language psychopathology, we call this openness – though some evil god defending the fragmentation of specializations might only see evidence of a mind like a butterfly. And who would reproach a Marxist researcher for setting up a system, establishing tables, and working only in terms of historical and dialectical materialism? If the materialist path avoids – and sometimes ignores – every epistemological site that is frequented by or under attack from "idealist ideologies," will it not become afflicted in some way by a relative lack? Is every construction, experiment, or production from an "idealist" framework really nothing but nonsense? This comment might be clearer in reverse: if one knows the disdain "liberal" science has for materialism, one begins to wonder what partial disarmament might look like.

Interdisciplinarity – even thought of simply, in a first approximation, as the juxtaposition of knowledges and specialties – expresses a will to go beyond objective limits, and sometimes even a hope that ideological barriers can be bracketed. Understood this way, it is a consequence of the hyper-specialization of fields, the extreme division of intellectual labor. It tends to be presented – but often with such artificial theatrics! – as the negation of a scattered character of knowledge, a kind of complementarity between scholars, and an attempt to restart scientific work in a more efficient way, with a more global and total understanding of the object it studies.

But before launching any interdisciplinary project, especially in education, it is useful to know exactly what we are saying, from what location, and why.

Science, techniques of analysis, outreach programs, and ideology: these are keywords – and also concepts – that recur frequently in our projects. They are seemingly clear, available for use and for reflection, and entirely irreducible as expressive values. Or at least, we think they are – and because of this, we can use them and integrate them into complex architectures that are difficult to understand or analyze. These concepts help us to situate ourselves, directly or indirectly: to objectify our personal dreams and transfigure them into a "collective" research project; or, in a fantastic demiurgy, to actualize fantasies that conveniently metamorphose into scientific work. What do they mean, these key terms and concepts? Specialized dictionaries are reassuring, as they almost always are: either they confirm our expectations, or, following tradition, they offer definitions by which we can easily rationalize the questions and motives that sparked our interest in interdisciplinarity in the educational sciences.

Perhaps to begin with we should know exactly what these sciences are, and in what precise sense they are science. Doctor Lacan takes an approach in book 9 of his *Seminar* that I find exemplary. He answers the essential question of whether psychoanalysis is a science with a thought-provoking detour: what kind of science would include psychoanalysis? In my opinion, by generalizing this approach we might free up what lies underneath or beyond the classifications that give each science its object, and is usually – almost as a rule – silenced.

Every specialist regularly demonstrates or exhibits the specificity of their approach. We are told that this is a matter of science rather than of ideology. It involves theoretical structures – or, eventually, concrete results obtained according to precise norms and specific methods – whose rigor is certified, which are more or less sanctioned, and which function smoothly, thanks largely to a few effective paradigms and productive hypotheses. To the question of what educational science is, for example, we could innocently respond by pointing to the terms of the question: why, it is the science that deals with education. This definition is circular, and seemingly facile. But is this not precisely the privilege of the specialist? A specialist can, on occasion, present definitions while being aware that the essential is somewhere else, that the definition might be nothing but an unfortunate facade, and that the science to be explained lies also, perhaps more so, in the use that is made of it.

I think of Lacan's impressive project, which I just mentioned. He uses a drive as the paradigm of his research, and develops it in a particular way through a play of complex metaphors, demonstrating, among other things, the antinomy of vision and gaze. By this he can reach and secure what he calls the fundamental register of Freud's thought: the register of the lost object.

The positions taken by the recently founded Society of Zairean Historians [Société des Historiens du Zaïre] – which are clearly ideological and explicitly identified as such – seem to me to follow a similar trajectory. In effect, the historians declared that they wanted to rediscover and describe a memory, a tradition, a past that was accidentally erased by the fact of colonization. Zairean sociologists and linguists then took this project up in turn. At their inaugural conferences both groups consecrated authenticity as a norm and paradigm, and affirmed the urgent need for projects that could shed light on the register and articulations of the lost object. These kinds of projects are launched because of disturbing factors present in our human and social sciences, which distort every objective, no matter how confident. Many of the methods, certainties, and approaches called scientific are in truth only equivocal but provisional and artificial coincidences between a number of objective factors and subjective elements, based on ethical, spiritual, or ideological correlations.

The human sciences are usually situated opposite the so-called exact sciences. This classical and traditional opposition is based on a presentation of simple differences: on the one hand, exactitude, objectivity, generalization, and laws; on the other, non-exactitude, subjectivity, tendencies rather than laws, and so on.

This lazy opposition goes far back in the history of science. In its principle it carries contradictions that, as Georges Gusdorf's monumental oeuvre has shown, would be better suited to describing the human sciences themselves. Today, in terms of rigor, what essential difference is there between methodology in linguistics and physics? The techniques used in both domains obey strict rules that involve complementary intervention by both inductive and deductive thinking. From a theoretical point of view, it is uncontroversial today to say that the physical and natural sciences always include a coefficient of probability analogous in nature to the one that affects work in linguistics. And at any rate – today more than ever, thanks to issues raised by atomic physics – would we not be justified in revisiting the concept and reality of objectivity, which is used as a criterion to differentiate disciplines? Only recently, as Gusdorf once wrote, the dualism of human sciences/physical and natural sciences gave (specialists in) both fields the comfort and security that result from mutual ignorance. Today, however, we should note, following Claude Lévi-Strauss, that what is difficult is to obtain a consensus on what a science *is not*. This is true not only within the social and human sciences – which cannot legislate with sovereignty, because in the end what is judged is their own scientific maturity – but also for representatives of the exact and natural sciences.

In sum, a change of perspective is called for; principally, to reconsider the classical organon and learn to think oppositions – after bracketing verbal and other violence – in terms of complementarity and interdisciplinarity. Thus: when mathematics and statistics "invest" the social and human sciences, they are not invaders but auxiliaries. By the exercise of open sovereignty, too, historians of the earlier periods on our continent can increasingly employ the conceptual armature of geology, or extremely elaborated techniques drawn from the most modern physics. And the movement is not unidirectional. Is it not significant – as Lévi-Strauss tells us – that today biological methodology increasingly employs linguistic models to support its concepts of code and genetic information? It also calls on sociological models, when it speaks of cellular sociology. And for physicists, phenomena of interference between the observer and the object of observation are now much more than a practical inconvenience for laboratory work. They provide an intrinsic model of positive knowledge that comes particularly close to certain branches of the social and human sciences; for instance, ethnology, which knows and accepts itself to be the prisoner of a similar relativism. I would add: at a conference held recently in Rome, what were initially extremely technical questions about probability in mathematics provoked an old philosophical debate: is probability objective or subjective?

These complementarities define and represent the configuration of real space for what I call interdisciplinarity in its second approximation. This space is determined by the same movements that ceaselessly organize and restructure the sciences that make it up, and so express the need for interdisciplinary contact and collaborations. They also announce the impending death of a particular type of scientific work: the classic work of the isolated scholar who is confined within a domain that she is master of, and nearly all of whose rules, norms, and techniques she knows.

As much as the other sciences and, from certain angles, more so, the educational sciences cannot maintain the precarious economy of definitively consecrated fields of knowledge. It is hard to present them as universal and immobile practices. Psychology, which Jean Piaget classifies, like pedagogy, as a nomothetic science, has always found itself in a situation a bit comparable to that of medicine: that is to say, he notes, it is forced to be applied before it possesses the experiential and above all the theoretical knowledge that would give it a sure foundation.[1] Is this a good or a bad thing – both for the science itself, and for the value of its applications? Without question, the lost object to be restored hides within the silent dynamic of research. Michel de Certeau remarks that

> As specialists, none of us claims to speak in the name of "reality." The good days of that assurance are long gone. We now have to recognize in every scientific result the value of a *product* – such as what comes off the conveyor belt of a factory – relative to institutions, to axioms, and to procedures. Far from uttering truths, it is thus inscribed in one functioning among others. It refers to a specific place and to its own causes. It is inscribed in the logic of a *technical production*.[2]

This text is of real use to me because I find in it, well synthesized, the principal problems that affect all contemporary scientific practice. In a specific field, that of education and teaching, it allows us to summarize facts that scientists often like to forget: that it is illusory to found a concrete practice on "eternal scientific norms," and that theories, like techniques, are highly dependent on the most diverse factors. Certainly, concepts like universalization and universality fulfill demands for unity. But these concepts mark above all a philosophical choice, which postulates that science should be situated or conceived as a project outside of time and space.

When it comes to education in Africa, apart from the enormous weight of the myth of science, we know and can easily name the most fundamental problems. I think they can be reduced to three principal issues: the temptation to produce one-dimensional persons, the appeal of a politics that promotes an aristocratic conception of the human, and finally the gap between scholarly culture and the real world.

For several years now, we have been conscious of the fact of our difference, and have interrogated the sites from which the things that define us as singular existences – economically, politically, and culturally – are elaborated. Our contradictions gave rise to ideologies – such as négritude, negrism, Pan-Africanism, and authenticity – that have contributed positively to the relativization of the canons of a same that, in total, is nothing but a subtle expression of cultural imperialism. Our quests and interrogations have had repercussions for education in the most general sense, and teaching in particular: new arrangements have been regularly introduced in an effort to express and assume the singularity of our sociohistorical experience.

But we also know today that, despite beneficial revisions, our education is and continues to be fundamentally reductive. Here as elsewhere, its goal seems to be the disappearance of strongly particularized individuals. At any rate, it is expressed as the imposition of a culture and abstract theoretical values that have been given once and for all. It is significant that, as Stefan Zolkiewski writes, we can "underscore the absence of fundamental criteria that might enlighten the predictions or reorientations now needed for a system increasingly proportioned to 'people who only want to have something' and decreasingly to those who 'want to be somebody.'"[3] Must we also note the hallucinatory mechanism that makes our teaching a process of objective dispossession? Its categories, concepts, language, instruments, norms, and references are "borrowed." Yes, I know, there is the violence of a sort of "universal" heritage. But I also see that ancient Greece appears to have taken up the contributions of pharaonic Egypt in a critical fashion, and so to have refined its own instruments.

This epistemological preeminence cannot be dissociated from the philosophy that implicitly runs through and upholds our system of education. The general organization of our teaching makes me think of an endless hallway. You enter one day, knowing that the road will be rough and that you will need to prove your "intelligence" at regular checkpoints; failure would mean losing any hope of seeing the light at the distant exit. The journey thus takes on a sacred value. At best, it will lead only from one step to the next: kindergarten, elementary, secondary, university. Of course there are escape routes in the hallway: they are there to "reorient" the "less good," the "deficient" – in short, those who are not of the same fiber as the "elect." But what is this exclusion about? In any case, to me it seems strikingly analogous to the banishment of the mentally disabled from society.

And so I think, taking up a wish of Michel Foucault's: perhaps one day we will no longer know what this academic incapacity was.

> Its form will have closed up on itself, and the traces it will have left will no longer be intelligible. To the ignorant glance, will those traces be anything more than simple black marks? At most, they will be part of those configurations that we are now unable to form, but

which will be the indispensable grids that will make our culture and ourselves legible to the future.[4]

The discrepancy between what is taught and the real environment is striking enough that it demands to be deciphered. Perhaps, here too, we will find that everything takes place as if it were impossible to undo the norms of the epistemological universe inherited from colonization.

The concept of interdisciplinarity, by teaching us to welcome contributions from other disciplines and showing us the relativity of our scientific theories and models, may help us better understand the order of repression by knowledge and teaching within which, and by which, we live. If it does this, it will also help us to set up "a humanism of refusal" (Althusser): a refusal of anything that, directly or indirectly, can hinder the advancement of the human, any human, in their singularity and truth.

6

Immediate History: An African Practice of Dialectical Materialism

Benoît Verhaegen's important work on the method of "immediate history" will attract curiosity and interest, and for more than one reason.[1] While *Introduction à l'histoire immédiate* [Introduction to Immediate History] offers a theoretical basis for Verhaegen's previous work on Zaire, he also wants it to mark the epistemological foundations of a new science. Or, more exactly, an new way of conducting research: synthetic, concrete, multidisciplinary, and situated proudly at the intersection of the social and human sciences. This practice is indissociably connected to the history of dialectical materialism. Its principal goal is to integrate the political and the scientific, and by this to promote the instability and contradiction necessary for all transformation.

Immediate history, according to its creator,

> refers to a set of scientific practices rooted in the materialist and dialectical philosophy of the nineteenth century, which can be found today as a critical current in most of the sciences. This discipline, at the confluence of history, anthropology, and sociology, is characterized by two traits: on one hand, it wants to reverse the traditionally unidirectional relation between scholar and object of knowledge, a relation founded on the object's passivity and maximal distance from the scholar. For this, it substitutes a relation of exchange that involves real participation by the object – as a historical actor with its own knowledge – and, at the limit, the disappearance of the scholar as an individual. On the other hand,

and correlatively, the method of immediate history is meant to be resolutely oriented toward social and political practice and engaged in a revolutionary transformation of the world.[2]

Alongside his empirical research on the history of Zaire from 1950 to 1965 ("my methodological reflection has followed the development of my empirical research more or less closely, sometimes behind and sometimes in advance of it, maintaining relations of opposition and reciprocal influences of a dialectical nature"), the progressive construction and organization of Verhaegen's epistemological universe has been guided, and almost dictated, by specific sociopolitical events:

> Having arrived in Zaire in 1958 to teach sociology and political science at the then-Lovanium University in Kinshasa, I was present at the launch of a movement of political and social transformation. Twelve years later, not all of its repercussions are visible. It seemed to me that the movement's general characteristics were: an over-politicization of reality after the thaw of colonial constraints; vibrant debate, with intense mass participation, about plans of action and political consciousness; an aggravation of the principal social contradictions and of political oppression; a situation of crisis that persisted throughout modifications to the social formation; and a recourse to the imaginary in the absence of exact consciousness of reality.[3]

Against this backdrop of more or less permanent crises, Verhaegen tells us, he has followed and tried to understand the rules and requirements of sociopolitical tensions. These are expressed eloquently in a history still to be written – that of the country's name. Between 1958 and today (1974), the country changed name four times (Belgian Congo, Republic of the Congo, Democratic Republic of the Congo, Republic of Zaire). It thus expressed on its own identity card the varying requirements of the real and imaginary environment.

Within the upheavals and delirium of languages finally set free from the colonial silence, and the general economy of a politics that according to some was not a politics at all – and that even in retrospect seems remarkably chaotic – attentive observation of this young independent society has allowed Verhaegen to note and name general frameworks. Taken as references, these help to explain apparent enigmas. He identifies three modes of structuring social reality: the tribal, whose context is the ethnic region; the national, affirmed as the frame of a state to be created; and finally the social, which seems to be determined by the reconversion and reorganization of social relations of production after independence. According to Verhaegen, they offer a structure to explain the scattered, varied, and contradictory events and political projects of the period. Events become connected by integration into these general frameworks. They take on values and establish an equilibrium that, while precarious, is logical enough to allow political behaviors that, at first glance, seem highly aberrant to be mapped onto the ideals that regulate them. They can then be linked, though often indistinctly, to tribal, national, anti-colonial, or social factors.

Verhaegen's analysis of these behaviors and the contexts in which they take place has been guided by his own inclinations and personal reading. He chooses a number of masters or guides, drawn from three different intellectual currents: the founders of Marxism; the Annales school; and various "leftist" philosophers and sociologists, such as Jean-Paul Sartre, Lucien Goldmann, Nicos Poulantzas, Henri Lefebvre, Georg Lukács, C. Wright Mills, Antonio Gramsci, etc. It seems likely that the use of theory to master empirical data is directed as much by intuition and personal temperament as by science, if not more so.

Verhaegen feels insecure about some of his references and the often unexpected roles he assigns to his reflectors. He repeatedly explains and justifies himself:

> I am aware that my influences are sometimes contradictory, and that there are often irreducible theoretical oppositions between the different authors ... I am not sure that I have succeeded in creating adequate coherence between these diverse borrowings and influences; what coherence there is results from my empirical method, because in the last instance that is what has determined my theoretical itinerary ... It may seem that I have deformed or truncated their thought in order to refer to them and claim their authority as my own. I believe that this is not due to any desire to construct myself as erudite or to align myself with celebrated authors. On the contrary, it involves a reflex of insecurity: I was worried that the involvement of intuition and personal creation would seem too great ... and would therefore weaken the cause I hope to defend.

* * *

Declarations like this – which also teach a way of being, today, a progressive Western academic in service to sub-Saharan Africa – prop up his essay from end to end. In a very classical structure, the book's six chapters are organized around two themes. The first, the place of immediate history within the social sciences, makes up the first part of the book. The second concerns the critical role of basic empirical knowledge and epistemological vigilance. A general conclusion draws lessons from his reflections: what is immediate history, what are the reasons for its existence, and how can it be practiced?

To summarize Verhaegen's book in a sentence, I would say that immediate history is a site where the social sciences intersect – a site that is frequented only by dialecticians (this last expression is from Georges Gurvitch).

This space turns out to be strange, surprising, and – as I will show later – overpopulated. Archaeologically, it is constituted by the most prominent strata of the discipline of history (the tradition of historical chronicles; the history of rationalist thought; and the philosophy of history – idealist with Hegel, materialist with Guizot, Thierry, Saint-Simon, and Michelet). But throughout, the atmosphere is clearly that of historical and dialectical materialism. The characteristics and ambiguities of immediate history can be easily seen in the way Verhaegen positions it with respect to historians' History, and to materialism. He writes:

> The field of immediate history is ... doubly limited in relation to classical history and historical materialism. It is limited in time, because it involves living history, which means it is still possible to speak with some of the actors and witnesses of the period under consideration. It is limited in terms of its object, because it considers only societies in movement. It should be further specified that this refers to not just any movement, since all human societies are, from their beginnings, evidently subject to a certain historical development. Historical movement considered as a possible object of immediate history can be qualified by the concepts of crisis, increased social awareness, and participation.[4]

In general terms, this project can be compared to the "Histoire immédiate" collection published by Éditions du Seuil in Paris. While classified as "History," it conducts a kind of instant history that belongs to what Pierre Nora would call a mixed or hybrid genre, an exploded genre.

In terms of methodology, Verhaegen acknowledges many relatives. These include Edgar Morin's concrete sociology, in which "observation unites the researcher and his object of research in a dialectical and multi-dimensional process. Hypotheses, facts, and interpretations are thus in constant exchange, each modifying the others and being modified in turn." Also mentioned are the methods and techniques that support the norm of "direct experimentation" in Jean Duvignaud's *Chebika* (1968); the scholarly, spare, and meaningful organization of Jacques Berque's *Histoire sociale d'un village égyptien au XXe siècle* [Social History of an Egyptian Village in the Twentieth Century] (1957); the complex structure of Charles Bettelheim and Suzanne Frère's *Une ville français moyenne: Auxerre 1950* [An Average French City: Auxerre 1950] (1950); and the macro-sociological logic and liveliness of Oscar Lewis's work. A similar approach can be found in Don Talayesva's *Sun Chief*, Jan Myrdal's *Report from a Chinese Village*, or Helena Valero's *Yanoama*. In all these different works, we encounter "a common technique: the use of the tape recorder and respect for the unrefined human document."[5] Among studies of sub-Saharan Africa, Verhaegen mentions Arnold L. Epstein (*The Network and Urban Social Organization*, 1961), Denise Paulme (*Femmes d'Afrique noire*, 1963), and Colin Turnbull (*The Lonely African*, 1968).

Verhaegen acknowledges similarities in viewpoint and concrete positions between immediate history and the nondirective approach in psychology and psychotherapy, as well as the more radical current of *anti-psychiatry* (R. D. Laing, Aaron Esterson, David Cooper). There as here, as Laing would put it, in the process of signification each party contributes to the completion or the destruction of the other; and both fields are concerned with "inter-experience." There is also methodological kinship between immediate history and Lourau and Lapassade's institutional analysis: according to Lourau, the object of this *counter-sociology* is above all "the concrete ways in which individuals, groups, and classes 'live' institutions. The inductive method so dear to classic empirical sociology is replaced by 'concrete analysis, if possible on-site.'"[6] This kinship exists, too, between immediate history and the Latin American *engaged sociology* of Orlando Fals Borda, which as a sociology of liberation is "theory and practice, idea and action ... synthesized – or in fruitful exchange – throughout a period of creative dynamism";[7] and between immediate history and R. W. Friedrichs's *dialectical sociology*: "Between the dogmatism of mechanical materialism and the abstract objectivity of the functionalists, dialectical sociology means to recognize and assume the inevitable impact of practice and subjectivity in all social sciences."[8] And lastly, between immediate history and the practice of *depth sociology* developed in the United States by Clifford Geertz and Johannes Fabian: "Their recourse to a methodology founded on intersubjectivity and dialectical exchange between subject and object is on this point [situated] in exactly the same current as immediate history."[9]

In sum, the site of immediate history is a contested and contentious space. Contested: "dialectical," "engaged," "spontaneous," "naive," or "immediate" sociology – whatever label is used – is attacked on one side by positivist sociology, which clings to the collection and description of facts "treated like things," and on the other by "scholarly" sociology, a "sociology of rupture" or of "detachment."[10] Contentious: going against "classical" theories, representations, and methods, this site affirms a new way of "studying" the other. It understands the other as person and difference – "sentiment and knowledge intertwine, the ego is subjectively present in experience" – and at the same time as a mirror where knowledge, rather than piling up, neutral, monumental, untouchable, and eternal, dissolves into action and lets action constitute itself in knowledge.

From knowledge to action, and from action to knowledge, what is constituted and defined is more a way of living and acting in society than a type of knowledge about it. And "science" – immediate history as "science" – is precisely this continuous movement:

> It is nothing other than a simple mediation between yesterday's practice of history and the political practice of tomorrow. It does not claim to retrospectively discover the meaning of history, or to sovereignly dictate to people their future line of conduct. It merely lets itself be traversed by the movement of praxis whose meaning, never completely revealed, connects or totalizes revolutionary action, the present consciousness of its actors, and the projects they form for the future.[11]

The thinkers who guide Verhaegen's methodology – the same ones who illuminate the site of immediate history – offer him a configuration that, despite a few vague spots, is relatively precise. All of them belong more or less to the same intellectual universe. The anarchists of the nineteenth century, Bakunin in particular, insisted on the "liquidation of science as a moral being existing outside of the social life of the world, represented by a body of credentialed scholars and diffused into the popular masses." Lukács wrote, magisterially: "For Marxism, there is ... not, in the final analysis, juridical science, political economy, history, etc., each autonomous; there is only one science, historical and dialectical, unique and unitary, of the development of society as a totality." Marcuse, on the one hand, shows Verhaegen "on the level of dialectical analysis and the use of Marxist categories ... the pathway to new developments and an adaptation to the real world of today"; on the other, by assigning "a liberatory and revolutionary role to new forces situated outside of the Western world, he confirms the possibilities of a privileged – if not exclusive – application of the method to Third World societies,"[12] and so provides values and norms that can explain some of Verhaegen's choices. From Goldmann, immediate history takes "the categories of totality and collective subject, and the concepts of collective consciousness and possible consciousness," but also the "conception of a genetic, materialist, and dialectical structuralism, which implies the dialectical unity of science and philosophy, of objective observation and values, and of theory and praxis, and the tendency toward identity between object and subject."[13] Lastly, and eminently, Verhaegen's project is profoundly marked by the norms Jean-Paul Sartre proposes for a structural and historical anthropology that would have a place within Marxist philosophy, integrating ideology and existence, as well as Sartre's "comprehensive" methodology.

Conscious of its power and limitations, objective and subjective – philosophers, Marx said, do not spring from the ground like mushrooms; they are products of their time – the methodology of immediate history sovereignly defines itself as a continuous act and posture of putting into question. It can have neither fully developed methods nor definitively established results. Verhaegen takes the idea of degrees of observation from Bachelard, and uses it to distinguish four moments in the process of knowledge. These different levels (empirical level, epistemological level, level of methodological elaboration, and level of application) act together each time a particular type of dialectical criticism is exercised. In his *Rationalisme appliqué* [Applied Rationalism], Bachelard distinguished three degrees of critical observation. First-degree observation is the critical consciousness of the subject who, by observing and studying an object, is able to "denounce errors and false appearances of understanding." Second-degree observation, or "observation of observation," "presumes a methodological elaboration that rationalizes the critical attitude of the first degree." Finally, third-degree observation "puts the method itself into question," and is considered "a moment in the development of the method." The critical attitude is thus affirmed as essential and constant, and the only possible well-founded resolution of a question is another question. But Verhaegen remarks, recalling the lessons of Marx, Lenin, and Mao, that "The relativism of dialectical criticism is nonetheless not absolute; its limit is fixed by praxis, whether this be voluntary experimentation in the physical sciences or historical social practice. To the permanence of critique must therefore correspond the permanent submission of knowledge to social practice, the only criterion of truth."[14]

The problem of every critical enterprise – despite the pitfalls of language, the detours and shadows of representations, and the ambiguities of circumstance – is to lead to the truth. In every type of consideration, the fundamental, insistent problem is to know the conditions under which a description in the social sciences can express the truth and authenticity of an experience. The fusion of philosophy and the social sciences that Marx called for leads Verhaegen from one philosophical order to another: Kierkegaard, Dilthey, Goldmann, and especially Sartre all encourage him to take up Robert Castel's plea:

> If the human sciences are condemned to remain cut up into a multitude of heterogeneous sectors, then positivism, whatever new name it may be dressed in, will have the final word, and the Sartrean project will be useless and empty from the start. If, on the contrary, something like a synthesis is thinkable, even in the future, then someone should attempt it, and everyone else should situate themselves in relation to this possibility.[15]

In sum, Verhaegen hints that he has attempted such a synthesis with immediate history – "whose object is the knowledge and comprehension of societies currently undergoing crisis and change, and whose method, founded on maximum identification between the object and subject, cannot be conceived outside of dialectical philosophy." Only this can provide an account of historical movement with its underlying contradictions, and synthesize the ensemble of forces and factors in play into a totalization that is both horizontal (structural) and vertical (historical) – the ultimate goal of "structural and historical anthropology."[16]

This remarkably presented problematic still leaves many question marks. The author explicitly acknowledges some of these, while others directly or indirectly flow from his hypotheses or methodological choices. It is possible that all of them can be reduced to two central methodological issues: the practice of scientific materialism today in the human and social sciences, and the ideological meaning of this practice in sub-Saharan Africa.

The goal of dialectical materialism is not only to constitute a climate where materialist orientations and pedagogies can flourish, endorsed by carefully chosen citations from Marx or Engels. Its goal lies in the determination of the general laws of movement, modification, and development of nature, society, and knowledge. As Leonov earlier noted with force, the study and determination of laws presupposes the total negation of finality in nature, and implies that the accident – that which occurs – is an effect of causes or givens that are both discernible and objective. Only in human activity, in effect, is there a finalism that is marked and cleanly conditioned by the concrete modalities of human existence in a given society. This is the primary and most essential fact, which concrete practices take their meaning from. Verhaegen knows this well, and he modulates it in generous and exemplary declarations. It may seem surprising that he makes frequent appeal to scholars whose works tend to challenge the force and logic of this perspective. But these minor inconsistencies are integrated well into the global project, which frankly echoes Engels's cry: "Natural scientists may adopt whatever attitude they please, they are still under the domination of philosophy. It is only a question whether they want to be dominated by a bad, fashionable philosophy or by a form of theoretical thought which rests on acquaintance with the history of thought and its achievements."[17]

What makes Verhaegen's project so seductive may also be – setting aside a relaxed and almost cavalier way of conducting materialism – an incessant and intelligent game of converting modes of reflection into provocations or, at least, a kind of voluntarist revolutionary action. I worry that, carried away by the implications of praxis in thought, he fails to distinguish rigorously enough between two phases in the process of knowledge: the one that goes from matter to consciousness and ends in sensation, and the one that begins from representations and sensations and is actualized in the production of the idea. Indeed, in a certain way Verhaegen underestimates the importance of theoretical thought; this might explain why he could at times be accused of a tendency to a sort of unilateral sensualism.

Nonetheless, Verhaegen's book is important; important enough that he can practically describe it as an African practice of dialectical materialism. We could, of course, ask for clarification: in particular, does this mean an African practice of materialism, or a practice of materialism in Africa? I am not trying to racialize anything – but, for example, I would like to know whether the space of representation is the same in both cases. And if not, what then?

Verhaegen's book is remarkable. On closing it we might, if we cared to, think of Lenin:

> "We should dream!" I wrote these words and became alarmed. I imagined myself sitting at a "unity conference" ... Comrade Krichevsky ... continued even more sternly ... "I ask, has a Marxist any right at all to dream, knowing that according to Marx, mankind always sets itself the tasks it can solve, and that tactics is a process of the growth of Party tasks which grow together with the Party?"[18]

7
The Price of Sin

Oh, the meanings of encounters and rifts between Africa and Europe! Could we not at long last change perspective, and forbid ourselves the use of the kind of statements that have let a great deal be said, but without ever offering anything that might help us each to assume our own particularity, with good will and in a mode other than that of alibis? Can the emotions (and neuroses) that have caused us to forget what it means to be other truly explain the kind of reasoning that – leaping over the necessary preliminaries – makes exclusive use of symbols that have value or meaning only as a result of a highly sympathetic conceptual effort?

These two questions show how troubling I find Jacques L. Vincke's text.[1] Although the argument is more a symbol and expression of lived fraternity than a rigorous explication of what are commonly understood as differences between African and European "traditions," it is posed from the start as a provocation, in terms of method as much as of the ideas it puts forward.

Unquestionably, when Africa is spoken of today the implicit model is a certain dated image of Africa. Vincke gives this as the reason for his insistence on privileging existence in Africa. I will therefore begin by asking whether the use of existence and essence as operating concepts does not in fact disorient his project's goals. Indeed, to define Africa and situate it against

Europe, why begin with categories that are so "charged" – so intimately connected with the Western tradition that they can be fully understood only within the twists and turns, the deletions and crossed-out glosses, of commentaries and texts that from the earliest Greek antiquity have been fascinated with the signified of the verb "to be"? A comparable image and example: how valid would it be to apply Galileo's law (the space traveled by a body falling vertically or along a parabola is proportionally related to the square of the duration of the fall) to the evolution in French of Latin short vowels in free position? Or, to take a more evocative imaginary situation: what relevance would Galileo's theory have when applied to marriage customs within a null set – for example, the class of garden peas who drink Coca-Cola, eat tires, smoke hemp, and live along a disused railroad?

What I am trying to say, trivially, is this: according to the most elementary operations of set theory, for the operatory play of the concepts of essence and existence to be valid when applied to African and European traditions there are two possibilities, and only two. Either, first, the African tradition is "contained" within the European tradition, and every element of the first actualizes an element of the second – unless the first is a null set, in which case its inclusion in the second would go without saying. Or else, second, there is a unification of the two totalities; that is to say, there exist elements of the African tradition that are elements of the European. Concretely, for example, the categories of essence and existence might be elements that belong to the intersection of the two sets (which would need to be demonstrated) – unless, again, the African tradition is a null set, in which case its effect on the unification would be entirely neutral.

But if, as Vincke tells us, differences exist between the two traditions – in particular norms and values that are consecrated in a particular way here but not there, and so belong to one set and not to the other – then, unless it can be demonstrated that the African tradition is a null set (presented graphically as neutral on the right and absorbing on the left), it would be best to note the properties of non-commutativity and non-associativity and draw the relevant conclusions.

I am not trying to affirm an irreducible gap between traditions, or between human societies. I am simply saying that the particularity of historical experiences is an obvious fact, and that each experience can be ascribed its own norms of intelligibility without requiring the intervention of instruments or categories privileged by another experience. Each time a transposition occurs, it runs the risk of influencing values and offering convincing but ill-formed discourses that teach facile myths, in an exquisite play of false convictions arising from the fantasies of the speaker or their culture.

Must I shout this? Any project that begins with a transposition of categories will be fascinating. There is an intoxicating temptation in analogies that can, by connecting, disseminate; or, by differentiating, cause theoretical areas of coexistence to appear. Whatever the limits of such a project – in particular: the indefinite work of continuous self-comparison, a misrecognition of the dynamisms and internal logics proper to every historical field, formal and other a prioris, etc. – to the human spirit it will lack neither charm nor grandeur.

This kind of theoretical construction, situated at the most extreme and fragile edges of a knowledge in movement, has advantages and disadvantages that have been first indiscriminately rejected, and then described quickly, far too quickly. To take a currently uncontroversial case, evolutionism in ethnology: this dream, which poured forth for decades, exorcised its own reductive violence by "scientifically" (and with such care!) mobilizing the fantasies of the West on the pretext (and with such perseverance!) of understanding the history and future of humanity. Critical perspectives, which came later, were sensitive in this fantastic corpus only to what betrayed cultural vanity and brought out methodological incongruity. By transplanting categories, it negated the diversity of historical paths under the guise of speaking a universality whose formulation, curiously, continued to affirm the preeminence of a particular history and thought erected as universal memory. An admirable obscenity, and one that any attempt at reduction might lead to?

But still, is it not by a similar play of disturbances (reductions, analogies, transpositions) that Mysticism tries to speak of God, who is infinite, in a finite language? What kind of enunciation, and what objective system of transcribing correlations between finite and infinite, give it a foundation when it speaks of a reality (essence and existence) outside of language, outside of space, outside of time? I say to myself that mystical "speech," the speech of love, is a limit-adventure of reduction: by putting God within the reach and call of man, and imposing concepts and categories derived from human history onto the divine, it establishes itself each time as an expression of confounding passion. By this remarkable violence, it seems to strike out whatever is excessive and (apparently) non-rigorous in the claim to live and translate the unsayable. But the fact remains: the discursive formations of mystical experience reduce the universe of the divine and divinity to a particular type of experience – a very human saturation of the passions – and in a very human language.

Returning to the text: It is easy to see that, while Vincke manages to avoid the reductionist traps the evolutionists fall into (this violence: a reified Other who has both history and memory taken away, and is then plunged into the night of hypothetical beginnings), the reasoning he describes seems to resemble a technics of matrimony. There is an expressed desire for self-annulment in the Other, at last (re)discovered; sweet tremblings and efflorescent urgency in the face of the Other's privilege; modest comments on the insignificance of the speaker's own flights of fancy; delicate (almost obliging) speeches and sublimating thought processes directed toward the sacred as understood by the Other, in an attempt to maintain the fervor of a friendship or a passion. From this, we come to words, meaning-effects, and "generous" demonstrations that are not used within "the tribe" itself. We find a speech that has become passionate through a process that demands closer attention: the rejection of any outside discourse. Rising above rumor (for example, the lack of clarity in ethnological works), it claims to say where the differences between African and European traditions reside, and on which side can be found the future of humanity.

Mutatis mutandis – as the preceding remarks have shown – Vincke speaks of "African Tradition" in the way that the mystics speak of God. I find this comparison shocking. It marks perfectly the limits of this "amorous" text (the price of sin!), which it would be a mistake to approach using the parameters of so-called scientific analysis. But as for the process of self-annulment that his discourse sketches out – if this is a problem, or poses one, it concerns only the author.

That said, faced with even the best-expressed passion, we still have the right to know whether the reality described by its sentimental outpouring is inflected according to the hyperbolic tastes of a lover, or the factual truth.

To begin with, a precise theoretical task: clarifying certain ideas or tools in the light of Vincke's principal interlocutor, Jean-Paul Sartre. This will show the urgent need for a different viewpoint.

Yes, to exist is to be free. And freedom, as Sartre has shown, can be reduced to existence: it is a whole that moves within a space of scarcity, in which it encounters many other practical organisms, at once similar and different – scarcity being a negative power that poses each organism as at once a human and an inhuman datum. The exercise of freedom, of my existence, merges in reciprocity and commutativity with the possibility that I am a surplus object produced by others, by the violence of the other. This constant tension and violence break forth at every occasion. A rigorous examination of dialectical experience as totalization will show that freedom is necessity. But I also know that my praxis is based and founded on the necessity of freedom – the opposite of the practico-inert, which I identify as the structure that was given to me, from before my birth, previously interiorized by the group I am born into. In this context, the exercise of my freedom is imperiously, if it is to be authentic, a victory over alienation. But I do not practice it within a field of freedom, but rather in an expanse restrained by the inertia of the group, an inertia that is felt and pledged.

In constant disequilibrium, my existence is freedom to the extent that it is defined and lived as a tension that, within a space of possibilities, can actualize only certain ones to the exclusion of others. But it is also lived as the projection of an other, which as anti-value must be kept at a distance. It is also clear that the action of freedom cannot avoid being violence. Commenting on Sartre, R. D. Laing and D. G. Cooper put it well:

> Free praxis can directly destroy the freedom of the other, or put it in parentheses, as it were, by mystifications and stratagems. Violence can also be action against the necessity of alienation, or be exercised against one's own or the other's freedom, in order to forestall the possibility of falling into seriality. Violence, whether against contra-man, against one's brother, as freedom to annihilate freedom, as terror-fraternity, etc. in every case is a reciprocal recognition of freedom and negation (reciprocal or univocal) of freedom by the intermediary of the inertia of exteriority.[2]

In my opinion, all of this shows that an essay in existential psychoanalysis would do better to start out from the concrete constellations of knots and conflicts sparked by freedoms in violent tension. To speak the singularity of the African tradition, we could begin with serial ideas,[3] and then see whether they resist an integrally objective analysis. This analysis would consist in bringing forth the rules that preside over the "equilibrium" of explicit or implicit infrastructural norms (the complex play of relations between work processes and social relations of production) and the type of determinations they exercise on the superstructures of the social formation. In short, it would be a question of defining one or several given spaces, and understanding the structural functions that directly or indirectly give meaning to the ideological signaling and determined speculative practices referred to by the term "tradition."

The initial formula is simple. It involves understanding the structures of interdependence that exist in every human setting between economic, political, and ideological spaces, independently of persons. Marx demonstrated this structure well. For example, he notes in the Preface to *Capital*, privileging the structure of the capitalist system:

> I paint the capitalist and the landlord in no sense *couleur de rose*. But here individuals are dealt with only in so far as they are the personifications of economic categories, embodiments of particular class-relations and class-interests. My standpoint ... can less than any other make the individual responsible for relations whose creature he socially remains, however much he may subjectively raise himself above them.[4]

The structure is primary, fundamental; it is characterized by its own rationality. Thus in the capitalist system, to quote Maurice Godelier:

> the rationalities of entrepreneurs and workers express their functions in the activities of production and distribution. The differences and inequalities of these functions are born from differences and inequality in the ownership of capital and the means of production. This inequality of function and ownership determines in turn the inequality of profit, and limits in advance the forms and possibilities of individual consumption.[5]

This illustration describes the "structure" that governs "function" in any formation whatsoever. Accordingly, it would be possible, and has been tried with unequal success, to elucidate relations between Africa and Europe using a theoretical practice that includes this idea. I alluded above to the theory of a space subdivided into three regions: the economic, which is determining in the last instance, and the political and the ideological, superstructures where theories and thoughts are determined in the form of echoes that reflect – perfectly or relatively well – relations in the fundamental region, the economic. The precise structures that operate within this vast frame obey the rules of the region that is determining in the last instance. On the infrastructural level, modeled after modes of production, there are particular relations between the processes and social relations of production. On the superstructural level, in the region of politics, there are relations between the organization of production and power on the one hand and political discourse on the other. In the region of ideology, there are relations between particular signals and speculative practices.

Ideology – our primary interest when we speak of tradition (think in terms of the "tradition" that makes us inheritors of the past!) – is not even an entity in itself. As Thomas Herbert has shown,[6] ideology cannot be considered merely as a determinable region within a social formation. It is thus theoretically impossible to consider it (along with its product, "tradition") as a group consciousness, a representation of the world, or a block of ideas valid for a society or a class that tend to be imposed together, as a unit of the type grasped by functionalism. This means that the question of ideology – and a fortiori that of "tradition" – cannot be posed or experienced except in light of relations between the three regions of every social formation.

Analysis of several contemporary African *Gesellschaftsformations* (see the work of Pierre-Philippe Rey, Claude Meillassoux, etc.) reveals an Africa characterized by the overlapping of different systems of productive forces and different social relations of production. The essential characteristic of these overlaps is to be the site of remarkable contradictions, where the structures of particular African lineage systems fit together with structural imperatives that result from the development of international capitalism. In this site, an exploiting or exploited ideology, conveyed by a humanism whose absolute theoretical foundation is the problematic of the essence (or the theoretical existence) of man, rationalizes the tensions that result from the difficult articulation of unstable Asiatic-type modes of production and the requirements of the capitalist mode of production.

If there are problems of comprehension or incomprehension between the ideological discourses of Africa and of Europe, they do not originate principally in cultural differences, but rather in the particular economic relations that unite the two worlds: expropriation and dispossession. One example is the polarization of colonizing and colonized countries into metropoles and satellites. In the colony this takes the form of the city – a more or less adequately Westernized enclave – as metropole, and the countryside as satellite. These structural limitations corresponded, and still correspond, to a process of permanent dispossession that contributes to the metropole's development, while demoting the satellite into underdevelopment. It is important to recognize, as Andre Gunder Frank points out, that "development and underdevelopment are not just relative and quantitative, in that one represents more economic development than the other; economic development and underdevelopment are relational and qualitative, in that each is structurally different from, yet caused by, its relation with the other."[7] From here we can understand the infernal dialectic. The movement from the satellized backcountry to the micro-metropolitan African city, and from there to the international macro-metropole that satellizes it, is a process of "development of development," while movement in the opposite direction is the "development of underdevelopment."

Confronted with the logic and infernal force of this structural alienation, philosophical and "scientific" languages are born, and especially the ones used in the human sciences. These languages sublimate reality. They modestly hide alienation under generous comments about the syntax of African political discourses, and dissertations on the economic takeoff of "developing" countries (an obvious counterfactual) or the originality of tradition, African communities, etc.

The reason these discourses (which do not only come from "outside") can be rejected, in my opinion, is because they are a "poverty" of conditioned intelligence. In truth, this poverty is a regime whose shape we can make out once we understand that it is fundamentally marked by the commonplaces of an opaque economic science. It is produced by rationalizations of the wanderings of a so-called liberal system, bogged down in its own arcana by presuppositions that go without demonstration.

These languages can also be rejected because they are expressions of a particular "madness." This is marked by a type of discordance, as when theories produced, worked, and sustained by a given Order are uncritically transposed and applied in a totally different context, where they are erected as "dogmas," "canons," and absolute "truths." Such a lack of correspondence between theory and reality – which many works of ethnology illustrate remarkably – makes one say, in the ordinary sense, "But this is madness!" Except that this ordinary sense of madness does not seem to me at all ordinary.

It is a fact: the discourses of the human and social sciences do not speak a "same," inoffensive and faithfully reproduced in its various expressions, after the model of logical systems. In their truth and their applications, they seem to be cut to fit, or made in the image of, certain modes of economic dependence.

In this case, do we need really need to show that processes of cultural self-affirmation, including movements to reject external languages, are never totally neutral?

An illustration will help show the kind of conflicts and contradictions that might explain speeches of self-affirmation. I quote a text of Sartre's, introducing additions as I go.[8] It discusses an exemplary relation: the one that connects the patient and the psychiatrist. "I am well aware that the 'patient' has to emancipate himself; his task is one of gradual *self*-discovery" (asserting the singularity of his tradition and his way of being). "The trouble ... is that it is understood *at the outset* that he will embark on this voyage of discovery *passively*, through a gaze that he cannot see and that judges him": the gaze of the doctor. Or similarly: the gaze of the master, a sovereign gaze on the needs and relations of the long term. For example: after a half-century of colonization, the Belgians, "model colonizers" (it was Senghor, I believe, who said something like this), found presumptuous a thirty-year plan developed by a teacher which proposed gradually directing their "Black pupils" to independence. But no! It always takes a great deal of time to be promoted by the gaze of the master who, with great patience, demands that we reflect back to him what he expects to see. The "patient," like the "colonized," must know how to wait and to continue, as he did in the past, to construct the universe that lies "ahead": "for several years, he has poured himself out, exposed himself, well aware that his apparently random and free-spoken remarks corresponded to a dark and hidden text that he had to construe rather than discover – a text contained in the spoken word in the sense in which, as Eluard said, 'There is another world, and it is inside this one.'"

"Is there not here a first important question? Is not the 'interminable psychoanalytic relation,' the dependence; the anticipated and induced transference; the feudal bond; the long confinement of a man lying prostrate ... reduced to the babbling of childhood, utterly drained – is not all this original violence?" The problem is neither the ambiguity nor the "problematic aspect" of a relation of dependence. It would be needlessly exhausting to wonder whether "it is psychoanalysis *as such* that has failed, or whether he would have been cured by a better analyst" – to ask whether colonization yesterday, neocolonialism today, and their discourses are a failure or not, and if their practices would have been more positive if they had been executed by better technicians.

The solution to the fact of dependence seems to flow from faith in oneself, from a conviction that "the road to independence (facing up to one's fantasies, and to other people) cannot pass via a situation of absolute dependence (transference and frustration; an at least tacit promise – I will cure you [I will liberate you; you will come to master knowledge]; waiting for 'authorization.'" The relation must explode. Between the "being-subject" of the "patient" or the "(neo)colonized" and psychoanalysis or another allegedly scientific language, the being-subject must be chosen. It must rebel and take up speech, if only for the blink of an eye! It will be asked to say what it is:

> Who is ... speaking? Is he no more than a blind psychological process, or is he the transcendence of this process by an act? I have no doubt that his every word and action could be given a psychoanalytical interpretation – provided he were reduced once more to his status as the object of analysis. What would vanish along with the subject, is the inimitable and singular quality of the scene – its synthetic organization, in other words the action as such. And let no one tell me it's a "patient" who is organizing it: I agree, I agree that he is organizing it like a *patient*. But he *is organizing* it, all the same. Psychoanalysis can explain the motivation behind someone who "acts out" his drama, but the acting itself, which interiorises,

surpasses and preserves the morbid motivations within the unity of a tactic, the act which gives a meaning to the meaning conferred on us – hitherto psychoanalysts have not bothered to take account of this.

By slightly rearranging the terms of this illustration, the "patient" and the "colonized" can be brought together in the same deviance, clearly showing the source and meaning of self-affirmative speech.

Within this framework, full of violence and truth, where can we situate Vincke's dissertation?

Don't tell me that by dwelling on these questions I have avoided taking the fundamental question head-on: what about tradition? I have already given my answer. To clarify, I would say: tradition, like the past, is in us and not behind us. My tradition, like my past, is in my present speech. And today this speech, which is marked by the concrete givens of my socio-economic space, makes me read my "history" subjectively, while in an inverse movement it reflects the archaeological field of my historical specificity. I am not saying that this field is untruthful in itself; I am merely stating that the discourses that claim to translate it often play a mystifying role. Strictly speaking, "tradition" is a beach cluttered with the present.

Finally, I think it is important to note that the "lesson of writing" that is invoked more and more frequently to differentiate African and European traditions is, at the very least, debatable. It emerged from the views of post-primitivist ethnologists, but today it can be encountered at every turn of philosophical or sociological works that touch, directly or indirectly, on non-Western societies.

I believe that Claude Lévi-Strauss first posed the problem in *Tristes Tropiques*, where he declared that

> the possession of writing vastly increased man's ability to preserve knowledge. It can be thought of as an artificial memory, the development of which ought to lead to a clearer awareness of the past, and hence to a greater ability to organize both the present and the future. After eliminating all other criteria which have been put forward to distinguish between barbarism and civilization, it is tempting to retain this one at least: there are peoples with, or without, writing; the former are able to store up their past achievements and to move with ever-increasing rapidity towards the goal they have set themselves, whereas the latter, being incapable of remembering the

past beyond the narrow margin of individual memory, seem bound to remain imprisoned in a fluctuating history which will always lack both a beginning and any lasting awareness of an aim.[9]

In my opinion, the rigor of this text – which is often cited as evidence, and seems to justify a parallel between the acquisition of writing and a dynamic model of structuring society – has no persuasive value. Besides the fact that the opposition between societies without writing and societies with writing is not especially viable – what exactly is meant by a society without writing? What does "writing" designate? – it is evident, as Lévi-Strauss clearly notes, that

> nothing we know about writing and the part it has played in man's evolution justifies this view. One of the most creative periods in the history of mankind occurred during the early stages of the Neolithic age, which was responsible for agriculture, the domestication of animals and various arts and crafts. This stage could only have been reached if, for thousands of years, small communities had been observing, experimenting, and handing on their findings. This great development was carried out with an accuracy and continuity which are proved by its success, although writing was still unknown at the time.[10]

But the chapter from *Tristes Tropiques* made a mark. Its dazzling hypotheses were quickly accepted, while its author's reservations were forgotten or ignored. For example, Lévi-Strauss remarks: "Although writing may not have been enough to consolidate knowledge, it was perhaps indispensable for the strengthening of domination." An example? "The fight against illiteracy is therefore connected with an increase in governmental authority over the citizens."

Manifestly, the lesson of writing is not the criterion par excellence. The lesson of production that follows it (the authorities, from which come the organization of power and of production) is the only norm that could lead to a categorization of traditions, or more simply of the history of peoples.

IV.
IN LIEU OF A CONCLUSION

What Murder of the Father?

(*The Other Side of the Kingdom*: response to Jean-Claude Willame)

The Other Side of the Kingdom, which aimed to reflect on the limits of the social and human sciences in Africa, provoked questions and criticisms. As we have seen, *The Smell of the Father* is merely an extension of this first essay. In different ways, it treats the same obvious fact with which *The Other Side of the Kingdom* begins: that the human and social sciences do not speak a "same," inoffensively and faithfully reproduced by each of its various expressions, on the model of logical systems; and that, in their applications, they seem to be cut to fit certain modes of dependence.

Of the various evaluations of my book, I would like to pause on the one by Jean-Claude Willame.[1] By responding to some of his criticisms, I hope to provide a justification for the orientation of my project, which I believe in more strongly than ever.

* * *

WILLAME: "The author acknowledges ... that his text 'often seems to make obvious propositions, which to some people may appear entirely useless, while to others they may go without saying.' What the author does not tell us, but can be read in filigree, is that what is fundamental on an *existential* level for him as a Zairean intellectual and alienated scholar is, for Western scholars, usually merely *theoretical*. We encounter here the contradiction of an intellectual elite that has discovered the 'secret of the elevator' and that, because of its elite position – he is not permitted to be marginal! – is subject to the conditioning of a neocolonial environment."

RESPONSE: Yes, I am still struck, as much today as when I put the final touches to *The Other Side of the Kingdom*, by the "obviousness" of my arguments. I would have engaged in serious self-questioning when I saw the book provoking interest and spite, except that I had already learned that the difficulties of a journey through the lands of science often have little to do, literally or figuratively, with that mysterious thing called "science." Indeed, it is clear that in these sites of passion – yes, a little-known fact: scientific practice is a passionate exercise! – what is received as true is not necessarily a scandalous proposition like "Africanist science has up to today been a glorious mystification," despite proofs offered in support. Instead it may be propositions that, while perhaps highly aberrant, are carefully constructed according to scientific "norms" and "references."

I affirm: we in Africa must rethink everything in the human and social sciences. We must interrogate "science" itself, beginning by asking what it is. Or, to use more palatable terms, we must reflect with extreme rigor on its practice and canons, and distinguish clearly between its aims and objectives (with the latter defined as the quantum of the aims). I would certainly hope that we would see in this the contradictions of an intellectual elite who have discovered "the secret of the elevator" and are entertained by the false paradoxes of the machine. I would hope, too, that to "possess" this secret would be liberating, in every environment. But my hopes are dampened, because I know the perversity of every elite in the eyes of the people. So why would I worry about something obviously trivial? Today, the African peasantry thinks of my work perhaps the same way that Francesca da Rimini (why not? she must be somewhere) would think of the genial farce offered to us by Frege and Russell: defining the natural number as a set of sets.

I would also like to say: it seems to me that "the revolutionary avant-garde," despite its existential anguish, has the air of an aristocratic caste. This is tiring, and needlessly depressing: they're the ones who understand Frege, Russell ... or Marx. Well then, what if we were to credit all human speech, the speech of every human, with its own "direct prophecy" and banal truth?

WILLAME: "Nowhere in the book do we find an analysis of the social formation that is Zaire. In this respect, we could turn back on the author his criticism of Gérard Leclerc's *Anthopologie et colonialisme* [Anthropology and Colonialism]: the history of imperialism is not addressed, even though it constitutes the hard kernel around which all the rest is organized in specific determinations."

RESPONSE: Bloch recalls a wonderful lesson from Leibniz according to which the past is pregnant with the future, and invites us to dream. Presented thus, the history of imperialism is an abstraction. What I mean to say is: a critical analysis of the human and social sciences as they are practiced today in Africa, or Bênoit Verhaegen's study of the rebellions in Zaire, seem to me to be very concrete ways of grasping the imperialist processes that also turn out to be the subtle means and techniques used by this monster called "imperialism."

When addressing the human sciences in Zaire, I had to deal with a still "living" past, that of colonial science in its full weight; and also with a present in which Verhaegen was scandalously trying to live out a singular practice of science rather than reproduce "a model." I was struck by the "recuperation" of colonial science, which was depriving young Zairean scholars of a possible revolution.

From my perspective, what sign and what system could be a better example of the contradictions of the social formation that is Zaire? Although, you will concede, this is a rather different horizon than the one Leclerc engages.

So then, for our dreams of the future, let "immediate history" be a hypothesis and a site of coincidence between scientific and political practice. In a word, let us have an engaged science whose central key is praxis; or, as Karel Kosik recently put it in his *Dialectics of the Concrete*,[2] the active unity of man and the world, of matter and spirit, of subject and object, of product and producer – this active unit that reproduces itself historically, constantly renewing and reconstituting itself in practice.

WILLAME: "Conscious of being myself a 'technician' who came up in the elevator, I set my discourse against the author's, backing him up against the wall. The specificity of the ideology of authenticity lies in the singularity of its project: its discourse pertinently translates the malaise of an elite trying to 'situate' itself. From this point of view, it is certainly not a fantasy created out of whole cloth by some oligarchy; but, like any ideology, does it not obscure things, if only by the choices it encourages?"

RESPONSE: What exactly is he talking about? Certain academics today show a strange prudishness around the concept of authenticity. Please understand me: this has nothing to do with the Zairean "farce." When authenticity is praised or deplored, an ideologically important fact tends to be forgotten: certain European philosophies of the nineteenth century – think of Germany, for instance – are philosophies of authenticity. Berque's works on "Arab authenticity," or Freire's early work on Brazil, no doubt belong to history or to sociology, but they can be grouped under a similar philosophical label. The questions that a contemporary German philosopher recently addressed, in an impressive book, to the philosophies of authenticity in German Romanticism could be rigorously applied to either of them.

My book, like every text, is heavy with spiritual and cultural references. But on this subject, it seems to me that what I have to say is directly and easily readable, without any need for a complex genealogy. The "traces" of Sartre are clear. Because of the sociohistorical context, I affirm the irreducibility of the subject and its right to speech. I find exemplary the words that Aimé Césaire wrote as he left the Communist Party: "No doctrine is worthwhile unless rethought by us, rethought for us, converted to us. This would seem to go without saying. And yet, as the facts are, it does not go without saying."[3]

A cult of difference? No, not necessarily. We are competent to judge the gap between the right to personality and demands of alterity that might lead to racism. What if we were to take Sartre's reflection on the Jewish question as an example and illustration? And then, Césaire taught me this: "Provincialism? Not at all. I am not burying myself in a narrow particularism. But neither do I want to lose myself in an emaciated universalism."[4]

And as I recall, Sartre, in his "Response to Lefort," says nothing different.

And what about ideology? From one end of my book to another, I speak of nothing else, for and against: in sum, following Thomas Herbert, ideology cannot be merely considered a definable region within a social formation. It is theoretically impossible to treat it as a group consciousness, a representation of the world, or a block of ideas valid for a society or class that tend to be imposed together, as a unit of the type grasped by functionalism.

WILLAME: "It is surprising that the author, although careful not to mark his unconditional accord with Marxism, admits that his argument is guided by materialism."

RESPONSE: In a note, Willame goes further. He thinks it significant that I refer "above all ... to two university 'Marxists,' Maurice Godelier and Louis Althusser," who Pierre-Philippe Rey apparently sees as the representatives of a new intellectual dogmatism: structuralist Marxism.

Guilty I am, then, of a non-orthodox practice of Marxism, for trying to make the case for a "just society" and "the advancement of man." Guilty, too, of moving on the level of ideology ("the level where Mudimbe places himself, as the starting point of what opens onto struggle") – and here I am *also* "driven" in the tracks of those dogmatic Marxists: the structuralists!

First of all, I will say simply: my reticence has a precise, practical meaning, which Césaire expresses very well in his "Letter to Maurice Thorez":

> It is the usage some have made of Marxism and communism that I condemn. That what I want is that Marxism and communism be placed in the service of black peoples, and not black peoples in the service of Marxism and communism. That the doctrine and the movement would be made to fit men, not men to fit the doctrine or the movement.[5]

I also think this, and I make the same demands, for example, of Christianity and of Islam.

And then, my dear Willame: like me, you know the remarkable force and the restrictions that come from an assiduous frequentation of Marx. You are familiar with too many of the appealing excesses and noteworthy insufficiencies of various uses of Marxist methodology today to tell me that, under analytical scrutiny, your *Patrimonialism and Political Change in the Congo* can be best explained by reference to Weber. Here, very concretely, we can understand Marx's quip: "I do not write recipes for the cook-shops of the future."

What, then, am I trying to protect by my prudence? Perhaps what I would imprudently call the "Tiresias complex": the ability to assume, in the virginity of a word and the madness of a hope, the activity and force of subjectivity confronting history. The dogmatism of Communist parties will not grant me this. Is this not because they more or less belong to the "lazy Marxism" Sartre speaks of in his *Critique of Dialectical Reason*? "This lazy Marxism puts everything into everything, makes real men into the symbols of its myths; thus the only philosophy which can really grasp the complexity of the human being is transformed into a paranoiac dream."[6]

WILLAME: "Here we land with both feet in the domain of utopia, more particularly the one recently defined by Baudrillard, for whom I know Mudimbe professes great admiration. In *The Mirror of Production*, Baudrillard speaks of a utopian violence that does not accumulate, but is lost: 'It does not try to accumulate itself as does economic value ... It does not grasp for power ... It wants only the spoken word; and it wants to lose itself in it.'"[7]

RESPONSE: Isn't there a misunderstanding here? Dr. Green's violent response to Dr. Lacan, which closes my book, provided the murder of the father as a convenient reference. The tendency has been to read *The Other Side of the Kingdom* only within this frame. But isn't it clear that this other violence, which I took from Baudrillard, is, all things considered, more essential: what did Marx have to say to the workers? He addressed himself to a (European) industrial bourgeoisie and, with "the dialectic," played tricks behind their backs.

With Baudrillard, I think that "utopia, for its part, would have nothing to do with the concept of alienation. It regards every man and every society as already totally there, at each moment, in its symbolic exigency."[8] Against the racism of perfection, of the completed stage of Reason that is a certain Marxism, let us return very attentively to Sartre, that little-known figure, to see if Baudrillard goes astray, and where, when he argues in his reflections that the worst misappropriation of the revolution was the enclosure of the "exploited" within only one historical possibility, that of taking power. Here we can see the depth to which the axioms of political economy have mined, invested, and rerouted the revolutionary perspective. Utopia wants speech against power, and against the reality principle, which is nothing but the fantasy of the system and its indefinite reproduction.

But I believe still more than this. In my book, I situated insurrection in the refusal Lacan calls *aphanisis*; that is to say, disappearance as represented by the *vel* used in symbolic logic. Perhaps, to better mark this powerful violence, it would be useful for me to note something that is important but goes unsaid: what Dr. Lacan names descends from Freud; but there are also Jones and Klein. And according to Jones, *aphanisis*, the disappearance of desire, is the object of a terror more remarkable than that of castration.

At present, I would like to know what exactly people mean when they speak to me of the "murder of the father." When I accepted this imagistic expression (in *Recherche, Pédagogie et Culture* 20), it was to speak of an infirmity, not to live it in a harmonious utopia. I never argued that with a mere cry we might attain a state of happy immobility; rather, I invoked the very violent type of movement that Freud speaks of in the conclusion of his analysis of the Wolf Man. And of course, as one knows, this latter has nothing to do with *aphanisis*. Really?

* * *

A very brief conclusion could be drawn from these quick remarks; one that is especially difficult to make understood, and which I will present in two propositions. The first I take from Baudrillard: the totalization of the subject is still the end of the end of the political economy of consciousness, sealed by the identity of the subject as political economy is by the principle of equivalence. The second is this: the abolition of this facility, which in addition is no doubt only a beautiful illusion, would imply a "revolution" that could lead to a new definition and another understanding of what it truly means to "be other" or "be oneself" – and, naturally, of what "might" then be a new scientific practice of the "one" and "its others."

From here, then, why shouldn't Africa, too, speak up?

Notes

Preface

1 *Partners in Development: Report of the Commission on International Development*, New York: Praeger, 1969.
2 [Translator's note: This book is not identified by Mudimbe, but is likely *De l'aide à la recolonisation: les leçons d'un échec*, Paris: Seuil, 1972 (translated as *From Aid to Recolonization: Lessons of a Failure*, New York: Pantheon, 1973)].
3 [Translator's note: This passage is slightly adapted from Michel Foucault, *The Archaeology of Knowledge and the Discourse on Language*, trans. A. M. Sheridan-Smith, New York: Vintage, 2010, p. 235.]
4 "Littératures et profils nègres" [Black Literature and Profiles], *Recherche, Pédagogie et Culture* 6 (33), 1978, p. 31. [Translator's note: Except where an English-language translation is cited, all translations of French-language sources are my own.]
5 Aimé Césaire, "Letter to Maurice Thorez," trans. Chike Jeffers, *Social Text* 28 (2), 2010, p. 152.
6 Jean-Bertrand Pontalis, *Après Freud* [After Freud], Paris: Gallimard, 1968.

I. Positions

1. A Sign, a Scent

1 *Essais d'ethnopsychiatrie générale* [Essays in General Ethnopsychiatry], Paris: Gallimard, 1970, p. xxi – translated as

Notes to pp. 4–10

Basic Problems of Ethnopsychiatry, trans. Basia Miller Gulati and Georges Devereux, Chicago: University of Chicago Press, 1980. [Translator's note: The English-language edition does not contain this introduction.]
2 Ibid., p. xxii.
3 Ibid., p. x.
4 This was on the subject of Devereux's *From Anxiety to Method in the Behavioral Sciences*, Paris and The Hague: Mouton and de Gruyter, 1967; see *Archives Européennes de Sociologie* 11 (2), 1970.
5 *Contrepoints* 5, Winter 1971, p. 189.
6 Devereux, *Basic Problems*, p. 1.
7 Ibid., pp. 1–2.
8 Ibid., p. 69. [Translator's note: The quotation is from Don C. Talayesva, *Sun Chief: The Autobiography of a Hopi Indian*, ed. Leo W. Simmons, New Haven: Yale University Press, 1942.]
9 See the *Iliad*, book 15.
10 Devereux, *Basic Problems*, p. 70.
11 V. Y. Mudimbe, *L'Autre face du royaume: une Introduction à la critique des langages en folie* [The Other Side of the Kingdom: An Introduction to the Critique of Mad Languages], Lausanne: L'Age d'Homme, 1973.
12 Michel Foucault, *The Order of Things: An Archaeology of the Human Sciences*, trans. Alan Sheridan, London: Routledge, 2002, p. 411.
13 [Translator's note: Not identified by Mudimbe, but likely *L'Ethnologue et son ombre* (The Ethnologist and His Shadow), Paris: Payot, 1968.]
14 Foucault, *Order of Things*, pp. xxii–xxiii.
15 Ibid., pp. xxiii–xxiv.
16 Stanislas Adotévi, *Négritude et négrologues* [Négritude and Négrologists], Paris: Union Générale d'Éditions, 1973.
17 Louis Althusser and Étienne Balibar, *Reading Capital*, trans. Ben Brewster, London: Verso, 2009, p. 168 [emphasis in the original].
18 Devereux, *Basic Problems*, p. 158.
19 Jean-Paul Sartre, "The Man with the Tape-Recorder," in *Between Existentialism and Marxism*, trans. John Matthews, New York: Verso, 1974.
20 Michel Foucault, *History of Madness*, trans. Jonathan Murphy and Jean Khalfa, London: Routledge, 2006, pp. 343–4.
21 See, for instance, the exemplary work of François Duyckaerts, *La Notion de normal en psychologie clinique: introduction à une critique des fondements théoriques de la psychothérapie* [The Concept of Normal in Clinical Psychology: Introduction to a

Critique of the Theoretical Foundations of Psychotherapy], Paris: Vrin, 1954.
22 Sartre, "Man with the Tape-Recorder," p. 202.
23 See Mary Barnes and Joseph Berke, *Un Voyage à travers la folie* [A Journey through Madness], Paris: Seuil, 1973, and the work of A. Esterson, R. D. Laing, D. G. Cooper, J. Heaton, H. Phillipson, J. D. Sutherland, and P. Senft.
24 Devereux, *Basic Problems*, p. 293.
25 Michel de Certeau, *Heterologies*, trans. Brian Massumi, Minneapolis: University of Minnesota Press, 1986, p. 135 [translation modified].
26 See, for example, W. H. R. Rivers, *Medicine, Magic and Religion: The FitzPatrick Lectures Delivered before the Royal College of Physicians London 1915 and 1916*, London: Kegan Paul, 1924.
27 Foucault, *History of Madness*, p. 528.
28 Gerard Buakasa Tulu Kia Mpansu, *L'Impensé du discours: "kindoki" et "nkisi" en pays Kongo du Zaïre* [The Unthought of Discourse: "Kindoki" and "Nkisi" in the Kongo Region of Zaire], Brussels and Kinshasa: Faculté de Théologie Catholique, 1973. See part III, ch. 3, below.
29 Buakasa, *L'Impensé*, p. 308.
30 Paul Diel, *Symbolism in Greek Mythology: Human Desire and its Transformations*, Boulder: Shambhala, 1980.
31 Gaston Bachelard, "Preface," in Diel, *Symbolism in Greek Mythology*, p. x.
32 Foucault, *Order of Things*, pp. 414–15.
33 Ibid., p. 415.
34 Bachelard, "Preface," p. viii.
35 [Translator's note: Ancient Greek *hupar* and *onar* are used to refer to waking life opposed to dream, but *hupar* can also refer to a "true" dream or vision as opposed to ordinary dream.]
36 Jean-Bertrand Pontalis, *Après Freud* [After Freud], Paris: Gallimard, 1968.
37 Ibid., p. 170.
38 See, for example, the Marxist critique: *La Nouvelle Critique*, June 1949 and December/January 1964–1965; C. B. Clément, P. Bruno, and L. Sève, *Pour une critique marxiste de la théorie psychanalytique* [For a Marxist Critique of Psychoanalytic Theory], Paris: Éditions Sociales, 1973.
39 Félix Guattari, *Psychoanalysis and Transversality: Texts and Interviews 1955–1971*, trans. Ames Hodges, Los Angeles: Semiotext(e), 2015, p. 275.
40 Jacques Lacan, *The Seminar of Jacques Lacan, Book XI: The Four Fundamental Concepts of Psychoanalysis*, trans. Alan Sheridan, New York: W. W. Norton, 1981, p. 8.

2. What Order of African Discourse?

1 L. S. Senghor, *Pierre Teilhard de Chardin et la politique africaine* [Pierre Teilhard de Chardin and African Politics], Paris: Seuil, 1962.
2 Michel Foucault, "The Order of Discourse," trans. Ian McLeod, in *Untying the Text: A Post-Structuralist Reader*, ed. Robert Young, London: Routledge and Kegan Paul, 1981, p. 65.
3 Ibid. [translation modified].
4 Ibid., pp. 65–6.
5 Ibid., p. 66.
6 Ibid., p. 52.
7 Ibid.
8 Ibid., p. 53 [translation modified].
9 Ibid., p. 55.
10 Ibid., p. 56.
11 Ibid., pp. 56–7.
12 Ibid., p. 57.
13 Ibid., p. 59.
14 Ibid., pp. 61–2.
15 Ibid., p. 62.
16 Ibid., p. 63.
17 Ibid., p. 64.
18 Ibid.
19 Ibid., p. 66.
20 Ibid.
21 Ibid., p. 67.
22 Ibid.
23 Ibid.
24 Frantz Fanon, *Black Skin, White Masks*, trans. Richard Philcox, New York: Grove, 2008, p. 205.
25 [Translator's note: As in the Preface, here Mudimbe is rephrasing a passage from Michel Foucault, *The Archaeology of Knowledge and the Discourse on Language*, trans. A. M. Sheridan-Smith, New York: Vintage, 2010, p. 235.]
26 Jean Baudrillard, *The Mirror of Production*, trans. Mark Poster, St. Louis: Telos Press, 1975, pp. 88–9.
27 Fanon, *Black Skin, White Masks*, p. 205.
28 Claude Lévi-Strauss, *Tristes Tropiques*, trans. John Weightman and Doreen Weightman, Harmondsworth: Penguin, 1976, p. 56.
29 Foucault, "Order of Discourse," p. 55.

3. Theoretical Problems in the Social and Human Sciences

1 [Translator's note: The designation of "science" is broader in French than in English, and the usual translation of "sciences sociales et humaines" is "social sciences and humanities." Throughout this book I have used the more literal translation "social and human sciences," since Mudimbe is centrally concerned with the "scientificity" of each of these disciplines.]
2 Raymond Aron, *Essai sur la théorie de l'histoire en Allemagne contemporaine* [Essay on the Theory of History in Contemporary Germany], Paris: Vrill, 1938.
3 [Translator's note: "World" and "Mind."]
4 Michel Foucault, *The Order of Things: An Archaeology of the Human Sciences*, trans. Alan Sheridan, London: Routledge, 2002, pp. 384–5.
5 Jacques Lacan, *Écrits*, trans. Bruce Fink, London: W. W. Norton, 2002, p. 730.
6 Jean Poirier, *Histoire de l'ethnologie* [A History of Ethnology], Paris: Presses Universitaires de France, 1969, p. 6.
7 Georges Politzer, *Critique of the Foundations of Psychology*, trans. Maurice Apprey, Pittsburgh: Duquesne University Press, 1994, p. 7.
8 See P. B. de Maré, *Perspectives in Group Psychiatry: A Theoretical Introduction*, Abingdon: Routledge, 2014, p. 124.
9 Jean-Paul Sartre, *Search for a Method*, trans. Hazel Barnes, New York: Knopf, 1963, p. 14.
10 Benoît Verhaegen, *Introduction à l'histoire immediate* [Introduction to Immediate History], Gembloux: Duculot, 1974, p. 91.
11 Pierre Lantz, "Critique dialectique et sociologie" [Dialectical Critique and Sociology], *L'Homme et la Société* 13, 1969, p. 142.
12 See, for example, Paul F. Lazarsfeld, *Philosophie des sciences sociales* [Philosophy of Social Sciences], Paris: Gallimard, 1970.
13 Anouar Abdel-Malek, "La notion de 'profondeur du champ historique' en sociologie" [The Notion of "Depth of Historical Field" in Sociology], in Georges Balandier, ed., *Sociology des mutations* [Sociology of Mutation], Paris: Anthropos, 1970, p. 54.

4. Christianity: A Question of Life?

1 Michel de Certeau, *L'Étranger ou l'union dans la différence* [The Stranger, or Unity within Difference], Paris: Desclée de Brouwer, 1969, p. 72.
2 V. Y. Mudimbe, *L'Autre face du royaume: une Introduction à la critique des langages en folie* [The Other Side of the Kingdom: An

Introduction to the Critique of Mad Languages], Lausanne: L'Age d'Homme, 1973, p. 37.
3 de Certeau, *L'Étranger*, pp. 73–4.
4 [Translator's note: In the language of Vatican II, *ad intra* refers to the internal working of the Church in itself, and *ad extra* to the Church's relations with the outside world.]
5 Robert Louis Delavignette, *Christianity and Colonialism*, London: Burnes & Oates, 1964, pp. 71–2.
6 Cf. *Maximum illud*, 1919. [Translator's note: This is an apostolic letter issued by Pope Benedict XV; following convention, it takes its title from the opening words of the Latin text.]
7 See the important work by Mudimbe-Boyi Mbulamwanza, *Testi e immagini: la missione del "Congo" nelle relazioni dei cappuccini italiani 1645–1700* [Texts and Images: The Mission to the "Congo" According to the Relations of the Italian Capuchins], 2 vols., thesis, Lubumbashi, 1977.
8 Ibid., pp. 329–91.
9 Jean Pirotte, *Périodiques missionnaires belges d'expression française: reflets de cinquante années d'évolution d'une mentalité 1889–1940* [Belgian Missionary Periodicals in French: Reflections on Fifty Years of the Evolution of a Mentality, 1889–1940], Louvain: Publications Universitaires de Louvain, 1973, p. 366.
10 [Translator's note: Jacques Dournes was a French missionary to Vietnam and a prolific ethnologist. He came into conflict with Church authorities for his disinterest in evangelization, and left the priesthood after he was removed from his missionary post in 1969.]
11 de Certeau, *L'Étranger*, p. 75.
12 Mudimbe, *L'Autre face du royaume*, p. 30: "Despite their declarations, it can always be shown that they were condemned only for political reasons; since, in fact, all religious witness also has a meaning and a role in the life of a state."
13 [Translator's note: "Toothing stones," in French "pierres d'attentes" (lit. "waiting stones"), refers in architecture to foundational stones designed to accommodate future additions. It has been used in Catholic discourse in Africa to refer to elements of African culture said to "anticipate" Christian doctrine.]
14 Michel Foucault, *The Archaeology of Knowledge and the Discourse on Language*, trans. A. M. Sheridan Smith, New York: Vintage, 2010, pp. 159–60.
15 Pope John XXIII, "His Holiness Replies," *Présence Africaine* 24–5, 1959, pp. 469–70.
16 The apostolic exhortation *Evangelii nuntiandi*, 1975, clarifies the problem: if pluralism is admitted, this is only under precise conditions, in order to maintain an "eternal truth."

II. Analyses and Tendencies

1. Society, Education, Creativity

1 Michel Foucault, *Discipline and Punish: The Birth of the Prison*, trans. Alan Sheridan, New York: Knopf Doubleday, 2012, p. 148.
2 Ibid., p. 138.
3 François Duyckaerts, *La Notion de normal en psychologie clinique: introduction à une critique des fondement théoriques de la psychothérapie* [The Concept of Normal in Clinical Psychology: Introduction to a Critique of the Theoretical Foundations of Psychotherapy], Paris: Vrin, 1954.
4 Georges Gurvitch, *Déterminismes sociaux et liberté humaine* [*Social Determinism and Human Freedom*], Paris: Presses Universitaires de France, 1963, pp. 160ff.
5 Michel Foucault, "The Order of Discourse," trans. Ian McLeod, in *Untying the Text: A Post-Structuralist Reader*, ed. Robert Young, London: Routledge and Kegan Paul, 1981, p. 55.
6 Ibid., p. 59.
7 Ibid., pp. 59–60.

2. Cultural Cooperation and Dialogue

1 [Translator's note: "Cooperation" is the standard term in French to refer to joint programs between countries, often between a wealthier and a less wealthy country. It includes what in English are often referred to as "aid" or "international development" programs.]
2 See V. Y. Mudimbe, *L'Autre face du royaume: une Introduction à la critique des langages en folie* [The Other Side of the Kingdom: An Introduction to the Critique of Mad Languages], Lausanne: L'Age d'Homme, 1973.
3 [Translator's note: Mudimbe gives no reference here, and I have not been able to identify the source.]
4 Michel Foucault, *The Order of Things: An Archaeology of the Human Sciences*, trans. Alan Sheridan, London: Routledge, 2002, p. 9.
5 Michel de Certeau, *The Writing of History*, trans. Tom Conley, New York: Columbia University Press, 1988, pp. 71–2.
6 [Translator's note: The last two sentences are a paraphrase of Foucault, *Order of Things*, p. 411.]
7 Herman Kahn and Anthony Wiener, *The Year 2000: A Framework for Speculation on the Next Thirty-Three Years*, New York: Macmillan, 1967; Herman Kahn and B. Bruce-Briggs, *Things to*

Come: Thinking about the Seventies and Eighties, New York: Macmillan, 1972.

8   A surprise-free projection is a projection which is not surprising to the author. It resembles the naive extrapolation of economics, though it is a somewhat more sophisticated concept and often more useful. In this so-called naive projection certain aspects of a situation are kept constant and others are permitted to continue or evolve in some prescribed manner – usually according to current trends. However, a surprise-free projection is often arrived at by using theories (or intuitions) that the author happens to believe or finds plausible. Therefore, if the analysis turns out to be true, he will not be surprised. This can also apply to multiple theories, even if they are contradictory – the author in this case is not sure which one is right but he will not be surprised if either one or the other comes out. (TC, p. 40)

9   The presentation and examples in the following are taken from TC (pp. 8–29), which will not be cited after each quote. [Translator's note: One modification has been made from the original, English-language report: the original point (6) has been moved to (13).] In my added comments, I repeat ideas and propositions of Dr. Kahn's, largely taken from two short unpublished works that he kindly shared with me.
10 Michel de Certeau, *Culture in the Plural*, trans. Tom Conley, Minneapolis: University of Minnesota Press, 1997, p. 106.
11 Jean-Paul Sartre, "Reponse à Lefort" [Response to Lefort], in *Situations VII: Problèmes du marxisme 2* [Situations VII: Problems in Marxism 2], Paris: Gallimard, 1965. [Translator's note: This passage is not found in the English translation of "Reponse à Lefort" (in *The Communists and Peace*, trans. Philip R. Berk, New York: George Braziller, 1968).]
12 Club Jean Moulin, *L'État et le citoyen* [State and Citizen], Paris: Seuil, 1961.

3. Universities: What Future?

1 *Actuel Développement* [Development News] 7, Industry Dossier, 1975.
2 [Translator's note: I have not located the original of this quotation.]
3 *Le Nouvel Observateur*, 25 January 1967.

4. Western Cultural Power and Christianity

1 A demand is only a call. If we wanted, we could experiment with understanding these, following Lalande's criticism, as something stronger, and something less intellectual and rigorously determined.

2 For a synthesis of these questions, see two excellent volumes by Guy de Bosschère: *Autopsie de la colonisation* [Autopsy of Colonialism], Paris: Albin Michel, 1967, and *Perspectives de la décolonisation* [Perspectives on Decolonization], Paris: Albin Michel, 1969.
3 Raymond Mauny, *Les Siècles obscurs de l'Afrique Noire* [The Dark Centuries of Sub-Saharan Africa], Paris: Fayard, 1970.
4 Ibid., p. 276.
5 These questions of syncretism could be expounded at length. I will limit myself to quoting Joel Schmidt's *Le Christ des profondeurs: chrétiens des premiers siècles* [The Christ of the Depths: Christians in the First Centuries], Paris: André Balland, 1970:

> If certain pagans heard of Christ, they would be able, if they knew the story of Krishna, to discuss at leisure the parallels between the cult and legends of Krishna and the cult and legends of Jesus. This was true to such an extent that certain exegetes suspected that Christ had visited the Indies during the obscure years of his existence, and had found the inspiration and vision for his Messianism in the story of Krishna, the Hindu Messiah.
> We should explore this last, and perhaps most surprising, point of syncretism, in order to fully explore what in Christianity can be reconciled with Paganism ...
> Krishna, incarnation of Vishnu, represents the second person of the Indian trinity, like Christ. Krishna descended from Yadou, whose name recalls that of Judah (Youda), father of the tribe to which Jesus Christ belonged. Like Christ, Krishna is of royal lineage. He was raised by Yasoda, also called Yasou-Mati, which could also be translated as "mother of Jesus." The shepherd Nanda passed for Krishna's father, just as the carpenter Joseph was Jesus's official father. But his true father was God, and Krishna's was Vasou-Deva (the god Vasou).
> Krishna is born in a cramped, poor, and desolate place, and Jesus in a stable. Both of them come into the world at midnight, and the two births are saluted in some way: the first by a meteor, the second by the gleam of the shepherds' star. Even the shepherds of Bethlehem and its region have their equivalent in the shepherds who came to offer gifts to the child Krishna.
> Krishna's parents have to hide their son from the fury of King Kansa, who orders the massacre of all newborns from the Yadou tribe, just as the flight into Egypt allows Jesus to escape the murder of the innocents of Judea by Herod's soldiers.
> When one day Jesus slips away from his parents and begins to act autonomously as the Son of Man, Joseph and Mary search for and find him. To their anguish and reproach – "Behold, your father and I have been searching for you" – Jesus responds: "Did you not know that I must be about my Father's business?" Similarly, after Krishna leaves his mother's roof, she hears her husband say: "O wife, no longer call Krishna your son; recognize him as your lord and adore him."

When St. Peter, followed shortly after by the Apostles, confesses Jesus's divinity by crying: "You are the Christ, son of the living God," he says the same thing as the shepherds who prostrate themselves before Krishna: "You are the creator of the universe, the one who erases the sins of creatures, Lord of the three worlds, be gracious to us, and today show us paradise."

Krishna and Christ perform very similar miracles. Krishna straightens the back of a hunchback, Christ that of a woman who had been bent in two for eighteen years. Both of them raise the dead. The Brahman hero can also be seen advocating some of the virtues the god-man came to teach to the world: humility, disdain for riches, forgiving wrongs, the obligation to love one's enemies and return good for evil, love for little ones and for the humble. While Krishna treats the Brahmans of his day harshly, Christ casts anathema on the pride and ostentation of the haughty Pharisees. Christ's triumphal entry into Jerusalem has a response in Krishna's majestic parade in the city of Mathura.

6 G. E. von Grunebaum, *Modern Islam: The Search for Cultural Identity*, Berkeley: University of California Press, 1962, p. 129.
7 Jean Pirotte, *Périodiques missionaires belges d'expression français: reflets de cinquante années d'évolution d'une mentalité, 1889–1940* [Belgian Missionary Periodicals in French: Reflections on Fifty Years of the Evolution of a Mentality, 1889–1940], Louvain: Publications Universitaires de Louvain, 1973.
8 In the following I systematically present Pirotte's quantitative study of ethnic characters.
9 Pirotte, *Périodiques missionaires*, pp. 180–1.
10 Ibid., pp. 239–40.
11 G. Defois, "Discours religieux et pouvoir social" [Religious Discourse and Social Power], *Archives de Sociologie des Religions* 32, 1971, p. 89.
12 Cited in Pirotte, *Périodiques missionaires*, p. 205.
13 See note 13, part I, ch. 4, p. 189.
14 Mudimbe-Boyi Mbulamwanza, *Testi e immagini: la missione del "Congo" nelle relazioni dei cappucini italiani 1645–1700* [Texts and Images: The Mission to the "Congo" According to the Relations of the Italian Capuchins], 2 vols., thesis, Lubumbashi, 1977.
15 Meinrad P. Hebga, *Emancipation d'eglises sous tutelle* [Emancipation of Churches under Guardianship], Paris: Présence Africaine, 1976, p. 9.
16 Ibid., p. 160.
17 Jean-Émile Charon, *De la physique a l'homme* [From Physics to Man], Paris: Gonthier, pp. 123–8.

III. Questions and Openings

1. "Niam M'Paya": *At the Sources of an African Thinking*

1 Placide Tempels, *Bantu Philosophy*, trans. Colin King, Paris: Présence Africaine, 1953, p. 119. Emphasis added.
2 [Translator's note: "Évolués," literally "evolved ones," was a term widely used to refer to French colonial subjects who had received a French education and taken on French cultural characteristics.]
3 Tempels, *Bantu Philosophy*, p. 118.
4 Ibid., p. 121 [translation modified].
5 Alioune Diop, "*Niam M'Paya*," in Tempels, *Bantu Philosophy*, p. 8.
6 Michel Foucault, *Discipline and Punish: The Birth of the Prison*, trans. Alan Sheridan, New York: Knopf Doubleday, 2012, p. 192.
7 Ibid., p. 209.
8 Ibid., p. 308.
9 Here one can consult Raymond Mauny, *Les Siècles obscurs de l'Afrique Noire* [The Dark Centuries of Sub-Saharan Africa], Paris: Fayard, 1970.
10 It is true that the slave traders spoke of Black races and ethnicities, but this was in the language of cattle merchants.
11 For edification on this point see, among other treasures of the genre, the volume *Voyages en Abyssinie et en Nubie* [Travels in Abyssinia and Nubia] from the "Christian Youth's Library, approved by Msgr. the Archbishop of Tours," collected and edited by H. Lebrun, Tours: Chez Mame, 1840.
12 Montaignes, *Essais*, book 1, ch. 31.
13 Michel Foucault, *The Order of Things: An Archaeology of the Human Sciences*, trans. Alan Sheridan, London: Routledge, 2002, p. 165.
14 Diop, "*Niam M'Paya*," p. 9.
15 Jean Chesnaux in Collectif, *Quel avenir attend l'homme? Rencontre internationale de Royaumont (11–20 Mai 1961)* [What Future Awaits Mankind? International Conference at Royaumont, May 11–20, 1961], Paris: Presses Universitaires de France, 1961, p. 56.
16 Diop, "*Niam M'Paya*," p. 11.
17 Chesnaux, in *Quel avenir*, p. 61.
18 Tempels, *Bantu Philosophy*, pp. 112–13 [translation modified].
19 See Senghor's preface to Eike Haberland, ed., *Leo Frobenius, 1874–1973*, Stuttgart: Franz Steiner, 1973, p. xi.
20 This is a question of point of view; we know under what conditions

and in what circumstances Western society represses voyeurism. The ethnology that derives from it was, and remains today, "a favor."
21 Foucault, *Order of Things*, p. 413.
22 Diop, "*Niam M'Paya*," p. 12.
23 Ibid., p. 7.
24 Ibid., p. 12.

2. On African Literature

1 D. Gilbert, *Le Droit de colonisation* [The Right to Colonization], Elisabethville: Lovania, 1956, p. 67.
2 Michel Foucault, *Discipline and Punish: The Birth of the Prison*, trans. Alan Sheridan, New York: Knopf Doubleday, 2012, p. 169.
3 Frantz Fanon, *Black Skin, White Masks*, trans. Richard Philcox, New York: Grove, 2008, p. 204.
4 Jean-Pierre Richard, *Littérature et sensation* [Literature and Sensation], Paris: Seuil, 1954.
5 It seems useful here to follow Paulin J. Hountondji's approach in *Sur la philosophie africaine*, Paris: Maspero, 1976 [translated as *African Philosophy: Myth or Reality?* trans. Henri Evans, Bloomington: Indiana University Press, 1983].
6 See, for example, the version edited by F. Michel, *Libri Psalmorum, versio antiqua gallica, e. cod. ms. in Bibl. Bodleiano asservato*, Oxford, 1860.
7 Pierre van den Bergh, "European Languages and Black Mandarins," *Transition* 34, 1968, p. 19.

3. Sorcery: A Language and a Theory

1 Gerard Buakasa Tulu Kia Mpansu, *L'Impensé du discours: "kindoki" et "nkisi" en pays Kongo du Zaïre* [The Unthought of Discourse: "Kindoki" and "Nkisi" in the Kongo Region of Zaire], Brussels and Kinshasa: Faculté de Théologie Catholique, 1973.
2 Benoît Verhaegen, "Préface," in Buakasa, *L'Impensé*, pp. v–vi.
3 Buakasa, *L'Impensé*, p. 8.
4 Ibid., p. 30.
5 See, for example, Robert Mandrou, *Magistrats et sorciers en France au XVIIe siècle: une analyse de psychologie historique* [Magistrates and Sorcerers in Seventeenth-Century France: A Historical Psychological Analysis], Paris: Seuil, 1968, pp. 75–120.
6 R. F. Fortune, *Sorciers de Dobu* [The Sorcerers of Dobu], Paris: Maspero, 1972.
7 Ibid., p. 167.
8 Buakasa, *L'Impensé*, p. 30.
9 Ibid.

10 Ibid., p. 59.
11 Ibid., p. 64.
12 Ibid., p. 70.
13 Ibid., pp. 71–106.
14 Ibid., pp. 107–52.
15 Ibid., p. 152.
16 Michel Foucault, *History of Madness*, trans. Jonathan Murphy and Jean Khalfa, London: Routledge, 2006, p. 251.
17 Buakasa, *L'Impensé*, p. 242.
18 Ibid., p. 280.
19 Ibid., p. 293.
20 Ibid., p. 295.
21 Ibid.
22 Ibid., p. 296.
23 See Reuben Osborn, *Marxism and Psychoanalysis*, New York: Dell, 1967, p. 112.
24 Buakasa, *L'Impensé*, pp. 8 and 297.
25 Louis Althusser, "Freud and Lacan," in *Writings on Psychoanalysis: Freud and Lacan*, New York: Columbia University Press, 1999, p. 7.
26 Ibid., p. 107.
27 Lucien Sève, "Psychanalyse et matérialisme historique" [Psychoanalysis and Historical Materialism], in *Pour une critique marxiste de la théorie psychanalytique* [For a Marxist Critique of Psychoanalytic Theory], Paris: Éditions Sociales, 1973, p. 260.
28 Buakasa, *L'Impensé*, p. 70.
29 Ibid., p. 307.
30 Ibid., p. vii.
31 Ibid., p. 308.
32 Serge Leclaire, *Démasquer le réel: un essai sur l'objet en psychanalyse* [Unmasking the Real: An Essay on the Object in Psychoanalysis], Paris: Seuil, 1971, p. 11.
33 Ibid., p. 23.
34 See Karl Vossler, *Geist und Kultur in der Sprache* [Spirit and Culture in Language], Heidelberg: Carl Winter, 1925.
35 Jacques Lacan, *The Seminar of Jacques Lacan, Book XI: The Four Fundamental Concepts of Psychoanalysis*, trans. Alan Sheridan, New York: W. W. Norton, 1981, pp. 44–5.

4. And What Will God Become?

1 Laënnec Hurbon, *Dieu dans le Vaudou haïtien* [God in Haitian Voodoo], Paris: Payot, 1972.
2 Ibid., p. 47.
3 Ibid., p. 48.

4 Ibid., p. 50.
5 Ibid., p. 125.
6 Ibid., p. 173.
7 Ibid., p. 190.
8 See note 13, part I, ch 4, p. 189.
9 Hurbon, *Dieu dans le Vaudou*, p. 174.
10 Ibid., p. 239.
11 Ibid., p. 17.
12 Karl Marx with Friedrich Engels, *The German Ideology*, Amherst: Prometheus Books, 1998, p. 44.
13 Louis Althusser, "Crise de l'homme et de la société" [Crisis of Man and Society], *Lumière et Vie* 93, 1969, p. 29.
14 Hurbon, *Dieu dans le Vaudou*, p. 255.

5. Interdisciplinarity and Educational Science

1 Jean Piaget, *Epistémologie des sciences de l'homme* [Epistemology of the Human Sciences], Paris: Gallimard, 1970, p. 234.
2 Michel de Certeau, *Culture in the Plural*, trans. Tom Conley, Minneapolis: University of Minnesota Press, 1997, p. 125.
3 See ibid., p. 102.
4 Michel Foucault, *History of Madness*, trans. Jonathan Murphy and Jean Khalfa, London: Routledge, 2006, p. 541.

6. Immediate History: An African Practice of Dialectical Materialism

1 Benôit Verhaegen, *Introduction à l'histoire immédiate* [Introduction to Immediate History], Gembloux: Duculot, 1974.
2 Ibid., p. 190.
3 Ibid., p. 13.
4 Ibid., p. 69.
5 Ibid., p. 79.
6 Ibid., p. 84.
7 Ibid., p. 87.
8 Ibid., p. 88.
9 Ibid., p. 90.
10 Ibid.
11 Ibid., p. 190.
12 Ibid., p. 102.
13 Ibid., p. 108.
14 Ibid., p. 132.
15 Ibid., p. 188.
16 Ibid.
17 Friedrich Engels, *Dialectics of Nature*, trans. Clemens Dutt, in Karl

Marx and Friedrich Engels, *Collected Works*, *Vol. 25*, London: Lawrence and Wishart, 1988, p. 491.
18 Vladimir I. Lenin, *What Is to Be Done? Burning Questions of Our Moment*, Beijing: Foreign Languages Press, 1973, pp. 171–2.

7. The Price of Sin

1 Jacques L. Vincke, *Le Prix du péché: essai de psychanalyse existentielle des traditions européennes et africaines* [The Price of Sin: Essay in Existential Psychoanalysis of European and African Traditions], Kinshasa: Éditions du Mont Noir, 1974.
2 R. D. Laing and D. G. Cooper, *Reason and Violence: A Decade of Sartre's Philosophy*, London: Tavistock, 1964, pp. 172–3.

3 The serial *idea* is not a conscious moment of action, that is, a unifying revelation of objects in the dialectical temporalization of the action, but is a practico-inert object. The evidence of a serial idea is in my double incapacity to verify it or to transform it in the others. Its opacity, my powerlessness to change it in the other, my own and the other's lack of doubt about it, are offered as evidence of its truth. (Ibid., p. 125)

4 Karl Marx, *Capital: A Critique of Political Economy*, *Vol. 1*, trans. Ben Fowkes, London: Penguin, 2004, p. 1.
5 [Translator's note: I have not been able to locate the source of this quotation.]
6 Thomas Herbert, "Pour une théorie générale des idéologies" [Toward a General Theory of Ideologies], *Cahiers de l'Analyse* 9, 1968.
7 Andre Gunder Frank, *Capitalism and Underdevelopment in Latin America*, New York: Monthly Review Press, 1967, p. 9.
8 Jean-Paul Sartre, "The Man with the Tape-Recorder," in *Between Existentialism and Marxism*, trans. John Matthews, New York: Verso, 1974.
9 Claude Lévi-Strauss, *Tristes Tropiques*, trans. John Weightman and Doreen Weightman, Harmondsworth: Penguin, 1976, pp. 391–2.
10 Ibid., p. 392.

IV. In Lieu of a Conclusion

What Murder of the Father?

1 Jean-Claude Willame, "L'autre face du royaume ou le meurtre du père"[The Other Side of the Kingdom, or the Murder of the Father], *Genève-Afrique* 15 (1), 1976.
2 Karel Kosik, *Dialectics of the Concrete*, Dordrecht: Springer, 1976.

3 Aimé Césaire, "Letter to Maurice Thorez," trans. Chike Jeffers, *Social Text* 28 (2), 2010, p. 150.
4 Ibid., p. 152.
5 Ibid., p. 150.
6 Jean-Paul Sartre, in *Search for a Method*, trans. Hazel Barnes, New York: Knopf, 1963, p. 53.
7 Jean Baudrillard, *The Mirror of Production*, trans. Mark Poster, St. Louis: Telos Press, 1975, pp. 166–7.
8 Ibid., p. 165.

Index

Abdel-Malek, Anouar 39
Abelin, Pierre 79
abnormal, concept of 5
academic system, structure of 58
active sociality 60
adaptation 4, 51, 52, 59
Adotévi, Stanislas 8
Aeterni regis clementia (Sixtus IV) 87
affluence 72–3
Africa
  annulment of memory 108
  books and museums 98
  break from the West 28
  concepts of nationality 123
  dated image of 162–3
  discursive policies 37
  dispossession 76, 90
  education 149–51
  empirico-positivist sociology 37
  erasure of collective identities 108
  erasure of individualities 108
  ethnology and 8
  formalist sociology 37
  independence 97, 98
  modernity 98, 111
  mythical 112–13
  new image 113
  organization and production 86
  political independence 76, 119
  post-independence 86
  practical modalities 76
  priorities
    African culture 85, 86
    economic sphere 85, 86
  reconciliation of programs 85
  reduced to a uniform region 88
  ripe for conquest 87
  rupture 90
  science 98, 178
    from within 40
  social and human sciences 17, 20, 21, 31
    alienation of specialists 39
    considerations for researchers 40
    contradictions of 64–5
    problems 39
    remaking of 40

silence 65
Westerner's gaze 39
tradition 162, 163
violent contact with the West 90
Western ideologies 68
Westernization of 51
Africa of Nations 97
African Christianity 41, 51–2, 91
  Africanization of Christianity 98–9, 101
  churches 51, 92
  colonization and colonizing program 96
  cultural change 91
  education 90
  integration 50
  integration into Africa 50, 106
  for a post-missionary era 98, 99
  Tempels's view 112
African culture 28
  aestheticization of 28–9
  autonomy 98
  essence of 77
  language 77
  noble status 113
  present and future 77
  prioritizing 85, 86
  promotion of 85
  in reference to African tradition 77
  specificity of 77–8
  Western cultures and 86
African *Gesellschaftsformations* 168
African language(s) 98
  replacing European language 30–1
African literature 115–23
  in African languages 121
  critics of 119
  cultural nationalities 120
  defining 120
  diversity of 120
  economic constraints 122
  in French 122–3
  function and role 119–20
  musicians 121
  oral literature 120–1
  unanimist prejudice 88, 120
  written literature 121
African liturgy 53
African religions 138
African theology 53, 54
African thinking, Foucault's model 26–7
African universities
  adaptations 82
  cooperation between Africa and Euro-America 83–4
  copies of Western mother-universities 81–2
  creativity 83
  enduring spirit 83
  evolution 82–3
  inheritance of Western models 82
  operational model 83–4
  own path of 82
  profitability 82, 83
  rigor
    political 83
    scientific 83
  Verhaegen on 82
Africanity 124
Africans
  claiming the rights of 20
  engaging with science 17–18
  image of 115
  sensitivity toward Western languages 91–2
  true meaning of 20
  unblocked thinking 26
  see also Black Africans
After Freud (Pontalis) 17
alienation 77, 111, 166, 169, 182
Allen, S. 67

Althusser, Louis 9, 10, 140, 181
  ideology 141
  on psychoanalysis 132
  on theological thought 141
Ampère, André-Marie 33
ancient Greeks 31
animist religions 99
anthropology 20, 29, 116–17
anti-psychiatry 156
aphanisis 183
Applied Rationalism (Bachelard) 159
Aristide, Achille 137
Aron, Raymond 33
authenticity 179–80
authors 23
An Average French City: Auxerre 1950 (Bettelheim and Frère) 156

Bachelard, Gaston 14, 16, 158–9
Bakunin, Mikhail 158
Bantu Philosophy (Tempels) 105–6, 112, 113, 137
Basic Problems of Ethnopsychiatry (Devereux) 3–4, 5, 6
Bastide, Roger 3, 4, 138
Baudrillard, Jean 28, 29, 182, 183
being-subject 171
Belgian Missionary Periodicals in French: Reflections of Fifty Years of the Evolution of a Mentality, 1889–1940 (Pirotte) 92
Benedict XV, Pope 48, 96
Berque, Jacques 180
biological methodology 148
biology 65
Black Africans
  characterization of 109
  docile bodies 107
  European contempt for 87
  faults and imperfections 92–3
  freedom 118
  ideal tableau 107
  Jesuits' judgments of 92–3
  positive characteristics of 92, 93
  reviving 95
  role to play in history 112
  Scheutist missionaries' judgments of 93
  self-affirmation 20
  stereotypes xvi
  traits 92–3
  violence against 110
Black alienation 111
Black Orpheus (Sartre) 118, 119
Black Skin, White Masks (Fanon) 119
Bonnet, Charles 109
Borda, Orlando Fals 156
Boulaga, Eboussi 137
bourgeois order 35, 38
Buakasa Tulu Kia Mpansu, Gerard 13, 124, 133–4
  dialectical thought and psychoanalysis 131–2
  discourses 126
  Freud and 131
  Kongo refrain 132
  Marx and 131
  scientific method 124, 125
  see also sorcery; *The Unthought of Discourse* (Buakasa)
Buddha, birth of 89

Calame-Griaule, Geneviève 136–7
Capital (Marx) 8, 167
capitalism
  functions 167, 168
  structure of 167, 168
Capuchin Fathers 48–9, 96–7
carceral city 107
carcerality 110
Castel, Robert 159

Index

Catholic Church, discourses 95–6
Catholic mission 45
Catholic religion 94
catholicity 96
Certeau, Michel de 12, 41
  on African culture 77
  on historians 69
  on missionaries 43, 50
  on products 149
Césaire, Aimé 117–18, 180, 181
change
  cultural 91
  experiential 91
Charon, Jean-Émile 99–100, 101
Chebika (Duvignaud) 156
chemistry 9
Chesnaux, Jean 110–11
China 75
Christian churches 45–6, 94
Christian culture 46
Christian experience 47
Christian Faith *see* Faith
Christian museums 45
Christian proselytism 96
Christian society 94
Christian West 47
Christianity 41, 46
  in Africa *see* African Christianity
  diverse contributions 89
  Eastern origins 98
  ethics and aesthetics 43
  Faith in Jesus Christ 51, 52
  glory of 87
  ideological phenomenon 140
  as an ideology 141–2
  missions *see* missions
  openness 53
  paganism and 44
  spirit of 47
  tropicalizing 51, 52
  Western imperialism 97
  Westernization of 99
  see also missionaries; missions

Christianity and Colonialism (Delavignette) 47
Christianization 94, 97, 106
Church Fathers 52
civilization 95, 96, 112
  law of 87
  phases of evolution 117
class struggle 38
Club Jean Moulin 78
Club of Rome 75
colonial enterprise 39
colonial politics 96
colonial science 179
colonization 20, 86, 95, 96, 109, 170–2
  American 138
  Belgian 170
  right of 116
commentary 23
committed sociology 37
complementarity 89, 91, 148
Comte, Auguste 29, 36
concepts 5, 67, 149
conceptual blocks 9
conceptual grid 108, 111
concrete sociology 156
conquistadores 116
consciousness 109, 118
Conté, Claude 4
conversion 42–3, 94
Cooper, D. G. 166
cooperation 64, 80
  colonizing approach 69
  Euro-American specialists in 69
  historical sovereignty of European thought 69
  programs of 68, 69
creativity 62, 63
  in African universities 83
  definition 57, 59–60
  disciplined errors 60
  double negation of 62
  education and 62
  invention 62

critical consciousness 159
critical enterprise 159
Critique of the Foundations of Psychology (Politzer) 35
cultural codes 7–8, 48–9
cultural confrontations 140, 141
cultural cooperation *see* cooperation
cultural imperialism 37, 149
cultural relativism 19
culture(s)
  complementarity 89, 91
  contacts between 85–9
  dialogue of 77–8
  differences 49, 53, 77
  exchanges between 88, 89
  foreignness to others 88
  Foucault on 7–8
  function of 77
  fundamental codes 7
  independence and 83
  individual personality of 88
  inheritance between 68
  as lived experience 4
  as a mirror 88
  nature and 69
  originality and autonomy of 88
  psychiatric perspective 5, 6
  psychoanalysis and 3
  sensate 71
  truth and 5–6
  universality 89
  see also African culture; Western culture

Damas, Léon-Gontran 117–18
Defois, G. 95–6
degrees of observation 158–9
  critical consciousness 159
  method 159
  observation of observation 159
Delavignette, Robert Louis 47
delirium 3–4
Delphi method 70
demands 86–91
  epistemological 90
  historical 86–9
  political 89–90
dependence
  absolute 171
  relation of 170–1
depth sociology 157
development
  of Africa 119–20
  of development 169
  economic 169
  metropole and satellites 169
  of underdevelopment 169
Devereux, Georges 3
  child psychology 10
  culture-in-itself approach 6
  ethnopsychiatry 3–4, 5, 6, 11
  logical discourse 11
  on psychoanalysis and ethnology 11
  positive aspects of method 6–7
  scientific concepts 9
  universality 5, 6, 11
dialectical criticism 159
dialectical materialism
  African practice of 152–61
  goal of 160
  history of 152
dialectical thought, psychoanalysis and 131–2
Dialectics of Nature (Engels) 160
Diel, Paul 14
Dilthey, Wilhelm 159
Diop, Alioune 105, 106, 108, 109–10, 111, 112, 113, 114
Diop, Cheikh Anta 28, 30
direct experimentation 156
Discipline and Punish: The Birth of the Prison (Foucault) 107–8
discipline(s) 23–4, 59, 60
  Foucault on 58, 59, 61–2, 107–8

means of 108
norms and rules 107
power from Church to state 61
discontinuity, principle of 25
discourse(s) 14
   authors 23
   Buakasa 126
   Catholic Church 95–6
   commentary 23
   doctrinal norms 24
   elision of the reality of 21–2
   Foucault on 21–2
   logical 11
   organization of disciplines 23–4
   procedures of control 22–5
   rituals 24
   of social and human sciences 61, 170
   social appropriation of 25
   societies of 24
   sorcery 127
   subjection of 22–5
   Western 28
   see also The Unthought of Discourse (Buakasa)
discursive police 60
dispossession 76, 90, 169
division of madness 22–3
docile bodies 59
   Black 107
   European 107, 110
doctrinal norms 24
dreams 133–4
   ancients 135
   Tempels's 113
   theocratic 47
Dumézil, Georges 4, 137
Durkheim, Émile 29
Duyckaerts, François 59–60

economic development and underdevelopment 169
economic power, centralization and concentration of 71–2
economic science 29
economic space 168
Éditions du Seuil 155
education 25, 57
   in Africa 149–51
   creativity and 62
   discipline 58–9
   European model 62
   growth 73–4
   Napoleonic system 58–9
   new political anatomy 59
   organization of 151
   reductive 151
   scholarly students 58
   uniformization 57, 58
educational sciences 148
Einstein, Albert 100
elites 71, 178
empirico-positivist sociology 37
engaged sociology 37, 156–7
Engels, Friedrich 8, 9, 160
Enlightenment 39, 87
Enlightenment progress 59
envelope forecasting 70
epistemological demand 90
epistemology 4
Essay on the Philosophy of Science (Ampère) 33
Essay on the Theory of History in Contemporary Germany (Aron) 32–3
essence, concept of 162, 163
ethnocentrism 7, 16, 109, 140
ethnological psychiatry 5
ethnology 4, 11, 14
   Africa and 8
   classical 15
   evolutionism in 164
   Foucault on 7
   founding of 35
   limitations of 6, 7–9, 14–15
   new beginning 113
   reuniting with psychoanalysis 15
   role and function 35

ethnology (*cont.*)
  singularity 14
  structural current 39
  volatilized 15
ethnopsychiatry 3–4, 5, 6, 11
  limitations of 8–9
  speech and context 6
Europe
  conquest of Africa 116
  disciplinizing 108
  elaboration of future 108
  misery of 110
  reducing African difference 108
  tradition 162, 163
  violent conquest of Africa 110
Evangelii praecones (Pius XII) 53
evangelization 50, 52, 87
evolution 109
exact sciences 32, 147
exclusion 30
  principle of 23
existence, concept of 162, 163, 166
Between Existentialism and Marxism (Sartre) 170–2
experience, types of 16
explication 67
exploitation 115–16
expropriation 169
exteriority, principle of 25

Fabian, Johannes 157
facts, system of 16
Faith 43, 45, 46, 60–1, 94
  science and 61–2
Fanon, Frantz 26, 30, 119
fathers of négritude 117
Femmes d'Afrique noire (Paulme) 156
fetishes 129
Fidei donum (Pius XII) 53
finalism 160
folklorization 113
formalist sociology 36–7, 38
Fortune, R. F. 127

Foucault, Michel 20, 27
  culture 7–8
  ethnology 7
  firm decisions 25
  methodological rules
    principle of discontinuity 25
    principle of exteriority 25
    principle of reversal 25
    principle of specificity 25
  procedures of control over discourse 22–5
  prohibited speech 22
  as a symbol 26
  views and comments on authors 23
  commentary 23
  discipline 58, 59, 61–2
  discipline-blockage 107
  discipline-mechanism 107–8
  discourse 21–2, 24, 25
  doctrinal norms 24
  ethnology and psychoanalysis 14–15, 15
  identity 51
  images 67
  madness 12–13, 22–3
  organization of disciplines 23–4
  rituals 24
  Romans 116
  sciences of man 34
  Western thought 21
  will to truth 23, 60
founding subject 21
Frank, Andre Gunder 169
free representation 43
freedom 77, 166
Freire, Paulo 180
Freud, Sigmund 3, 16, 131, 132, 183
  psychoanalytic theory 16–17
Friedrich, R. W. 157
Frobenius, Leo 112
functionalism 168

Future Shock (Toffler) 75
futurology 75

Galileo 60, 62, 163
Geertz, Clifford 157
Geistesgeschichte 134
genies 129, 130, 131
The German Ideology (Marx) 141
giant cities 73
Gilbert, D. 115–16
global metropolis 72
God 94, 99, 139–40
God in Haitian Voodoo (Hurbon) 136–7
  gazes 137
Godelier, Maurice 167, 181
Goldmann, Lucien 154, 158, 159
Gospels 43, 46, 52, 94
Gramsci, Antonio 154
Greek mythology, symbolism in 14
Grosse, Ernst 117
Grunebaum, G. E. von 91
Guattari, Félix 17
Gurvitch, Georges 60, 155
Gusdorf, Georges 147

Hahn, Eduard 117
Haiti 136
  see also Voodoo
Haitians 138
Hebga, Reverend Father 98, 99
Hegel, Georg Wilhelm Friedrich 33, 116
Helmholtz, Hermann von 33
Herbert, Thomas 168, 180
heresies 60, 61
heretical reforms 61
Heusch, Luc de 66
hierarchy of peoples 117
historians 69
historical demand 86–9
historical materialism 125, 132, 155, 158

history 35, 157, 172
  center of 132
  critical reading of 88
  force of subjectivity 182
  as mirror 86
  redefining 87
  searching for norms 87–8
  see also immediate history
History of Madness (Foucault) 12–13, 128, 150–1
Homer 6
Hudson Institute 70–4, 75, 76
human behavior 14
human nature see nature
human sciences 34, 66, 147, 159, 169, 179
  see also social and human sciences
human subject 132
human subjectivity 33
hupar 16
Hurbon, Laënnec
  confrontation 140, 141
  toothing stones approach 140, 142
  views and comments on
    Bantu Philosophy 137
    confrontation 140
    God 139, 140
    human meaning 142
    new approach 137–8
    universality 142
    Voodoo 136–7
  hermeneutic approach 139, 142
  phenomenological approach 138–9, 142
  structural approach 139, 142
  studying 140–1
  theological approach 141
  see also *God in Haitian Voodoo* (Hurbon)
hypotheses 62

idealist ideologies 145
identity 51
ideological space 168
ideological systems 13
ideology 37, 141, 168, 180–1
  definition 38
The *Iliad* 6, 117
immediate history 152, 155, 179
  characteristics and ambiguities of 155
  as a contested and contentious space 157
  definition 152–3
  depth sociology and 157
  dialectical sociology and 157
  engaged sociology and 156–7
  institutional analysis and 156
  intersection of social sciences 155
  methodology 156
  synthesis 159–60
imperialism
  cultural 37, 149
  Euro-American 86, 87, 97
  history of 179
  search for goods 86
  spiritual 99
industrialization 72, 112
infrastructural norms 167
institutional analysis 156
institutionalization 72
intellectual elites 178
intellectual métissage 30
intellectuals 74
Inter coetera (Callixtus III) 87
interdisciplinarity 144–51
  benefits of 151
  presentation of 145
  second approximation 148
  understanding of 145
interference, phenomena of 148
international capitalism 168

Introduction to Immediate History (Verhaegen) 152, 154–5, 157, 159
Isis 89

Jahn, Janheinz 117, 121, 124
Jesuits 92–3
Jesus Christ 46, 89, 99
  transfiguration of 89
John XXIII, Pope 53

Kagamé, Reverend Father Alexis 27, 121, 137
Kahn, Herman 70–4, 75, 76
Kant, Immanuel 4, 66, 117
Kantianism 65
Kesteloot, Lilyan 117
Ki-Zerbo, Joseph 28, 83
Kierkegaard, Sören 159
kindoki 124–9, 130, 133
  event 130
  gardens 130
  indetermination 130
  revelation 130
  social game 134
  theory 128
  see also nkisi
knowledge 23, 30
  European tradition 68
  parallel 33
  process of 68, 158, 161
  reorganization of 31
Kongo 125–6, 127, 130–1
Kosik, Karel 179

Lacan, Jacques 18, 135, 146, 183
  sciences of man 34
Lachelier, Jules 33
Laing, R. D. 36, 156, 166
laissez-faire 72
language(s) 129, 134
  African 30–1, 98
  of missionaries 92, 95–7

philosophical 169–70
    of religions 100–1
    scientific 169–70
    theological 100–1
    value of 17
Lantz, Pierre 38
Lapassade, Georges 37
Lavoisier, Antoine 9
Leclaire, Serge 134
Leclerc, Gérard 179
Lefebvre, Henri 154
leisure 72–3
Lenin, Vladimir Ilyich 161
lesson of writing 172–3
Lévi-Strauss, Claude 4, 30, 66, 147, 148
    on writing 172–3
Lewis, Oscar 156
liberal science 145
linguistic relativism 88
linguistics 147, 148
Lisieux, Thérèse de 43
literacy 73–4
logical thought 43
The Lonely African (Turnbull) 156
Lopes, Duarte 87
lost object 146–7, 149
Lourau, René 37, 156
Lufulwabo 27
Lukács, Georg 154, 158

madness 12–13, 170
    division of 22–3
magic 127
mana 137
Mandeville, Bernard 68
Marcuse, Herbert 158
Marx, Karl 8, 9, 10, 131, 132, 159, 181
    philosophers 158
    views and comments on
        capitalist structure 167
        materialism 141

Marxism 154, 158, 181
    lazy 182
materialism 28, 67, 132, 141, 145, 160, 181
    see also dialectical materialism; historical materialism
matter 100
Mauny, Raymond 86–7
Maximum illud (Benedict XV) 53, 96
Mbiti, John 27
medicine 12
Mendel, Gregor 62
Mens 33
metaphysics 66
Métraux, Alfred 138
metropoles 169
military capacity 74
Mills, C. Wright 37, 154
The Mirror of Production (Baudrillard) 28, 182
misery
    of Europe 110
    of the intellectual 109–10
missionaries
    biblical themes 97
    Capuchins 48–9, 96–7
    Certeau on 43, 50
    distancing and detachment 42
    double duty 45
    encounters with Africans 92
    enunciations 46–7
    Faith 45, 46
    gaze and judgment 92–4
    incarnating the truth 43
    Jesuits 92–3
    The Message 46
    paternalism 49
    program *ad extra* 45, 46–7
    projects of conversion 108
    propaganda literature 48–9
    questions for 48
    reflectors 43
    relations 48–9

missionaries (*cont.*)
  Relations 97
  Scheutist 93
  speaking and writing 44
  speeches 45–6, 49–50
  superiority of 93
  truth 43
missionary complex 44
missionary encyclicals 53
missionary languages 92, 95–7
missions
  ambiguity of 44
  Belgian Catholic 92
  building complexes 47
  conversion 41, 42–3
  explicit projects 94–5
  meaning of 43
  as a multivalent field 50–1
  philosophy of 51
  questions about 50
  relation to the other 44
  rupture 41, 42
  salvation 50
  voyage 41, 42
modernization 72
modes of production 168, 169
Montaigne, Michel de 109
moral regeneration 95
moral sciences 32, 33
morality 68
Morgan, Lewis Henry 117
Morin, Edgar 156
Mulago, Vincent 27, 137
multifold trend 70, 71, 74
Mundus 33
Mwondo Theatre 121
mysticism 164–5

naming, power of 16
Napoleonic education system 58–9
nativity 89
natural sciences 33
nature 17
culture and 69
objectivity of 33
Nègre 115
négritude 19, 20, 118, 119
  movement 117–18
The Network and Urban Social Organization (Epstein) 156
nkisi 129–31, 133
  formation and organization 130
  readings 130–1
  social game 134
  see also kindoki
nkulu 130–1
Nkuruse 121
non-Westerners, behaviors of 12
Nora, Pierre 155
normal, concept of 4

Obenga, Théophile 28, 30
Oedipus complex 3
onar 16
The Order of Things: An Archaeology of the Human Sciences (Foucault) 7–8, 14–15, 21–4, 67
organization of disciplines 23–4, 30
The Other Side of the Kingdom (Mudimbe) 177–83

paganism 44
pagans 41
  missionaries' perception of 48–9
Panoff, Michel and Françoise 7
papacy 87
papal bulls 87
passive sociality 60
Pereira, Pacheco 108
philological transcription 122
philosophers 158
philosophical languages 169–70
philosophical project 65

philosophy 66, 67, 98, 159, 160
  see also Bantu Philosophy
    (Tempels)
phlogistic theory 9
physics 147, 148
Piaget, Jean 148
Pierre Teilhard de Chardin and
    African Politics (Senghor)
    20
Pigafetta, Antonio 87
Pirotte, Jean 92, 93, 96
Poirier, Jean 29
political demand 89–90
political economy 76, 182–3
political independence 111
political power, centralization
    and concentration of 71–2
political space 168
Politzer, Georges 35
Pontalis, Jean-Bertrand 16–17
population growth 73
positivism 159
positivist sociology 36, 38, 157
Poulantzas, Nicos 154
praxis 17–18, 18, 37, 158, 159,
    161, 166, 179
Présence Africaine 106
Price-Mars, Jean 138
The Price of Sin (Vincke) 162,
    165–6
"the primitive" 40
primitivism 95
Princeps pastorum (John XXIII)
    53
principle of discontinuity 25
principle of exteriority 25
principle of reversal 25
principle of specificity 25
problems of conscience 36
production 86, 168
  modes of 168, 169
  relations of 76, 168
program ad extra 45, 46–7
prohibited speech 22

propositions 62
psychiatric ethnology 5
psychiatry 10–11
psychoanalysis 3, 6, 11, 14
  Althusser on 132
  case studies 14
  contemporary language 16–17
  dialectical thought and 131–2
  limitations of 14–15
  product of Freud 16
  redefining 15
  reuniting with ethnology 15
  see also Freud, Sigmund
psychoanalytic anthropology 113
psychology 35, 156
  as a nomothetic science 148
psychotherapy 156

quaternary industries 73
Quranic school 63

Rabemananjara, Jacques 117
rationality 74
Reason and Violence: A Decade
    of Sartre's Philosophy
    (Laing and Cooper) 166
reason, scientific 61, 62
relations
  of ideology 76
  between infrastructures and
    superstructures 76
  of power 76
  of production 76, 168
religions
  antagonisms between 101–2
  diversity and number of 101
  dogmas of 101
  images and symbols 101
  languages of 100–1
  personal 101
  postulates 101
  social 101
  see also African Christianity;
    Christianity

Report from a Chinese Village (Myrdal) 156
Rerum ecclesiae (Pius XI) 53
revealed God 99
revelation 43, 51
reversal, principle of 25
Rey, Pierre-Philippe 181
Richard, Jean-Pierre 120
Ricoeur, Paul 65
The Right to Colonization (Gilbert) 115–16
rituals 24
Romans 116
Rousseau, Jean-Jacques 117
Rubbens, Antoine 105
rule of Christ 94
rule of God 94
rupture 42, 90

Sacred Congregation of the Propaganda Fide 48
Saint-Simon, Henri de 29
St. Bonaventure 61
St. Thomas 61
salvation 94–5
Sane clarissimis (Martin V) 87
Sapir-Whorf hypothesis 88
Sartre, Jean-Paul 10–11, 154, 158, 159, 180, 182
  comments and views on "the gaze" 78
  lazy Marxism 182
  patient and psychiatrist relations 170–2
  freedom 166
  négritude 118–19
Satan 95, 96
satellites 169
"the savage" 35, 40, 109
savage mind 66
scarcity 166
Scheutist missionaries 93
Schmidt, Joel 192–3n5
scholarly sociology 157

scholars, of African history 30
science(s) 60
  Africanization of 29
  ambiguities within 29
  colonial 179
  complementarity and interdisciplinarity 148
  definition 146
  discourse of 61
  economic 29
  educational 148
  exact 32, 147
  Faith and 61–2
  history of 147
  ideology of 9, 65, 66
  interrogation of 178
  isolated scholar, obsolescence of 148
  liberal 145
  methods and approaches 147
  moral 32, 33
  natural 33
  rationalist motivations 29
  reductionism 16
  revolution 10
  terminology 16
  theoretical structures 146
  traditional motivations 29
  see also social and human sciences; social sciences
sciences of man 34
scientific blocks 8–9
scientific knowledge 72
  de-Westernization of 66
scientific languages 169–70
secret societies 24
self-affirmation 170, 172
self-annulment 21, 165
The Seminar of Jacques Lacan (Lacan) 18
Senghor, Léopold Sédar 19, 20, 27, 112, 117
serial ideas 167, 198n3
Sève, Lucien 132

Index

sin 162, 165–6
Slama, Alain-Gérard 4
sociability 60
social and human sciences 8
  discourses of 170
  vs. exact sciences 32
  hallucinatory ethnocentrism 16
  rethinking 178
  scientific materialism 160
  theoretical problems in 32–40
  see also Africa, social and human sciences
social appropriation of discourse 25
Social History of an Egyptian Village in the Twentieth Century (Berque) 156
social knowledge 38
  universality of 39
social order 36
social phenomena 39
social planning 74
social progress 110–11
social reality 154
social relations of production 168
social sciences
  contradictions 35–6
  divisions within 32–6
  economic and political power 39
  ideological 38
  lines of demarcation 35
  missions of practitioners 37
  newness 32
  recognition 32
  uncertainty of 32
socialization 57, 62–3
societies of discourse 24
Society of Zairean Historians 146–7
society(ies) 60
  current tendencies 70–6
  ethnocentric decision 75
  general movement of 76
  hierarchization of 39
  social structure 129
sociologists, categories of 36
sociology 29, 35
  birth of 38
  committed sociology 37
  concrete sociology 156
  contradictions 36
  definition 36
  depth sociology 157
  empirico-positivist 37
  engaged sociology 37, 156–7
  formalist sociology 36–7, 38
  founding of 35
  positivist sociology 36, 38, 157
  scholarly sociology 157
  as a science of "Order" 38
sorcery 124–35, 132, 133
  as a coded language 134
  combatting 127
  discourse of 127
    African 127
  for explaining other phenomena 128
  understanding 128–9
  Western considerations of 127
Soriano, Marc 12
souls 95
specialists 146
specificity, principle of 25
speech 6, 22, 45–6, 49–50, 178
  prohibited 22
stages of humanity, theories of 117
state, disciplining power of 61
structural Marxism 181
structuralism 65–6, 67
  concept of structure 67
suburbanization 73
Sun Chief (Talayesva) 156
superstructures 168
syncretism 99–100, 138

technical knowledge 72

Tempels, Reverend Father Placide 105–6, 112, 113
terminology 10, 16
 system of 16
tertiary industries 73
theological languages 100–1
theology 53–4
theories 149
 reality and 170
therapeutics 13
Things to Come (Kahn) 70–4
thought and reality 66, 67
Tiresias complex 182
toothing stones approach 96, 140, 142
tradition 162, 163, 167, 168, 172
transcription 122
translation 14
transpositions 164
trial of meaning 108, 109, 111
Tristes Tropiques (Lévi-Strauss) 30, 172–3
tropicalization 51, 52–3
truth 5–6
 will to truth 23, 30, 31, 60, 95

underdevelopment 40
 economic 169
uniformization 57, 58
universal cultural model 4
universal mediation 21–2
universality 5, 6, 11, 27, 142–3
 culture 89
 papacy 96
universities
 as a business 80
 as an ivory tower of culture and research 80–1
 political imperatives 79
  economic contract 79
  imperial and ideological vocation 79–80
  profitable programs and structures 80
 as productive enterprises 80, 81
 recycling of cadres 81
 as sites of ongoing education 80, 81
 socialist and leftist demands 81
 see also African universities
The Unthought of Discourse (Buakasa) 13, 135
"Kimputu case" 127–8, 131
kindoki 124–9, 130, 133, 134
nkisi 129–31, 133, 134
social reality 133
social relations 133
urbanization 73
utopia 68, 182, 183

van den Berghe, Pierre 122
Verhaegen, Benoît 36–7, 37, 133, 160–1, 179
 influences on 154, 158
 methodology 157–8
 sociopolitical events 153–4
 sociopolitical tensions 153–4
 structuring social reality 154
  national, the 154
  social, the 154
  tribal, the 154
 theoretical thought 161
 views and comments on African universities 82
 insecurity about influences 154
 kindoki and nkisi 133
 sorcery 124–5
 see also dialectical materialism; immediate history; *Introduction to Immediate History* (Verhaegen)
vice 68
Vincke, Jacques L. 162, 163, 165–6, 172
 "African Tradition" 165
 see also The Price of Sin (Vincke)

violence 78, 115, 164, 165, 166
Virgin Mary 89
vital force 137
voluntarism 89–90
voluntary activity 43
Voodoo 136–7
  class relations 138
  dialecticalization of the social 138
  hermeneutic approach to 139, 142
  history of 138
  as an ideology 141–2
  phenomenological approach to 138–9, 142
  structural approach to 139, 142
  studying 140–1
  theological approach to 141
Vossler, Karl 134
voyage 41, 42
  symbolism of 43

Western Christianity 51
Western civilization 22
  civilizing mission 39
Western cultural power 85
Western culture 28, 66
  and other cultures 39
  perspectivization of 29
  superiority of 87, 93
  values and ideology 78
Western discourse 28
Western philosophical thought 21
Western values 72
Westerners
  exploitation of Africa 115
  imposing models on non-Westerners 11
  methods of 12
  violence 115
What Is to Be Done? (Lenin) 161
White Man's School 37, 126
will to truth 23, 60
  African 30, 31
  particular version of 95
Willame, Jean-Claude 177–83
writing 172–3
Wundt, Wilhelm 43

Yanoama (Valero) 156
The Year 2000 (Kahn) 70–4

Zaire 124, 146–7, 152, 153, 179
  human sciences 179
  social formation 179
Zolkiewski, Stefan 150